W9-BIK-532

ONE HUNDRED VICTORIES

ALSO BY LINDA ROBINSON

Tell Me How This Ends:
General David Petraeus and the Search for a Way Out of Iraq

Masters of Chaos:
The Secret History of the Special Forces

LINDA ROBINSON

ONE HUNDRED VICTORIES

SPECIAL OPS AND
THE FUTURE OF
AMERICAN WARFARE

PublicAffairs | NEW YORK

Published in the United States by PublicAffairs™,
a Member of the Perseus Books Group

PublicAffairs books are available at special discounts for bulk purchases in the US by corporations, institutions, and other organizations. For more information, please contact the Special Markets Department at the Perseus Books Group, 2300 Chestnut Street, Suite 200, Philadelphia, PA 19103, call (800) 810-4145, ext. 5000, or e-mail special.markets@ perseusbooks.com.

Book Design by Janet Tingey

Library of Congress Cataloging-in-Publication Data
Robinson, Linda, 1962–
One hundred victories : special ops and the future of American warfare /
    Linda Robinson.—First edition.
pages cm
Includes bibliographical references and index.
ISBN 978-1-61039-149-8 (hardback)
ISBN 978-1-61039-150-4 (ebook)
1. Afghan War, 2001—Campaigns. 2. Afghan War, 2001—Commando operations—United States. 3. Special operations (Military science)—United States. 4. Counterinsurgency—Afghanistan—History—21st century. 5. United States—Armed Forces—Afghanistan—History. 6. Taliban. 7. Afghanistan—Politics and government—2001. 8. Afghanistan—History, Military—21st century. I. Title.
DS371.412.R62 2013
958.104'78—dc23
2013016787

First Edition
10 9 8 7 6 5 4 3 2 1

"To win one hundred victories in one hundred battles is not the acme of skill. To subdue the enemy without fighting is the acme of skill."

—SUN TZU

CONTENTS

CAST OF CHARACTERS   ix

INTRODUCTION   xiii
   "You'll Have to Kill a Lot of Men Like My Father"   xiii
   Missed Opportunities   xvi

CHAPTER 1: Hitting Targets   1
   On the Hunt   1
   Reeder's Epiphany   9

CHAPTER 2: Into the Villages   21
   The Battle for Buy-In   21
   Miller's New Idea   25
   From Black Ops to Village Ops   31

CHAPTER 3: The Taliban's Home   39
   "Who Will Go with Me?   39
   Maiwand   44
   Summer of Assassinations   59

CHAPTER 4: Paktika   65
   Chamtu   65
   Catastrophic Success   80
   To Pirkowti Again   86

CHAPTER 5: On the Border   93
   ODA 3316   93
   Fighting Uphill   101
   Operation Sayaqa   103

CHAPTER 6: The Burdens of Command   117
   "Who Is Going to Take the Blame?"   117
   Growing Pains   124

CHAPTER 7: On the Same Team ... or Not   137
   Hugger and Slugger   137
   "We're Not Going South, Are We?"   148

CHAPTER 8: SEALs Do Foreign Internal Defense, Too   159
   SEALs Take Charge   159
   Commandos Raise the Bar   170
   The Fallen   175

CHAPTER 9: Good Enough?   181
   West Paktika   181
   Aziz Leads   192

CHAPTER 10: Highway One   203
   Uprising   203
   Expulsion   208

CHAPTER 11: Will the Valley Hold?   217
   A Band of Brothers   217
   The Last Team   225

CHAPTER 12: The Endgame   241
   Unity of Command at Last   241
   Whither Local Police?   249
   Afghan Special Ops to the Fore   257

CHAPTER 13: The Future of Special Operations and
American Warfare   261

AUTHOR'S NOTE   269
NOTES   275
SELECTED BIBLIOGRAPHY   297
INDEX   303

The photo insert appears between pages 136–137

CAST OF CHARACTERS

(Listed in order of appearance. Military ranks are current as of July 2013.)

INTRODUCTION

Maj. Gen. Christopher Haas—CFSOCC-A commander, 2011–2012
Bismullah Khan Mohammedi—Tajik leader, minister of interior, minister of defense
Col. Mark Schwartz—CJSOTF-A commander 2011–2012

CHAPTER 1: HITTING TARGETS

Maj. Gen. Edward Reeder—CFSOCC-A commander, 2009–2010
Lt. Col. Brad Moses—CJSOTF-A operations officer
Col. Pat Mahaney—battalion and deputy CFSOCC-A commander
Maj. Christopher Castelli—company commander

CHAPTER 2: INTO THE VILLAGES

Maj. Gen. Scott Miller—CFSOCC-A commander, 2010–2011
Command Sgt. Maj. J. R. Stigall—CFSOCC-A command sergeant major
Capt. Geno Paluso (Navy)—CFSOCC-A chief of staff
Brig. Gen. Don Bolduc—CJSOTF-A and deputy SOJTF-A commander

CHAPTER 3: THE TALIBAN'S HOME

Col. Chris Riga—Special Operations Task Force South commander, 2010–2011
Brig. Gen. Abdul Raziq—Afghan police general in Kandahar

CPT Dan Hayes and ODA 3314—team in Maiwand, 2010–2011
Jan Mohammed—Afghan Local Police commander in Maiwand
Maj. Scott White—company commander at Camp Simmons
Col. Bill Carty—Special Operations Task Force South commander,
   2011–2012

CHAPTER 4: PAKTIKA

Maj. Mike Hutchinson and ODA 3325—team in Paktika, 2010–2011
Commander Aziz—Afghan Special Squad leader in Paktika

CHAPTER 5: ON THE BORDER

Cpt. Matt and ODA 3316—team in Kunar, 2011
Nur Mohammed—Afghan Local Police commander in Kunar
Maj. Eddie Jimenez—company commander at Camp Dyer
Lt. Col. Bob Wilson—Special Operations Task Force East commander,
   2011–2012
CW2 Mike and ODA 3313—American team partnered with Afghan 1st
   Commando Kandak

CHAPTER 6: THE BURDENS OF COMMAND

Gen. John Allen—ISAF commander
Col. Heinz Dinter—CFSOCC-A operations officer, 2011–2012
Capt. Wes Spence (Navy)—CFSOCC-A chief of staff, 2011–2012
Cdr. Alec McKenzie—CFSOCC-A staff officer in charge of ALP program

CHAPTER 7: ON THE SAME TEAM … OR NOT

CPT Brad Hansell and ODA 7233—team in Maiwand, 2012
Captain Najibullah—Afghan Special Forces team leader
Lt. Col. Richard Navarro—Special Operations Task Force South com-
   mander, 2012
Command Sgt. Maj. Brian Rarey—SOTF-S battalion sergeant major
Maj. Angel Martinez—company commander at Camp Simmons
Sgt. Maj. J. R. Jones—company sergeant major at Camp Simmons

CHAPTER 8: SEALS DO FOREIGN INTERNAL DEFENSE, TOO

Cdr. J.R. Anderson—Special Operations Task Force Southeast commander, 2011
Commander Mike Hayes—Special Operations Task Force Southeast commander, 2012
Abdul Samad—Taliban leader
Lt. Marshall—SEAL platoon leader partnered with Afghan 8th Commando Kandak
Lt. Col. Ahmadullah Popal—8th Commando Kandak commander

CHAPTER 9: GOOD ENOUGH?

CPT Jason Russell and ODA 1114—team in Paktika, 2012–2013
CPT Jae Kim and ODA 1411—team in Paktika, 2012–2013

CHAPTER 10: HIGHWAY ONE

CPT Terrence Jackson and ODA 1326—team in Ghazni
Lt. Col. Chris Fox—Special Operations Task Force East commander, 2012–2013
Maj. John Bishop—SOTF-E operations officer

CHAPTER 11: WILL THE VALLEY HOLD?

Maj. Kent Solheim—company commander at Camp Dyer
ODA 3131—team in Kunar, 2012–2013
Asim Gul, Wazir and Gudjer—ALP commanders in Kunar
Maj. Ben Hauser—company commander at Camp Dyer
Col. Tony Fletcher—CJSOTF-A commander, 2012–2013

CHAPTER 12: THE ENDGAME

Maj. Gen. Tony Thomas—SOJTF-A commander, 2012–2013
Brig. Gen. Sean Swindell—NATO Training Mission-Afghanistan deputy commander
Gen. Sher Mohammed Karimi—chief of Afghan army general staff

INTRODUCTION

"YOU'LL HAVE TO KILL
A LOT OF MEN LIKE MY FATHER"

Chris Haas was one of the first Americans to arrive in Afghanistan after the 9/11 attacks on New York and Washington. A shaved-bald special forces officer with a hoarse voice and a love of cigars, Haas is easygoing but essentially private, careful and skeptical while maintaining an outward affability. He bowed his head before each meal, but did not speak of religion. His reserve contrasted with the effusive warmth of his Texan wife, Betty, whose smiling picture he tacked to the bulletin board by his desk.

Haas flew in on October 26, 2001, on one of the first helicopters that made it over the Hindu Kush following 9/11. At the time he was a lieutenant colonel, and he would be in command of the first four special forces teams to soldier through the winter weather and link up with Northern Alliance militia leaders. He would work side by side with CIA veterans of the Afghan-Soviet war of the 1980s, who would reforge their ties with the Northern Alliance, dispensing suitcases of cash for Afghan salaries, equipment, and fuel. The three who arrived first were Agency pros and a pleasure to work with, qualities not shared by some of the whippersnappers the CIA would later send out. They included "Doc," who had been a special forces medic before joining the CIA; Gary Schroen, a former field officer; and Gary Berntsen, a former CIA station chief.

Haas's most important duty was serving as liaison to the Northern Alliance leadership, the Tajik-led militia that had been fighting the Taliban for years and was the only armed group with the ability to

topple the regime and oust its Al Qaeda allies. The "G chief," or
guerrilla leader, was Bismullah Khan Mohammedi, a wily, determined
Northern Alliance leader who was highly beholden to his Tajik faction, the second largest of the groups making up Afghanistan's ethnic
mosaic. As he grilled Haas in his headquarters at Jabal Saraj, he sought
to put his would-be patron on the defensive. "Are you ready to lose
men? There will be fighting," he said to Haas and his operations
officer, Mark Schwartz. "Is the United States going to abandon us
again?" he continued, referring to the abrupt end of America's interest
in Afghanistan after the Soviet departure in 1989. Haas knew it was a
test. Bismullah Khan—or BK, as he would come to be known in the
years ahead, when he went on to become Afghanistan's army chief of
staff, interior minister, and then defense minister—was trying to level
the playing field. The Northern Alliance certainly wanted American
help, and it desperately needed the firepower that Haas had at his
disposal. But BK wanted to stay in the driver's seat. The Northern
Alliance wanted American help in order to throw out the Taliban and
take control of the country.

From his training, Haas knew that managing this relationship was
crucial. He could not change BK or his group's objectives, but he
could not become captive to them either. Over the weeks and months
ahead, he and BK became friendly, but Haas never gave in. "Haas
would call him on that righteous talk," Schwartz later recalled. "He
would talk to him straight."

The basic objective—toppling the Taliban and getting Osama
bin Laden—was clear, but the details were complex. Haas was to
strengthen the Northern Alliance militia while simultaneously restrain-
ing it from sweeping south to capture Kabul, Afghanistan's capital,
and wreaking vengeance on the Pashtuns—who formed the largest of
Afghanistan's ethnic groups. He was to stall the alliance until a multiethnic power-sharing agreement had been forged in Bonn and a leader
had been chosen. Meanwhile, he was to keep tabs on feuds among
the various militia leaders of the north as well as among the Pashtun
factions jockeying for control over Kandahar, the second largest city
in the country after Kabul.

During his eventful first tour in Afghanistan, Haas experienced first-hand the difficulties and limitations of warfare with guerrilla allies, first in the drive to capture Kabul, which was complete by November 2001, and then in the December pursuit of Osama bin Laden and Al Qaeda fighters as they fled into the Tora Bora mountain stronghold, bound for Pakistan. At Tora Bora, special operations teams joined up with Pashtuns from eastern Afghanistan who proved dubious allies, as some of them sold safe passage or turned a blind eye as Al Qaeda slipped through the 14,000-foot peaks and across the border.

Next, Haas received a stark and lethal lesson in the fog of war as he led the main attack against the Al Qaeda remnants in Operation Anaconda in March 2002, when his teams trained and led Zia Lodin's Pashtun force into what became a bloody battle. The battle, which took place following a three-week course of instruction to instill some basic discipline and infantry tactics into the motley band, was complicated by overturned trucks, a collapsed bridge, lack of promised US air support, and precisely ranged mortar, artillery, and machine-gun fire from Al Qaeda fighters dug into the mountains. Zia's forces suffered a 14 percent casualty rate, including a friendly-fire attack from an AC-130 Spectre gunship that also killed US Army Chief Warrant Officer Stanley Harriman.

One loss particularly stung Haas and reinforced the treacherous nature of guerrilla politics. Just east of the Anaconda battleground lay the Khost-Gardez Pass—a key mountain pass to the eastern border region. It was guarded by a notorious Pashtun strongman named Pacha Khan Zadran. A young special forces soldier named Nate Chapman was killed by his militia, and Haas never forgot what one of Pacha Khan Zadran's sons, who served as an interpreter for US forces, later told him: "You'll have to kill a lot of men like my father before Afghanistan will change."

Afghanistan was in the throes of a cultural and generational transition that would go on for many more years. Strongmen would continue to hold sway, and assassination would remain a common method of settling political disputes. Ethnic factions and Cold War–era alliances led by septuagenarians trumped many of the wishes and aspirations of younger, more educated Afghans. The twelve years after 2001 did see enormous progress—as well as a tremendous amount of killing—but the overall character of Afghan politics remained stubbornly feudal. The rule of the fist, the Tajik-Pashtun divide, and the grip of the few over the many would change only slowly, as the old men and the old ways passed from the scene. Pacha Khan Zadran became a member of the Afghan parliament, but he remained the strongman of the Khost-Gardez Pass.

MISSED OPPORTUNITIES

Special operations forces achieved an amazing feat, toppling the Taliban with about 350 operators, a handful of CIA operatives, and Afghan militias. They justly received kudos for this unalloyed success: they had had to improvise after 9/11, and overcome Afghanistan's ferocious obstacles, including terrain, weather, and internecine political machinations. But the special operations forces also missed a huge opportunity in this period—and it was not the failure to catch bin Laden at Tora Bora. Once he had retreated to his mountain lair, it was highly unlikely he could have been found without reliable Afghan partners. No American troops knew their way through the labyrinthine mountain passes, and none were acclimated for trekking and engaging in battle at 14,000-foot altitudes.

The real opportunity missed was the chance for special operators, those first in, to define a game plan, a way ahead that would envision a conclusive endgame to the Afghan conflict. Time and again, the United States has mistaken the decapitation of a regime or a terrorist network as victory, a tactical triumph as the decisive point after which only mopping up remains. Especially in the case of Afghanistan, where the complex political and physical terrain created many possibilities for a rural insurgency—allowing it to survive, thrive, and come back to fight another day—the capture of the cities and the installation of the new government of Hamid Karzai did not constitute a sufficient conclusion to the problem.

Special operations forces were in the lead initially, but they did not capitalize on this moment to design a plan to put Afghanistan definitively on the road to stability. True, the diplomats of the United Nations, the United States, and the North Atlantic Treaty Organization (NATO) were all meeting in Bonn to divvy up responsibilities for police, army, counternarcotics, and demobilization, as well as the political tasks of holding elections and writing a constitution. But the special operations forces, by dint of their intensive engagement with the gritty realities on the ground in those first six months, might have made a major contribution, not only on the security front, but to a framework that would provide stability for the 76 percent of Afghans who lived outside the cities. It was a failure that was eventually addressed, but only after eight years.

The biggest reason for the missed opportunity was an institutional one. Although US Central Command (CENTCOM) had handed special operations forces the lead after 9/11, special operators had no fully staffed, theater-level command ready to step up to the task. John F. Mulholland Jr., a colonel, came forward and performed admirably in an emergency situation. But his 5th Special Forces Group had never prepared, trained, or staffed itself to be a battlefield headquarters. A variety of other special operations commands were sent to Afghanistan, but none of them were up to the task, and none was given the overarching responsibility of coordinating all special operations, let alone the entire military effort. The ball then passed to the conventional forces, and special ops never got it back.

In the event, the conventional forces did no better. They were not at the time schooled in counterinsurgency, and they had no particular knowledge of South Asia. Furthermore, although NATO provided a welcome broad umbrella of political support for a coalition that grew to include forty-two countries, it led to a highly problematic bifurcated command structure for the war. The International Security Assistance Force (ISAF), a NATO-led international peacekeeping force, wanted little to do with combat, and a separate US command focused almost entirely on hunting terrorists on the eastern border with Pakistan. ISAF's purview was initially limited to the capital and overseeing the coalition members' nation-building duties as apportioned at Bonn.

Neither command paid much attention to the south, which was the Pashtun heartland, the area that had been and would again become the Taliban's home. As incredible as it may sound to students of military history, none of the constantly changing cast of commanders even bothered to write a campaign plan for Afghanistan until 2009.

Until 2009, the entire US military effort was overly focused on hunting down individuals considered to be problematic. This was a diversion from doctrine, in which counterguerrilla operations are merely a subset of activity, something to be nested within a wider approach that, depending on the circumstances, is termed "counter-insurgency," "foreign internal defense," or "stability operations." They are all aimed at supporting the indigenous government and enhancing its ability to perform the basic functions of government. Because the essential fact of supporting the locals was forgotten, ideas of employing ever greater numbers of US troops gained traction. This flaw should have been noted by special operators, but the hard, cold reality was that they were unprepared to carry out this role except at the most tactical level. They were not employed correctly, and they did not have the opportunity—after that brief initial window—to employ themselves correctly.

Haas was aware of this deficit, and when he returned to the United States after his next deployment to Iraq, he wrote his master's thesis at the US Army War College fleshing out a proposal for the creation of a special operations forces command structure able to plan and lead such campaigns. But there was no fix in place when he next returned to Afghanistan, in 2006. He came back as a colonel and commander of the 3rd Special Forces Group, which was thrust into a role for which they were still not ready. Whereas a colonel in charge of a conventional army brigade would be expected to plan and execute combat operations for 3,000 to 5,000 men in a province or state-sized area, the special forces groups were put in charge of the full range of special operations conducted across the entire territory of Afghanistan (an extremely rugged land of mountains and desert considerably larger than France, with one of the world's poorest road systems). It was all they could do to manage the tactical and logistical tasks of fighting in a terrain as forbidding as this.

There was another factor, a more existential question of what special operators were for, that became increasingly cloudy over the decade in Afghanistan, and for that matter in the "global war on terror." Were they meant to work with tribes and local forces, or were they meant only to hunt and kill? And were they clear enough in their own minds about how they should be used to win wars, or at least how they were to successfully hand them off to others? Many old-timers felt that special operations forces had lost their way at the very moment they burst into the limelight, becoming poster boys for counterterrorism. Haas, along with his comrade Edward M. Reeder Jr. and a black ops special operator, Austin Scott Miller, wrestled with this question as they became generals and returned to Afghanistan, entrusted with leading special operations teams minted after 9/11. It was up to them, as senior special operations generals of their generation, to discover what special operations forces were for and what they could really achieve. In the course of their arduous and fitful journey, they struggled to craft a strategy that would define not only special operations forces deployments for the years ahead, but the essence of US military force abroad in a new era—an era of leaner budgets and ballooning skepticism from all sides about mass military deployments in foreign adventures.

CHAPTER ONE

HITTING TARGETS

KANDAHAR 2007–KABUL 2010

ON THE HUNT

Pat Mahaney could not believe it. When he arrived in Afghanistan on his fifth tour, in March 2007, as the special operations battalion commander based in Kandahar, he found that the Taliban had made a spectacular comeback. A fearsome one-legged Taliban fighter named Mullah Dadullah Lang was leading the charge. Dadullah had championed the use of suicide bombers, previously almost unheard of in Afghanistan. He had recruited 141 Afghans who had blown themselves up in 2006.[1] He had risen to become the senior military commander through the use of brutality, ordering assassinations and adopting bomb-making techniques from Arab Al Qaeda members holed up in Pakistan. He also adopted beheadings as one of his personal signatures, taking a page from Abu Musab al-Zarqawi in Iraq. He had ordered the decapitations of Afghan soldiers, and even of followers who disobeyed him. When an Italian reporter was taken hostage, it was Dadullah who ordered that his Afghan driver be beheaded. All of

I

these deeds he liberally publicized on Al Jazeera and through DVDs he had made in Quetta, Pakistan, his base.

By 2007 the Taliban had regained control of large areas of the south—Dadullah claimed twenty districts and a fighting force of 12,000 men.[2] They had begun to shift from a guerrilla war to massing in large numbers to attack bases and towns, slowly drawing a noose around Kandahar City, the capital of Kandahar Province in the Pashtun south, from which the Taliban had ruled Afghanistan in the late 1990s. Taliban roamed freely from Helmand, the province due west of Kandahar, across northern Kandahar and into Zabul Province.

Recognizing the deterioration, NATO decided to send a small Canadian task force to Kandahar in mid-2006 to supplement the small British footprint in Helmand. The emboldened Taliban had heavily mined the perimeters of the British outposts, and the Canadians were thrust suddenly into unfamiliar terrain and a hotter war than they were ready to fight. Mahaney led the only American force in the south— an undermanned battalion of three companies with eighty-two men apiece—one of which he sent to Herat, the westernmost province under his command. One battalion of the 82nd Airborne Division, the 1-508, was on call as a reserve force in case they got into trouble.

Mahaney could see that dramatic action was called for. A student of Sun Tzu, he realized that he would need to make up for his force's small size with innovative tactics that would surprise the enemy. He cooked up a scheme with his staff and then sold it to the Canadians and the British, who made him the commander of the operation.

The reason for being in Afghanistan was never theoretical for Lieutenant Colonel Patrick J. Mahaney Jr. On the door of his tactical operations center at Kandahar Airfield, he had hung a photo of a New York firefighter at the World Trade Center. His father, a forty-one-year veteran of the city's fire department, had been at the towers on 9/11. Mahaney lost six friends and a cousin that day. "We were not out for revenge," he wrote in an email later. "It was about civilization versus barbarity." Over four tours, he had developed ties to Afghans and became deeply committed to seeing the country succeed.[3]

Mahaney launched Operation Nish on April 4, 2007. The goal was to wrest control of the town of Sangin, in Helmand, from the Taliban's grip. It was the base from which the Taliban was launching attacks into neighboring provinces. Dadullah had easy access to it, traveling freely across the flat land of the Helmand-Pakistan border. Mahaney threw out standard military doctrine, which called for forces to travel in small units to avoid air and artillery attack. The Taliban had neither aircraft nor artillery beyond short-range mortars. He assembled all the available forces—Canadian troops, an Afghan army battalion from the north, Afghan police, and logistical support—in one long convoy that stretched for nearly five kilometers. The ISAF command in Kabul thought he was crazy, calling his convoy the "fireworm" as its headlights lit up the predawn sky. As it traveled through the streets of Kandahar City to get to Highway One west, the convoy was attacked by a handful of Taliban. The troops returned fire, killing three attackers, and proceeded west down Highway One into Helmand. There Mahaney did another unexpected thing: instead of turning north onto Highway 611, he turned the "fireworm" off the road, due east into the desert. He knew the Taliban would have seen their approach and heavily mined the road north to Sangin. His staff had studied the terrain and could move off-road quickly with little risk of ambush or accident. When the convoy was parallel to Sangin, it made a sharp encircling turn, and it flooded into the town exactly at noon, just as Mahaney had planned. His forces handily took the town without a single casualty. Infiltrating piecemeal up the highway would have surely cost them dead or wounded. The enemy was caught off guard by the flanking maneuver.

The coalition seized control of Sangin, but the Taliban continued to mass and attack elsewhere, including in Helmand, Kandahar, and Uruzgan. So Mahaney went on the offensive again. He did not have the numbers to overwhelm these concentrations of Taliban fighters, but he did have good human intelligence from an Afghan network that had been developed over the past five years. "This was year six of the war," Mahaney reflected. "By year six, World War II was over." Successive special forces battalion commanders, relying on the same interpreters, had gotten to know Afghans all over the country. "We could find out what was going on one hundred miles away by having someone call his cousin," Mahaney said.

When the Taliban fighters felt they could attack with impunity, they would mass and thus present a good target. Mahaney used various deception tactics to encourage this. "We would draw them out to attack us, to make them think they were winning," he said. By presenting a small force—a twelve-man team and some Afghans—he would encourage the Taliban fighters to come out of the villages to attack. Once they were out in the open, away from the civilians, Mahaney's men would call in the aerial attack. At times, Mahaney would divert units to unexpected targets to catch the Taliban unawares. Or he would have units converge from different firebases. The Taliban, and even the special ops' own Afghan partners, never knew who was going to show up where—or when.

Mullah Dadullah came to Helmand on May 12 to shore up his forces. A special mission unit had been sent by Lieutenant General Stanley A. McChrystal to help track Dadullah by tapping into the communications of his brother, who had been captured in Pakistan but later released. Upon learning that Mullah Dadullah was planning to reenter Afghanistan, the special mission unit passed the tip to British special operations units in Helmand. The British commandos killed Dadullah after a fierce four-hour battle—to prove it, the Kandahar governor displayed his body to the local media.[4]

Dadullah's death did not, however, cause the violence to abate. His fighters regrouped and moved east into northern Kandahar and Uruzgan. Mahaney's force continued to encounter large Taliban formations, even after unleashing air attacks against them and inflicting heavy casualties. The special operators fought through enemy defenses to retrieve the bodies of eight dead troops whose Chinook was shot down at the end of May by a man-portable missile near Kajaki. In another major battle in Herat's Zerikow Valley, Mahaney counted 136 killed. The official battle damage assessment done by military intelligence later concluded that more than 200 were killed, including 4 senior Taliban leaders. Mahaney was amazed at how the Taliban continued to come out in droves, battle after battle.

President Karzai's brother Qayum, a member of the Afghan parliament, came to see Mahaney. He was extremely concerned about the Taliban massing in northern Kandahar. They were taking over towns and, he believed, would soon conduct an assault on Kandahar City itself. The Kandahar governor, who had been wounded in an assassination attempt in late May, also appealed to Mahaney, asking him to break the Taliban's grip on the highway that connected Kandahar City to Uruzgan, the province to the north. A small Dutch-led task force there was cut off and could only receive supplies by air. The Canadians were also keen to gain control of the highway—which the military called Route Bear—so they could finish reconstruction of the Dahla dam, which irrigated most of Kandahar and was a high-profile project. Security on Route Bear had been provided mostly by an unofficial highway police force run by Matiullah Khan, from the Karzais' Popalzai subtribe. But in the face of the Taliban onslaught, his checkpoints were being overrun and his men killed. Six years after the fall of the Taliban, Afghanistan was a patchwork of provinces barely held together.

Mahaney and Robert "Chris" Castelli, his company commander in Tarin Kowt, Uruzgan's capital, drew up a plan and began to install field artillery sites and conduct reconnaissance. In late June they launched Operation Adalat ("Justice," in Pashto) to break the Taliban's hold on the Shah Wali Kot Valley and derail the planned offensive on Kandahar City. Castelli was the officer in charge on the ground, but, as in Sangin, they assembled a combined force to bottle up the enemy. It was highly unusual for special operators to lead an ad hoc armored task force, but that is what the circumstances required. The Canadians supplied 6 Leopard tanks, 13 light armored vehicles, and 13 support vehicles, along with about 200 troops. They also supplied 3 M-777 howitzers with 155 mm rocket-assisted artillery. Special operators were going to war with heavy metal against a dug-in Taliban force. All told, they had assembled a force of 1,200 for what would be, for many of them, the largest fight of their careers. Castelli's intelligence indicated that up to 900 Taliban fighters were entrenched along this key artery and the surrounding mountains and valleys to facilitate their movement and operations in a swath stretching from Helmand through Kandahar into Zabul and north into Uruzgan.[5]

There were only three exits from the valley. Castelli and his men would establish a blocking position to the north, and another team would block the second exit. A third force moving up from Kandahar, special forces and Canadian armor, would attack and push the Taliban into the blocking forces' waiting fire. As the operation began, Castelli dropped artillery rounds in unpopulated areas to warn civilians and push them out of the planned engagement area. In the event, a mass exodus of women and children headed due south, directly into the path of the oncoming tanks. To ensure that the civilians evacuated to a safe area, Castelli sent Afghan soldiers and police into Shah Wali Kot's district center.

With his four gun trucks, Castelli then assaulted uphill, directly into the Taliban's well-defended mountain position. The American special operators and Afghan forces drove through the Taliban lines, firing their weapons furiously, and then turned to attack again, pinning in the insurgents. Facing the armored force on the south, which was pounding them with tank and artillery fire, the insurgents opted to flee east. Monitoring the radio traffic, Castelli heard the Taliban requesting motorcycles to evacuate their leaders. Castelli called for air support, but the Dutch aircraft could not identify the target and would not drop below their mandated ceiling to do so. "You are cleared hot to engage," Castelli repeated. But they would not. Frustrated, Castelli asked them to clear the airspace above his battlefield. If they were not going to stop the fleeing Taliban, he needed someone who would. His SATCOM (satellite communications) exchange with the Dutch and his call for additional air support were heard by units around the country. A Black Hawk on a logistic resupply "milk run" diverted and came to his aid, hitting targets that the operators marked with their laser designators or by sight until Apache attack helicopters, armed with Hellfire missiles, arrived from Kandahar.

The battle lasted two days, and in the end, four hundred Taliban were killed. The official battle damage assessment count came in at more than five hundred. The coalition forces had killed two Taliban commanders; a third had escaped on a motorcycle during the kerfuffle with the Dutch. All this they learned during the detailed searches of surrounding villages in the subsequent days. Matiullah Khan and his highway patrolmen had scooped up all the Taliban weaponry from caches they discovered. Castelli was mildly annoyed that he had to bargain with them to turn the weapons over, but working with MK's force was worth the hassle. "They were the most reliable [Afghan] guys," Castelli said—more reliable than the Afghan army—"and they were absolutely feared by the Taliban." Castelli had been coming to Uruzgan since 2002; he had built the special operators' original small firebases at Tarin Kowt and De Rawood.

Operation Adalat blunted the Taliban's summer offensive. There was no mass attack on Kandahar City. Route Bear was reopened to Afghan and coalition traffic, and Uruzgan began receiving supplies. The route was never closed again.

That did not mean the Taliban was defeated. The diehard remnants moved further east to a target they thought they could overrun, Firebase Anaconda in eastern Uruzgan. It was the most vulnerable of the four firebases in Uruzgan, and perhaps of all the fifteen bases Mahaney's men occupied. Almost every time his team members left the gate, they were in a firefight. Castelli took his sergeant major to visit and observe the base. The team's tactics were textbook, and they had welded additional armor around their gun turrets and rear gunner positions. But "that base should never have been built," Castelli concluded. The terrain the base was located on simply could not be properly defended. There were only two exits, one of which was through a narrow pass and a bridge. The outpost was surrounded by high ground and dry riverbeds, or *wadis*, which gave natural cover to approaching forces. The closest Afghan homes were barely one hundred meters away. When he was on patrol there, Castelli's vehicle was hit by rifle fire or shrapnel nineteen times. He decided the base must be closed or moved.[6]

In early August, before he could carry through with this move, at least seventy-five Taliban fighters laid siege to Anaconda. They brazenly camped outside, lobbing their mortars into the compound.

Then, on August 8, to the astonishment of the soldiers inside, the Taliban attacked them head on. The insurgents believed the firebase contained only one special forces team and some Afghan troops, when in reality there were about thirty westerners, including Australians, and about fifty Afghan army and police troops, some of them fairly experienced. To Mahaney, this frontal assault in broad daylight suggested the insurgents were mad, or even drugged. But the Taliban had been probing and testing and attacking this vulnerable spot for weeks on end, and they thought it was now ripe for taking. Waves of bearded guerrillas rushed the outer checkpoints and the gates from three directions, firing AK-47s, grenade launchers, and mortars. The men inside unleashed a barrage of machine-gun fire and fired their own mortars while calling in the Apache helicopters based at Tarin Kowt. When the dust settled, more than twenty of the Taliban lay dead and the rest were scattered. Two Afghan girls who lived nearby were wounded, as were two Afghan soldiers.[7]

Mahaney reviewed the situation as his battalion prepared to leave in November 2007. During a 217-day tour, the battalion had been in 287 combat engagements with the Taliban. The official count of enemy killed in action by 1st Battalion, 7th Special Forces Group, was 3,407—more than the total for all the other units combined in Afghanistan in the same time period. The battalion had lost twelve men, and twenty-four others were wounded, including special operators and six embedded trainers attached to their units.[8]

The battalion had fought hard and smart and had achieved enormous battlefield successes. The operators had not just killed a lot of Taliban, but had also thrown themselves into information operations, setting up ten radio stations from which to broadcast programs to locals, distributing 2,000 radios, and forming Afghan army psyop (psychological operations) units. A flood of press releases countered Taliban claims, including attempts to smear Afghan allies. Mahaney had thoroughly investigated the claims against the Kandahar governor, Asadullah Khalid, and Matiullah Khan. "I don't want to be working with any war criminals," he said. He found no evidence for the accusations, but plenty of what he considered unsubstantiated claims were nonetheless incorporated into United Nations and diplomatic reporting without any attempt to check, corroborate, or source them. Mahaney was particularly concerned to dig into alleged human rights abuses, including any torture, mistreatment, or killing outside of battlefield combat. He found no evidence for any of it that he considered solid. Corruption, however, was another matter.

Mahaney, forty-one, had spent most of the past six years in Afghanistan—nearly half of his career in special ops—and although he was leaving, he believed he was likely to be sent back once again. Over the next year at the NATO Defense College in Italy, he continued to think about the Afghan war. He felt something was missing. In the early years of the war, the word "counterinsurgency" had been all but banned. Then Mahaney recalled that "for years we talked about clear, hold, and build. *Hold?* We had never done it—and we weren't going to do it without locals."[9]

REEDER'S EPIPHANY

In the early days, special operations forces were consumed with hunting Taliban, and their use of local Afghans was largely expeditious to this purpose. As one special forces officer said, "we'd round up our indig [operator slang for their indigenous fighters] to go hit targets." The special forces teams were arrayed all along the Afghan-Pakistan border in a series of firebases that were guarded by an Afghan militia force—or AMF, as it was called—and these militiamen also often went along on raids. In the view of many special forces, including John Mulholland, this approach had locked down the border pretty well and kept the Taliban on the run. The militia force had been formed in the first six months of the war when there was no Afghan army, and at that time there had been no one out in the bush except the special operations forces and the CIA. But as time went on, others began to look askance at the AMF, seeing it as an irregular force that did not have any connection to the nascent Afghan army.[10]

There was also little continuity in approach from one commander to the next. The colonel in charge of the Combined Joint Special

Operations Task Force–Afghanistan (CJSOTF-A) changed every seven months. In 2006–2007, Chris Haas and Ed Reeder swapped places twice. In terms of personality, Ed Reeder was a study in contrast with the taciturn Haas. Big as a bear, garrulous, but fiercely competitive, his nickname was Silverback. He had come to know the Afghans well on four tours, two in Kandahar in 2002 and 2003 as a battalion commander and two in 2006. Reeder had been an adviser in El Salvador in 1988, early in his career, as that small Central American nation was battling a Soviet-backed Marxist insurgency, and later participated in the first major US military operation since Vietnam, the invasion of Panama in 1989 to oust dictator Manuel Noriega.

In Afghanistan, Reeder bonded with various Afghan leaders with zeal, burrowing deep into the Pashtun world. They invited him to live in their homes, gave over their homes for safe houses, and asked him for advice. Few Americans had such an extensive network among the southern Pashtun leaders. The special forces had been the only American forces in southern Afghanistan from the earliest days of the war, when they met up with Hamid Karzai, who had come across the Pakistani border with a few guys on motorcycles. And they kept returning—not just the units, but the same individuals, first as captains, then as majors, then as lieutenant colonels or colonels. Sergeants kept coming back, on teams and in companies and battalions. Once cell phones came to Afghanistan, Afghans kept their numbers on speed dial and their photos as screensavers.[11]

During his back-to-back tours in 2002 and 2003 in southern Afghanistan, Reeder got to know Karzai's close friend and mentor, Jan Mohammad Khan, whom Karzai appointed governor of Uruzgan. Reeder lived in his house for a time. He came to know Karzai's half-brother Ahmed Wali Karzai and his brother Qayum well, too, while also befriending Gul Agha Shirzai from the rival Barakzai tribe. Shirzai had raced to Kandahar ahead of Hamid Karzai in 2001, moving into the governor's palace and forcing Karzai's hand. Karzai eventually eased Shirzai out by appointing him governor of Nangahar in the east. Shirzai's brother remained as the apparently permanent commander of the Kandahar Airfield, a perch from which he and his son oversaw the family's burgeoning trucking and contracting business, fueled by the influx of troops and dollars. Reeder's friendships with these men extended beyond his tours in Afghanistan. They paid him visits at Fort Bragg and stayed in touch by phone. Shirzai sought his advice as Karzai dangled offers of cabinet positions to dissuade him from running for president in 2004. In the end, the clever Karzai managed to keep the wheeler-dealer Shirzai out of the race and then left him in his post at Nangahar.

From his first tours in 2002 and 2003, Reeder and his men had been heavily engaged in targeting Taliban. Although the senior Taliban and Al Qaeda leaders had left for Pakistan, a lot of local Taliban remained. By his own admission, Reeder had not spent a lot of time thinking about how to stand up a good Afghan government or security force. Like Mahaney's battalion later on, Reeder's one battalion of special forces teams was spread out across the three provinces, with virtually no conventional forces in the south—and one reserve brigade was divided between Kandahar Airfield and Bagram. The training of the Afghan army had barely begun. In these circumstances, the special operators relied very heavily on the Afghan militia force they had recruited and hired. "They were a very effective force because they were local," Reeder said. "They knew the people and the terrain." After Reeder decided to cross-load Afghan and special forces personnel in each other's vehicles, the ambushes stopped. "The locals did not want to kill a local guy," he noted.

When Reeder returned as the commander of the CJSOTF-A in 2006, his troops still focused on targeting Taliban insurgents, but they also assumed more training and advisory missions. They were partnered with thirteen Afghan army battalions, called *kandaks*. Reeder's boss back at US Central Command in Tampa, Brigadier General Frank Kearney, wanted him to build an Afghan special forces unit, but Reeder persuaded him that the Afghans' skill level was still too immature. Instead he proposed they start a light-infantry commando unit. The first one hundred were selected and sent to Haas's 5th Group forces in Jordan for training. These Afghans became the training cadre for the commandos, and in 2007, the first two commando kandaks were formed and fielded. Reeder viewed the commandos as one of the US special operations forces' most successful contributions to the Afghan project. The commandos received an extra $50 a month in pay and double food rations, but he believed the secret to their 99 percent retention rate was a predictable deployment cycle and regular leave. After returning from leave, the commandos would live and train with the special operators at Camp Morehead outside Kabul before heading back into combat alongside a US special operations team.

By then, a training command had been created for the Afghan army and police, although the police, always an afterthought, still lagged behind badly. The overall US commander, Lieutenant General Karl Eikenberry, ordered Reeder to demobilize the 11,000 members of the Afghan Militia Force. "Tell them to go into the army," Eikenberry said. "And get them out of [battle dress uniforms]." Reeder was crushed, but this edict had been percolating for a while. As Afghanistan's formal army stood up, both the tolerance and rationale for unofficial and competing armed formations not under the control of the Afghan government waned. The reach of the Afghan government was still limited, but the fear of wayward militias was a legitimate concern and a legacy of the tumultuous 1990s. There was no simple solution, however. This issue exemplified the ongoing tension between those who wanted expedient solutions and those who aspired to more idealistic results. The operators tended toward the practical. Reeder knew from conversations with the AMF members that they had no desire to serve in an Afghan army unit far from their homes. Few would volunteer. Instead, many militia members transitioned to a paid security force, which was confined to guarding the perimeter of the special operations forces' firebases.[12]

Two weeks before the end of his tour in 2007, Reeder watched Mahaney's troops crush the Taliban in Operation Adalat. "It was like shooting fish in a barrel," Reeder said. The battalion had been hugely successful in blunting the Taliban's drive to retake the south.

As he packed up to go home, the champion of the counterguerrilla fight had an epiphany. How many times had special forces done this? To what end? Reeder asked himself. They simply were not getting anywhere with the constant raiding approach. They could conduct raids for the next one hundred years and not finish off the Taliban. "It seems like every time I come back here, the security situation is worse," he thought. "Maybe we need to do something different."

Before leaving the country, Reeder had several long talks with the CIA station chief in Kabul, who was also a friend of his. They discussed how the Taliban, a force of maybe 20,000, was managing to affect a country of 33 million. The Taliban had no trouble recruiting fighters, albeit largely inexperienced ones. The destabilizing cycle could go on forever. It was going to take a different approach to change this pattern. How had the Taliban taken control of Afghanistan in the first place? And now, how had they managed to make a comeback in 2005–2006, despite averaging only 10 percent support in public opinion polls conducted within Afghanistan? Admittedly, those polls primarily measured the views of urban Afghans and those in easy-to-reach, and therefore non-insurgent-dominated, areas. But what were the Taliban doing right—and could the special ops forces learn from it?[13]

Reeder spent the next year working as the executive officer for Admiral Eric Olson, the four-star admiral in charge of US Special Operations Command in Tampa, and continued to think about his experience in Afghanistan. He concluded that he could have done things differently. First, he realized, special forces needed to have a better understanding of the tribal dynamics of the country. The Taliban had used their knowledge of those dynamics to win over smaller tribes and subtribes by supporting their grievances against the bigger or more powerful tribes. Second, there was a need for a greater emphasis on defense, and especially on helping Afghans protect their own homes. To date, the special operations forces had focused on using Afghans as offensive tools to attack suspected Taliban enclaves, whether because they wanted to fight or because they were eager for the paycheck. Civilian self-defense was not a new idea for special operations forces; US special forces had conducted the largest such effort to date in Vietnam among the highland tribes, in what was called the Civilian Irregular Defense Group. The Marines had a similar village defense focus in their Combined Action Program.

Reeder was introduced to a political scientist named Seth Jones who had spent the past five years researching a book on Afghanistan. Jones had examined how the Taliban had taken power after the end of the Soviet occupation in 1989, and he had found that they had recruited one tribe and village after another through a series of deals, eventually taking over the entire countryside before closing in on Kabul in 1996. Looking further back in history, he found that the five decades of the Musahiban dynasty's rule had been largely stable, in part because the monarchs struck agreements with rural Afghans to maintain security in their own areas. The Pashtuns, in particular, were far more inclined to police themselves than they were to allow others to run their affairs. Thomas Barfield, an American anthropologist who had studied the country for more than forty years, characterized its social history as relying on a decentralized model of security and governance in which the ruler in Kabul traditionally controlled the pursestrings, doling out money and patronage to regional power centers that in turn were expected to keep the peace in their areas.[14]

Meanwhile, Admiral Olson had been pushing for the creation of a special ops command in both Afghanistan and Iraq led by a general instead of a colonel. He realized that a command in the region led by a colonel was simply not adequate. Each colonel that had headed it had struggled with a short staff, haphazardly filled with a few additional personnel. The churn was also a problem: the staff turned over every seven months. Most of all, a colonel simply could not get into the room where the big decisions were made. The number of generals and admirals in Afghanistan had steadily increased, and it took a quantum leap in 2009 when a new three-star operational command was created. That command, the ISAF Joint Command (known as the IJC), eventually tripled in size, to 3,000 staff and 19 generals and admirals.[15]

The four-star general in charge of the Afghan war, General David D. McKiernan, agreed with the petition of Olson and others. Combined Forces Special Operations Component Command–Afghanistan (CFSOCC-A) was created in 2009, and Olson recommended Reeder as its first commander.

When Reeder arrived in Kabul, he found that McKiernan had already approved and launched a local defense experiment called the Afghan Public Protection Program, or AP3. The pilot was implemented in Wardak, a critical province bordering Kabul, in January 2009 by Brad Moses, a special forces company commander. Afghans would recruit candidates who would be approved by the local *shura*, or consultative council. Recruits were vetted by the National Directorate of Security (NDS), the Afghan intelligence service performing internal security functions—the Afghan equivalent of the FBI. Given uniforms and paid half the salary of policemen, the recruits, following training, would be put to work as security guards at mosques, schools, bazaars, and other sites chosen by the locals. The AP3 volunteers were paid and armed with AK-47s through the Ministry of Interior, with the special forces providing the initial three-week training program.

The initial pilot was approved with a ceiling of 1,200 recruits, but this number was expected to increase to as many as 10,000 if the pilot was successful. According to Brad Moses, the effort got off to a good start. But then it went sideways, owing to two main factors. First, the recruiting, vetting, training, and oversight role was handed off from special operations forces to the conventional unit in the province in mid-2009, and they did not spend enough time with the newly minted defenders to properly mentor them. The force then morphed from a self-defense effort into a highway police force defending Highway One. Recruits from other provinces began filling the ranks, setting the stage for AP3 to morph again, this time into a bribe-taking shake-down operation. Second, a local Wardak figure, Ghulam Mohammad Hotak, a former Taliban commander, switched sides. Moses regarded Hotak as highly nefarious and refused to involve him with the program during his tenure. But in December 2009, the Afghan government permitted Hotak to form his own lightly supervised AP3 contingent.[16]

Reeder discussed expanding the AP3 program with McKiernan, but the latter doubted that NATO would agree. "They will think you are promoting warlords and militias," McKiernan said. Reeder believed his idea would get off the ground only if influential Afghans embraced the effort. He went to see Sibghatullah Mojaddedi, the president of the Afghan Senate who had been president of the country in 1992. An important Sunni religious figure, Mojaddedi embraced the idea. "The only way you are going to protect the population is to arm them," he said. "But you must put the special forces in the villages to prevent ethnic or tribal cleansing."[17]

Reeder also set his staff to work on a slightly different concept from AP3, which they dubbed the Community Defense Initiative. Mahaney, who had come back for a sixth tour as Reeder's operations officer, enthusiastically embraced this pivot to putting local Afghans in charge of securing their villages. As if the scales had fallen from their eyes, he and his 7th Special Forces Group veterans saw that they had applied this self-help approach for years in Latin America, first in El Salvador and then in Peru and Colombia. Their emphasis had to shift to assisting rather than leading Afghans, and in a very deliberate and carefully structured way. Civil defense was not a replacement for the national army or a local police force, but an adjunct to them. Reeder's staff began to do the rigorous evaluation of Afghanistan's tribal mosaic that had been lacking. It was the beginning of a campaign approach guided by an overarching concept and plan.

Reeder thought the best model was a volunteer defense force with villagers taking shifts. He believed this approach would prevent any one faction from dominating other members of the community. He also wanted the defenders to bring their own guns, and he wanted to limit the US contribution to training and development projects. In his view, these limits would mitigate the risks. If the men were paid, and the pay ran out, a disgruntled armed local would be more likely to turn to nefarious activity than someone who was a volunteer to begin with. He wanted the solution to be something the Afghans could sustain. The interior minister, however, insisted that they be paid, and so they were.

On May 11, 2009, US Defense Secretary Robert Gates asked for McKiernan's resignation. McKiernan was a thoughtful general, but not decisive enough, or so the Obama White House concluded as it completed its yearlong review of Afghan policy. Stan McChrystal, the hard-charging special ops counterterrorism chieftain, was picked as the next commander and promoted to four-star general. He had gained fame in the inner circle of national security leaders from his days in Iraq, where he had turned his unit into a ferociously effective, relentless machine to hunt down Al Qaeda and Sunni insurgents.

Shortly after McChrystal arrived in June, Reeder and Jones went to talk to him about local defense. Reeder asked him what he wanted to do about AP3. McChrystal was noncommittal. "I don't want to kill it, but let's reassess in six months," he said. They described the fledgling Community Defense Initiative and the development projects. "We have to get Karzai to ask for it, to ask the US to do it," Reeder said. "It has to be an Afghan program or it won't work. It will just be seen as another Western program."[18]

The next day, McChrystal raised the idea with Karzai over breakfast at the presidential palace. When he returned he sent the message through his staff: "Tell Reeder thumbs up." Reeder proceeded to launch the Community Defense Initiative in July, but he noted that there was no overt sign of support from Karzai.

Reeder directed his special operators in the field to be on the lookout for spontaneous anti-Taliban activity. They would find it in Gizab in 2010, a village overrun by the Taliban a few years earlier. It was pure serendipity that the team was in the area, however. Reeder planted the seeds by sending a team to Day Kundi Province, 25 miles from Gizab, after its governor came to see him. The governor complained that his province did not reap any benefits in aid or attention because it was not a hotbed of insurgency. "I want a PRT," he said, referring to the provincial reconstruction teams that brought development projects and government training to provinces. A building had been built, but no development workers had ever arrived. Day Kundi was not a priority because it was peaceful. Its population was ethnic Hazara, Shia Muslims who had been brutally persecuted by the Taliban. Reeder sympathized with the governor, but he had no authority over PRTs. He offered instead to send a twelve-man special forces team, ten naval construction workers (called Seabees), and a "radio in a box" manned by psyop soldiers. They would hire local Afghans as deejays to produce programs and play music. The grateful governor burst into tears.

The team settled into the PRT building and began getting to

know the neighborhood. Several months later, the residents of Gizab decided they had had enough of the Taliban. When the uprising in Gizab occurred, the team moved in to help. Reeder also made sure the Shia religious leaders knew what they were doing to help the Hazaran Shia, who were the majority population in this area. Iran was heavily courting Afghan Shia to build its own avenues of influence. Reeder went to see the senior Shia cleric in Kabul, Ayatollah Shaikh Mohammed Mohseni, who was surprised by the overture. Reeder insisted on taking his boots off at the mosque door, and the cleric later invited him to come on Sundays to pray after his own Christian tradition. Like most other Afghans, the ayatollah thought that all special operators did were night raids, so Reeder kept him apprised of their projects such as renovations of mosques and provision of medical care. He sent him a CNN report on the team providing first aid for a Shia child who had been medivacked to Kandahar for surgery, and the cleric rebroadcast the information on his own television show.

Reeder's burgeoning Afghan Rolodex led other commanders to his door. They used his Pashtun network to help tone down Karzai's periodic anti-American tirades. At McChrystal's request, Reeder asked the powerful Karzai ally Jan Mohammad Khan to meet with outraged elders following a devastating special ops raid in Uruzgan in February 2010 that mistakenly killed twenty-seven civilians. When Private Bowe Bergdahl went missing in Paktika Province, Ed Reeder called the former governor of Uruzgan, a former Taliban deputy minister who had joined the government. The latter's contacts said that the soldier had been taken across the border to Miran Shah in Pakistan. A week later, in response to Reeder's appeals for information, Qayum Karzai, the president's brother, visited Reeder in Kabul and gave him a note from the kidnappers demanding $19 million and the release of twenty-five prisoners at the Guantanamo Bay detention camp in exchange for Bergdahl's release. He also gave him a video, the first proof that Bergdahl was still alive. Karzai had obtained both via a Pashtun who had traveled to Miran Shah. Reeder later received a second message, which lowered the ransom demand to $5 million and dropped the demand to release detainees, but to his surprise, none of his superiors followed up on it.[19]

Did Reeder's close relationships wind up empowering Afghan leaders and powerbrokers? Probably, at least in some cases. Reeder's perspective was that he had to deal with the Afghans who wielded significant influence. His ties no doubt helped the United States understand the machinations going on at any given moment within Afghanistan, but a lot of Afghan skullduggery was overlooked in the name of friendship, leaving open the question of whether more tough love would have reined in some of the corruption. As the massive flow of US funds ratcheted up the corruption to new heights, the coalition formed a task force aimed at peeling apart the web of money and influence in order to stop malfeasance and worse. Contract procedures were tightened, but very few insiders went to jail.

By the time Reeder left in March 2010, special operations teams had formed local defense groups in seven sites around the country. Some of the sites did not work out—in Achin in Nangahar Province, for example, an anti-Taliban uprising devolved into tribal and land conflicts. In Arghandab, just north of Kandahar City, however, Karimullah Naqib eagerly sought a special forces team to come to his valley to push out the Taliban. This would become one of the most successful and enduring sites. That bond had been forged in 2007, when Naqib had credited Mahaney's men with saving his life after he had come under attack as the newly anointed head of the Alikozai subtribe. Local defense was still nascent, but it was now more than an idea.

The year 2010 marked a pivot for special operations forces as they turned away from pure combat operations to embrace local defense as a viable way to bring security to a largely rural society. Before this new direction could get off the ground, however, there would be more turmoil at the top.

CHAPTER TWO

INTO THE VILLAGES

KABUL 2010–KUNDUZ 2011

THE BATTLE FOR BUY-IN

Scott Miller, the special ops general who took over in March 2010 after Reeder's departure, would take up the torch of civil defense and add his own, significant twist during his year and a half at the helm. But first he needed to bring the rest of the military, the US embassy, and the Afghan government on board. Civil defense may have been an old idea that special operators had just rediscovered, but it was controversial in Afghanistan. The biggest objection was the fear that any such effort would empower the warring militias that had viciously torn apart the country in the 1990s. Proponents of the idea emphasized that what they had in mind were small, village-based defensive groups. Historically, Pashtun tribal elders had raised *lashkars* or *chalwesti*, armed defense groups from the community, to respond to threats and then disbanded them when they were dealt with. This was quite different from the large militias, some numbering 30,000 or more, that were formed in the 1980s by Afghan mujahideen and warlords to fight the Soviet occupation.[1]

This Afghan history was complicated by the succession of programs the United States had backed or started since arriving in 2001, none of which had calmed concerns, and which led many to assume that the same ad hoc, offensive-minded, and manipulation-prone results would ensue this time. Opposition extended from Afghans—although Karzai had periodically favored the idea of self-defense for Pashtuns, and his brother Qayum certainly did—to nongovernmental organizations, such as human rights groups, to retired general Karl Eikenberry, whom the Obama administration had appointed as ambassador to Kabul. Reeder thought Eikenberry would support the Community Defense Initiative because these groups were to be strictly defensive, but a ninety-minute meeting failed to persuade him.[2]

Eikenberry's skepticism extended to the entire US venture. He doubted that Hamid Karzai was "an adequate strategic partner," as one of his leaked cables put it. The debate over local defense was only one element of a remarkable and crippling struggle over US policy that continued even after the Obama administration completed its extended policy review in 2009. The administration defined the US objective narrowly—preventing the restoration of an Al Qaeda safe haven in Afghanistan—and gave the US military 33,000 troops and two years to achieve it. The bureaucratic warfare raged on, pitting those who felt the policy goal could be achieved by hitting Al Qaeda targets as they popped up against those who believed it required an Afghan government and security force capable of defending its territory from terrorists and other threats. McChrystal (in a somewhat paradoxical evolution, given his background as the master black ops terrorist hunter) became a vocal proponent of the latter counterinsurgency approach. An additional cohort believed that the Karzai government's corruption and parochialism were a principal cause of the reborn insurgency and that reform should be the central focus.[3]

McChrystal devoted a lot of time to building a relationship with Karzai and devising ways to promote better governance and economic development. He remained somewhat lukewarm about local defense—

perhaps because he and Reeder never got along well—until the arrival of Reeder's successor, Brigadier General Austin Scott Miller, in March 2010.

Miller had been serving as director of the Pakistan-Afghanistan Coordination Cell (PACC) at the Pentagon, which made him McChrystal's primary link to Washington. A rising star in the special operations community, Miller had earned McChrystal's trust as the commander of the Delta task force under McChrystal's Task Force 714. Miller's quiet manner contrasted with the brasher egos of his club, but his pedigree spoke for itself: he was a Delta Force veteran of the 1993 "Black Hawk Down" battle in Somalia, and he had commanded Delta Force in Iraq during the raging years of the Iraq War. He had helped to hunt down the number-one target in Iraq, Abu Musab al-Zarqawi, who was killed in June 2006. Miller's sincerity exerted a charismatic force that drew people into his orbit.

After 9/11, McChrystal and Miller had revolutionized special mission units. These units were already known as the most proficient shooters and rescue forces in the US military before 9/11. But the most difficult part of hunting terrorist leaders is finding them, not killing them, so McChrystal and Miller introduced three changes. First, they brought technical intelligence and intelligence analysts into their fold; second, they replaced a hierarchical command-and-control structure with a flatter organizational model that fostered constant communication and encouraged subordinates to take the initiative. Then they set a relentless pace powered by the first two changes.[4]

Miller took the same meticulous approach as he prepared to take over for Reeder: assembling the expertise, building a network, and preparing it to work overtime. The secret to special operators' tactical prowess was constant training and careful preparation of their kit, and Miller believed in the same zealous attention to detail as a commander. He was keen to prove himself on a new mission in a new theater. Although he was known to Delta, as well as to Rangers and SEAL Team Six, for the first time he would be leading a force that included other SEAL, special forces, civil affairs, and psyop units. He was acutely aware that some in the special forces hierarchy viewed him as an interloper from the "black side" of special ops and were discouraging those who wanted to join his team. Miller recognized that special forces were trained to work with indigenous populations and had spent the past decade in Afghanistan, and he augmented their expertise with social scientists and created a program called Afghanistan-Pakistan (AFPAK) Hands to produce a deeper bench of knowledge.

When he arrived in Kabul in March 2010, Miller had ideas for the local defense program aimed at increasing its chance of success and decreasing the risk that it would spawn out-of-control militias. First, he needed to bring McChrystal fully on board. Shortly after arriving, Miller gave him a briefing that one aide described as "transformative." McChrystal, now fully convinced of the need to address Afghanistan's conflict at the village level, agreed to seek Karzai's formal and public concurrence so the machinery could be created for a full-fledged government program.[5]

McChrystal did not carry the ball very far down the field, however. His military career came to an abrupt end following the publication of a *Rolling Stone* article on June 22, 2010, in which he and his aides were described and quoted as criticizing the White House and Vice President Joe Biden in scathing terms. McChrystal flew to Washington with a resignation letter in hand, which Obama accepted on the spot. The next day, Obama asked General David Petraeus, then the head of Central Command in Tampa, to take the post, which he did on July 4.[6]

Petraeus did not need to be sold on local defense; he believed it was a potential game changer in a war that was going badly. Given that most Afghans lived in villages, Petraeus felt that "bottom-up" efforts would temper the highly centralized government system in which all provincial governors, mayors, district subgovernors, and generals were appointed by the president. Petraeus had done something similar in Iraq with his Sons of Iraq initiative, which started in Anbar as the "Sunni Awakening" and which he extended throughout greater Baghdad in 2007 and 2008. But the Sons of Iraq movement had been undertaken rapidly, with few guidelines and—most important—without the endorsement of the Iraqi government. Iraq's

Shia government later largely reneged on its commitment to incorporate Sons of Iraq into the regular police or army—a commitment extracted under duress and late in the game. By making the Afghan local police an Afghan government program from the start, Petraeus hoped to avoid those pitfalls.[7]

Before deciding whether to endorse the program, President Karzai presided over several contentious meetings at the presidential palace, which was nestled in a wooded park a few blocks from the yellow and burgundy mansion that housed ISAF headquarters. It took the single-minded Petraeus only ten days to secure Karzai's agreement to the local defense initiative, which was renamed Afghan Local Police (ALP). On August 16, Karzai signed a formal decree spelling out the specific terms of the program.

Karzai insisted on a key feature: that the Afghan Ministry of the Interior would administer the program. The ministry would validate Afghan Local Police guardians, who would be recruited and vetted by local Afghan shuras, and they would report to Afghan police chiefs. Americans would train the recruits and pay their part-time salaries of $120 monthly plus a $65 food voucher until they were put on the ministry payroll. The ministry would provide pay, weapons, ammunition, uniforms, and radios. The program would sunset in three (later extended to five) years. The total force was to be capped at 30,000, and no more than 300 defenders would be recruited from any one district. These provisions were intended to ensure that the force would be carefully formed and closely overseen.[8]

MILLER'S NEW IDEA

Miller's mission was to ensure that the program worked as intended and that the many pitfalls were avoided so that the local defense effort would contribute to a turnabout in the war. Ironically, Miller pushed the local defense concept even further than its original framers had envisioned. "It took a black ops guy from [the special mission units] to understand the limits of kill and capture," his command sergeant major, J. R. Stigall, commented.[9]

Miller's new idea was village stability operations: that Afghan local policemen by themselves were not sufficient to bring peace to rural Afghanistan, and the country had to be stabilized from the village level up. He got the idea while reading about pacification in Vietnam in a 1999 book by Lewis Sorley, *A Better War: The Unexamined Victories and the Final Tragedy of America's Last Years in Vietnam*. Miller renamed the program "Village Stability Operations/Afghan Local Police," or VSO/ALP. The name was cumbersome, but he wanted to stress that the goal was community mobilization, to help villages identify and address the problems that were creating conflict and instability in their area. Special operations teams were ordered to focus on village stability operations as a first step, and only if and when the villagers decided they needed and wanted to form a local police group would they proceed to do so. Under the Community Defense Initiative, development assistance had been provided to villages, but this new approach made governance and development coequal legs of the triad. The closest parallel in recent special operations history had been the deployment of special forces teams to villages all over Haiti after Haiti's military junta was ousted and the elected government restored in 1994.[10] Miller's plan was to rebuild Afghan stability one village at a time. It was nothing if not ambitious.

Miller wanted to find an enduring solution, not quick fixes that would later unravel because teams were relying on dubious characters or had failed to understand village dynamics. He tapped development experts from the United States Agency for International Development (USAID) and RAND social scientists whom he invited to join his staff. It was his trademark move, to create a big tent of diverse talent. He had done this in Baghdad when he had convened a weekly video conference of all the conventional brigade commanders in order to share what his Task Force 16 operators were up to and to exchange information. For years special operators had not shared information with each other, let alone with their conventional brethren, who were, after all, the "battlespace owners" working there every day. This practice quickly reduced the tension and grudges that had built up in four years of night raids by the door kickers. In a similar move, when Miller set up the Pakistan-Afghanistan Coordination Cell in the Pentagon, the walls were literally taken down in the national military command center in the bowels of the building to create an open bay of cubicles where the intelligence, plans, and operations staffs were relocated to work side by side. Every Friday, he presided over what was probably the largest regular video teleconference in the US government. At these "Federation Forum" meetings, a think-tank researcher or another expert would present new analysis, and McChrystal or his deputy and a dozen or more outposts in Afghanistan would tune in to give updates and join the discussion. The Pentagon conference room was crammed with an assortment of academics, analysts, and officials, with the White House, State Department, USAID, and multiple other agencies on the video link.

Miller used his network of experts and operators to figure out exactly what needed to be done, how to do it, and where to do it, and—perhaps most important—to design measures to ensure continuity of effort as units and commanders came and went. It was vital to stop the churn and ad hockery that had characterized special operations and prevented them from achieving lasting impact. First, a four-step process was fashioned that teams were directed to follow: shape, build, hold, transition. An SOF team was first to tour an area to gauge whether there was potential support for such a program. The "shaping" phase would usually entail some combat operations to reduce the insurgent presence and to create breathing room for villagers to begin to take charge of their affairs, but the combat was to be carried out by other forces—commandos or Afghan soldiers, or, if none of these were available, another coalition force. Only a few operations or detentions might suffice: Taliban domination was due in many cases to the absence of any government security force, officials, or services in much of rural Afghanistan. After the shaping operations, the SOF team, if invited, would move into the village or in the vicinity to begin phase two, building the program. As the villagers began taking ownership of their own security and resolving their issues, ideally with the help of the local district government, the effort would move into the third, or "hold," phase. Finally, the SOF team would transition the area to local control, while returning for regular visits to provide some fallback support.

Four basic criteria were developed for selecting the villages in which to embed the special ops teams. First, since the program's premise was helping Afghans who wanted special operations assistance, the teams would have to be invited in. Second, the villages should be ones that had already demonstrated the desire to resist the Taliban. Third, the location had to be logistically sustainable so that the teams could receive food, water, fuel, and ammunition. Fourth, the location should be consequential to the overall fight. This criterion was difficult to define and was interpreted in various ways. The basic idea was to look for and support resistance to the Taliban in the corridors and sanctuaries that led directly to population centers—in the words of one operator, "where the ratlines met the population."[11]

To avoid duplication of effort, the staff planners intended for the teams to avoid areas where conventional forces were already operating. But in some areas conventional forces might seek help, because they rarely reached below the level of the district center—which was equivalent to the county seat—to the villages where most Afghans lived. The same was true of the civilian coalition presence, where the lowest-level entity was the district support teams (DSTs) manned by personnel from the State Department, USAID, and sometimes the US Department of Agriculture. Fewer than fifty districts had DSTs. At the height of the surge, 1,040 civilian officials were sent to Afghanistan, but most of them remained in Kabul, or, at best, provincial capitals. Even where DSTs did exist, their ability to reach villages was limited by safety rules imposed by the US embassy. The essential difficulty in combating a rural insurgency resides in its dispersed nature, which requires commanders to make accurate decisions about where to place scarce manpower. It was easy enough to ascertain which of Afghanistan's thirty-four provinces mattered most in terms of insurgent threat, population, and political-economic value. The Taliban dominated a broad swath of rural Helmand, northern Kandahar, Uruzgan and Zabul, and the eastern border provinces, which were laced with ratlines that intersected population centers of varying size. Highway One, the major artery running from Kandahar through Zabul, Ghazni, and Wardak to Kabul, was bisected by many valleys where the Taliban rested and resupplied themselves and through which they moved. The difficulty lay in deciding where to focus within the key provinces: Which of Afghanistan's 398 districts and 30,000 villages ought to be the focus of the teams' efforts?[12]

The list of districts that special ops teams would scout for willing villages was determined in conjunction with the newly appointed minister of interior, Bismullah Khan Mohammedi (BK). One hundred districts were initially agreed upon. The majority of the districts on the list were in the south and east, where the vast majority of the insurgents were located, but approximately one-third of the districts BK endorsed were in the north and west. Local defense was justifiable in some strategic and vulnerable spots—for example, the districts around the Salang Tunnel, the principal transportation artery to the northern border, or critical passes in the west. And in the largely Tajik and Uzbek north, some pockets of Pashtuns had become insurgent havens. But BK and Vice President Mohammed Qasim Fahim Khan saw the program not so much as a tool to combat insurgents as an opportunity for a jobs program for their Tajik constituents, and perhaps a way to rebuild militias that had been demobilized in 2002 and 2003. Even if the insurgency was largely in the Pashtun south and east, they were not keen to create a force of 30,000 armed Pashtuns.

Implementing the program would take all the special forces, SEALs, and Marine special operations teams the United States could muster. A few teams remained partnered with the Afghan commandos, and the Task Force 535 units remained focused on counterterrorist raids. Admiral Eric Olson, the four-star admiral in charge of US Special Operations Command, pushed through requests for more army special forces teams as well as special operations civil affairs and military information support (psyops) teams. Between April 2010 and March 2011, the number of special operations forces assigned to the mission doubled, increasing from 2,900 to 5,900.[13]

Even with the extra special operators, Petraeus saw that they would not have enough manpower for the widely dispersed rural sites. In

November 2010, he asked the army for a conventional army infantry battalion that he would place under Miller's operational control. The army was not enamored of this idea, but Petraeus insisted that it was critical to the success of his campaign. The army was loath to chop conventional units away from their chain of command to work under special operators. Even more unpalatable was that the battalion's squads were to be parceled out to help secure the teams' remote sites and thicken their patrols. It was a huge responsibility to levy on young platoon and squad leaders, and discipline would be at risk. Moreover, the battalion commander's career path could be compromised, because he would not be leading an intact unit in the traditional way.

On short notice, 1-16 Infantry Battalion of the 1st Infantry Division at Fort Riley was sent to Afghanistan in January 2011. Petraeus requested a second battalion, and the 1-505th of the 82nd Airborne Division arrived in June 2011. The latter battalion had the advantage of a longer lead time to prepare for the unusual mission, and since it was based at Fort Bragg, it linked up immediately with the US Army Special Operations Command and the 3rd Special Forces Group for training. The 82nd Airborne tapped one of its best young officers, Lieutenant Colonel Curtis Buzzard. He selected those of his battalion he believed were best suited for the task. Many soldiers who had served in Iraq during the surge had rotated through small outposts, but this time they would be serving an extended tour out in a very primitive, rural environment. It was to be a round-the-clock, months-long experience of going native. Young soldiers used to Wi-Fi, Facebook, video games, chow halls, and regimented formations would have to adapt.

Buzzard was named the commander of Special Operations Task Force–North (SOTF-N) based in Mazar-e Sharif. Special forces battalions retained command of the teams in the south and east. Navy SEALs took command of a newly formed Special Operations Task Force–Southeast, covering Uruzgan, Day Kundi, and Zabul. The Marines and the 1st Special Forces Group traded command of teams in the west and southwest. Marine Special Operations teams made up the majority of teams assigned to the west and to Helmand, where

Marines had assumed control of the battlespace from the British in 2009.

All these battalion-level SOTFs reported to CJSOTF-A, now led by Colonel Don Bolduc, who in turn reported to Miller. Bolduc was every bit as driven and meticulous as his boss, although the personalities of the two men could not have been more different. Bolduc was outspoken—known to challenge men to pushup contests—and toyed with the idea of running for political office when he retired. He wrote articles and enjoyed attention, whereas Miller did not relish the limelight. The CJSOTF oversaw the tactical day-to-day operations and the resupply of the far-flung teams. Bolduc pushed authority down to the teams to conduct patrols as they saw fit within their designated "ops boxes," only requiring approval of about 8 percent of the missions where contact with other forces or combat was deemed likely.

FROM BLACK OPS TO VILLAGE OPS

For the emphasis on village stability to be more than rhetorical, Miller set up an apparatus to ensure an equal focus on the governance and development elements of the program. He knew that special ops teams would have their hands full focusing on the security leg of the triad. So he created Village Stability Coordination Centers (VSCCs), which were located alongside the battalion SOTF commands, and sent his trusted lieutenant, Lieutenant Colonel Scott Mann, who had been part of Reeder's original design team, to Kandahar as the first VSCC-South coordinator.[14] The VSCCs were not intended to do governance and development work themselves, but rather to help teams find governance and development resources in the Afghan government and the coalition. The VSCCs were to tie the "top down" to the "bottom up." They were expected to reach out to the regional commands and their civilian counterparts and find those with expertise, programs, or funds. In addition, they would engage with nongovernmental organizations and cull or produce analysis to better understand the specific districts. The VSCCs embodied the network ideas that Miller had employed as a terrorist-hunter.

Miller also formed a national-level node of the VSCC at ISAF in Kabul to reach out directly to the Afghan ministries responsible for local governance, rural development, and agriculture and help bring their programs to the districts once the teams had achieved sufficient security. The national coordinator, Colonel Randy Zeegers, the 20th Special Forces Group commander, formed an especially close relationship with the Ministry of Rural Reconstruction and Development, arranging visits for its officials to newly secure districts so they could assess the situation for themselves and authorize the formation of community development councils and the initiation of projects the villagers chose.

A third layer of the network consisted of the Provincial Augmentation Teams and District Augmentation Teams, dubbed PATs and DATs. These positions were manned by the AFPAK Hands program that Miller had launched while on the Joint Staff with backing from the chairman of the Joint Chiefs of Staff, Mike Mullen. Military personnel who volunteered to become AFPAK Hands were asked to commit to serving at least two tours in Afghanistan, and in return they were provided with language and academic training and stateside positions that would allow them to remain engaged in between their tours. The objective was to develop a cadre of expertise that had been lacking since the beginning of the war. Miller was the first AFPAK Hand, and many special forces officers signed up as well, in addition to Air Force and Navy personnel.

Miller stayed in Afghanistan longer than most commanders, from March 2010 until July 2011. His headquarters was located at the New Kabul Compound at the bustling traffic circle a block from the US embassy and the ISAF headquarters. Many Afghans thought the base was a prison because of its prominent guard towers and high walls, which were topped by green netting that obscured views into the camp. High-wattage lights mounted on poles glared out to the street all night long. But inside the compound, three drab beige and brown buildings were surrounded by a warren of Quonset tents and a two-story stack of "man cans," trailers that contained beds, flimsy wardrobes, and, occasionally, desks. The ground was covered with fist-sized gravel, which crunched under the booted feet of the troops. The grim, utilitarian military architecture of concrete walls and concertina wire did evoke a prison, an aesthetically numbing environment in which military personnel and contractors measured their days in chow hours and physical training (PT) breaks from their deskbound labors. In a bit of gallows humor, the gym in the basement of the main building was named the Dungeon.

Miller's diverse staff hailed from every tribe of the special operations community. His chief of staff, Geno Paluso, a SEAL captain, and his army command sergeant major, J. R. Stigall, ran a tight ship. His deputy commander was Pat Mahaney initially, and then Alex Krongaard, another SEAL captain who would soon be promoted to rear admiral. Describing Miller as "a shorter version of McChrystal," Paluso said, "There are a lot of general and flag officers here. Very few of them could've done what he has done." Paluso had arrived in December 2009 and would stay for two and a half long years. Miller inspired intense loyalty among his staff by working even harder than he drove them. Unlike his former boss, McChrystal, Miller did not post a sign, but the staff understood that the same rules applied: they were expected to work seventeen hours a day and use the other five for sleep, exercise, and meals.[15]

Miller brought two practices with him from his black ops experience, in addition to the punishing work pace: flat networks and communications. He convened VSCC and other video teleconferences that consumed hours each day: these kept Miller in touch with every echelon and allowed the lowest levels to raise concerns or express opinions he might not otherwise hear. "Over-communicate" was one of his mottoes. It was Miller's preferred method of command, whether he was hunting terrorists or stabilizing villages. He always checked in with Petraeus and other senior commanders before reaching out to their subordinates, and Petraeus increasingly trusted him to deal with senior Afghans.[16]

Miller was also determined to fix the problems of continuity that had plagued the special operations effort in Afghanistan until now. In addition to holding commanders conferences that cast a wide net, he and Scott Mann institutionalized a week-long predeployment course in the United States called SOF Academic Week. It offered up an extensive curriculum on the methodology they developed for local police and village stability as well as a rich menu of Afghan, Pashtun, and Islamic expertise, with native speakers, experts, retired intelligence officers, and returning operators. It was open to conventional units as well, and soon over a thousand soldiers and general officers were signing up to attend whenever these were held. Miller's staff and the RAND experts in his initiatives group produced videos, research papers, and manuals. One of the special forces officers who attended the SOF Week training voiced amazement at the degree to which Miller had embraced and elevated the standards of what building and advising indigenous forces should mean. "He gets it more than many of our own," he said.

Miller spent four or five days each week visiting his troops around the country. He wangled funds from Central Command for a fleet of a half-dozen Beechcraft 1900 contract planes to ferry special operations personnel around their bases. One of the most important functions of Miller's circulation was to try to ensure that his teams were receiving the support they needed from the two-star regional commands and their subordinate brigades, which were called the "battlespace owners." The special operations teams had their own chain of command straight up to the four-star ISAF headquarters, which did not include the conventional forces' regional commanders and their brigades, but the latter could exercise the "choke-con" of special operations forces by withholding airlift, attack helicopters, or convoys to resupply food, fuel, and ammunition. As a one-star general, Miller was a junior in a sea of generals, but his prior relationships with other commanders, many of them forged in Iraq, enabled him to have more influence than he otherwise would have had.

Miller traveled constantly—not only to stay in touch with the situation, but also to provide direct moral support. "What do you need?" was his constant refrain. Although many officers asked this question, the general had a way of making people feel like he genuinely cared. On one occasion, he flew to Mazar-e Sharif for a promotion ceremony and to award Purple Hearts and met with his battalion commanders from the north, south, east, and west who had flown in for the event. Later, Miller spoke frankly to his subordinates about the casualties that operators had incurred and demanded better attention to their needs. He then sat down for a briefing from the captain whose team was the partner for the Afghan commandos assigned to the north. Miller arranged for him to try out for Delta Force. Then he boarded a Chinook to fly east to neighboring Kunduz Province, where he attended a graduation ceremony for newly trained members of the Afghan Local Police, along with the German general who was the Regional Command–North (RC-North) commander. The Afghans sat uncomfortably under the blazing sun in red plastic chairs lined up before a stage as they were called up one by one to receive their diplomas. Miller, the introvert, was equally unhappy to be on stage, his smile more of a grimace. He had also wrenched his back lifting weights. He stood at attention as the team members—decked out in new, sharply pressed *shalwar kameezes*, or man jammies, as soldiers called them, and the wool muffin-shaped *pakol* hats commonly worn by the Tajiks of the north—shook hands with every new graduate.

Miller gained an education in the complex national political dynamics of Afghanistan as he spent an increasing amount of time on Tajik demands and reactions to any instability in the north. Hamid Karzai was a Pashtun, but he had struck key Tajik alliances. For most of Miller's tenure, BK ran the Ministry of Defense and Fahim Khan was one of the vice presidents. Both were Tajiks. Another Tajik, a rival Northern Alliance commander, the powerful Atta Mohammad Noor, was governor of Balkh Province, where Mazar-e Sharif was located. In addition, the top ranks of the Afghan army and police force, as well as the NDS, the Afghan intelligence service, were largely occupied by Tajiks from the Northern Alliance. For all intents and purposes, Tajiks ran Kabul, and thus the country, from a security perspective. Karzai had reinforced this power-sharing arrangement in his reelection bid by making Fahim one of his vice presidents, thus ensuring the support of this powerful, organized minority. Karzai maintained and controlled a shifting cast of ministers, commanders, and provincial and district governors through a heavily centralized constitution, which granted him authority to appoint all of these positions. Late in Miller's tour, after the police commander in the north was assassinated by a Taliban suicide bomber, he watched with concern as the Tajik leaders rallied former militia members to gird for the possible return of the vicious civil war of the 1990s. "They are getting the band back together," he muttered with foreboding.[17]

Miller did not sugarcoat the difficulty of what they were attempting. After a visit to Zabul Province, he said grimly, "There is not one district that isn't controlled by the Taliban," dismissing official reports that glossed over this inconvenient fact. But that did not mean he was pessimistic about the prospects for village stability and the local defense effort. He kept after the teams to be rigorous in implementing the procedures they had so painstakingly crafted. "The population will see if they do not pick the right leader or recruits," he said. So the ultimate failsafe would be for the teams to keep their ears and eyes open and to correct course if they got it wrong.

Miller had imposed a new standard for detailed planning and execution of special operations, but he understood that success or failure would ultimately be determined at the ground level. He could try to set the conditions for success, but the art of the endeavor was practiced by the teams. Although he had formed an analytical assessment cell to develop ways to measure progress or the lack of it, it would take time to know whether the teams were able to midwife stability in the villages, much less whether their efforts would have any impact beyond the immediate environment. Would the Afghan district and provincial police chiefs prove capable of overseeing the new force? Would the initiative in fact help turn the tide of the war, as Petraeus and others hoped? They might not know until long after they departed whether they had left Afghanistan better able to fend off the Taliban. All Miller could do was give the teams and their Afghan partners a fighting chance.

First, they would have to survive. Since the beginning of the war, army special forces teams had been living out in the hinterlands in about a dozen small firebases along the border and in parts of the rural south, but they were now going even farther off the grid. Not since Vietnam would so many special operators be scattered in small teams living in such remote, hostile places. Dozens of teams were moving into remote villages where they were much more exposed to ambush and attack. Their first line of defense was to get to know the Afghan villagers among whom they were now living, and quickly build a human intelligence network while practicing good security tactics. If that failed to deter attacks, the teams were equipped with an arsenal of ground-based power, including individual and crew-served weapons such as M-16s, M240 squad automatic weapons (SAWs), .50-caliber machine guns, and miniguns. If they were overrun, the teams' vital link to external defensive and offensive power was the Air Force combat controller from the special tactics squadrons who was assigned to each army, SEAL, and Marine team. He would talk to the overhead surveillance assets and call for air support. On high-risk patrols, he would request an air weapons team to be on call, and in emergencies he would place the 911 call to any birds in the area. The air weapons team might be attack helicopters from a conventional unit controlled by the regional command, fast movers such as F-16s or F-15s controlled by the theater command, and/or one of the special operations command's own AC-130 gunships, a lumbering plane that packed a fearsome array of firepower.

The catch was that all of this awesome firepower had to be applied in very precise conditions to avoid civilian casualties. Living among the villagers would severely constrain the team members. The special operators were no longer supposed to be conducting set-piece battles such as those Pat Mahaney had led, but rather, teaching the fishermen how to fish.

CHAPTER THREE

THE TALIBAN'S HOME

KANDAHAR 2010–2011

"WHO WILL GO WITH ME?"

The framers of the local defense initiative recognized that Kandahar was the single most important province, so it received the greatest number of special operations teams. It was also the hardest place in which to find willing volunteers, because it was the cradle of the Taliban—its spiritual home, where it had regrouped while the coalition was sleeping. Taliban leader Mullah Omar had ruled from Kandahar, and before the Taliban came to power he had taught at a madrassa west of the city. Once ousted, he took up residence in Quetta, Pakistan, just a few hours' drive away.

Kandahar Province's landowning khans had largely fled to the city of Kandahar, and tenant farmers, left to fend for themselves, were easily cowed. In 2010, Taliban influence in the province overshadowed the government almost everywhere outside of Kandahar City. The insurgency asserted itself as a ubiquitous presence through the use of threatening night letters, summary justice dispensed by shadow courts, and thugs on motorcycles carrying AK-47s or PKM machine guns. Even if most Kandaharis rejected this extremist version of Islamic rule, survival instincts dictated compliance. The Taliban was, for young men, a source of seasonal employment, especially after the cash crops of opium and hashish were harvested.

The natural landscape of Kandahar was far less intimidating than the rugged mountains that characterized most of the insurgent belt in the south and east. The province is mostly flat, with small humps of mountains springing up here and there on dun-colored plains. The irrigated land between the Arghandab and Helmand rivers serves as the breadbasket of the south and the opium capital of the world. South of the Arghandab, the blood-red Registan Desert runs in undulating ripples to Pakistan, crisscrossed by smuggling trails and nomadic Kuchi herders who camp in black cloth tents. The province's manmade landscape provides many guerrilla-friendly structures, such as arched grape-drying sheds dotted with tiny windows, which are perfect portholes for guns. Grape arbors made of chest-high walls of mud are impassable to Humvees and favor fighters on foot. Homemade bombs festoon their walls or the sides of the underground irrigation channels, called *karezes*, which from above look like holes bored by giant moles in a snaky line across the plains. Columns of insurgents can run underground and pop up miles away. Arched kilns, surrounded by high piles of freshly baked bricks, await customers and offer one more spot to hide.

In the summer of 2009, all of Kandahar Province was under siege, but there were few forces available to pull it back from the brink. In hindsight it seemed incredible that the United States had neglected the south, leaving it to small numbers of British and Canadian troops while Americans obsessed on the eastern border where bin Laden had last been seen. Realizing belatedly that the war was about to be lost, the Americans hastily threw the 5-2 Stryker Brigade into the fight. It was led by a man named Harry Tunnel who thought counterinsurgency was bunk. His troops proceeded to get chewed up in Arghandab District and then got even in Maiwand District, where a rogue "kill team" was subsequently prosecuted for extrajudicial killings. (Tunnel was investigated and absolved, but lower-level soldiers were eventually tried, and some were convicted.)

In November 2010, Major General James Terry arrived in Kandahar to lead Regional Command–South, the coalition headquarters, and attempt to turn the tide in his yearlong tour. His first order of business was to beat back the Taliban in an arc west of Kandahar City stretching from western Arghandab through Zhari and Panjwayi districts. Terry, who had fought here briefly with the Canadians in 2006, knew this was the epicenter of the Taliban insurgency in Afghanistan. The 2nd Brigade of the 101st Airborne endured heavy casualties in Zhari, suffering ninety killed and wounded, many of them multiple amputees. The perimeter around their base was so heavily mined that they used rocket-launched explosive mine-clearing line charges called "miclics" to blast open paths for vehicles or foot patrols.[1]

Unlike some conventional commanders, Terry was a big fan of special operations forces. He counted on them to provide a rural security blanket through the Afghan Local Police, because he did not have enough troops to do it himself. He practiced counterinsurgency with a blend of enemy- and population-centric tactics: after using clearing operations to dislodge the Taliban, he quickly brought district governors back to their districts to begin the "hearts and minds" work by providing essential services.

Terry met frequently with the special operations battalion commander, Chris Riga, who was the current occupant of the special ops' small patch of Kandahar Airfield. Special forces had claimed the cluster of blue and white buildings in 2001 and had been there ever since. Once part of the commercial airport, the long, low main building, with arched rooms and arcades, looked like a Hobbit motel. A few steps and a chain-link fence with a coded lock separated Riga's Camp Brown from Terry's headquarters, a building with a badly leaking roof surrounded by a stockade of two-story "man cans."

Riga had made quite a name for himself. Two months before Terry's arrival, at a provincial council meeting on September 14, the council chair and half-brother of the president, Ahmad Wali Karzai, announced that Afghan security forces would mount an all-out assault on western Arghandab. It would be led by a cocky and corrupt border policeman named Abdul Raziq. "Who will come with me?" Raziq asked. There was silence, and then Riga leaned forward. "I'll come with you," Riga said. Raziq got up from the table and started to leave. "When do we go?" Riga asked. "Are you ready? Let's go tomorrow," the itchy Afghan replied.[2]

Riga was primed for this scene. He had been called in by the British commander, Major General Nick Carter, a few days earlier. Carter explained to him that the Afghans were readying another offensive that was similar to the operation they had just launched in Malajat. Raziq had outpaced the conventional forces partnered with him in Malajat. This time, Carter said, the Afghans were prepared to go on their own, on orders of their president. "Can you partner with him?" Carter asked Riga. "Yes, we can partner with anyone," Riga told him. He had been coming to southern Afghanistan since the beginning of the war; this was his sixth tour. Carter was a bit surprised when he saw Wali Karzai and many other Afghan officials and council members greet Riga with hugs and kisses at the council meeting. Riga had met Raziq on a previous tour in Zabul as a company commander, but he had not worked with him before. He knew that Raziq had been accused of a tribally motivated killing of thirteen Afghans in 2006 and was alleged to have made a lot of money from the bustling commerce at his base in the border town of Spin Boldak.[3]

Riga and Raziq left the council meeting and repaired to another room in the municipal building to plan the first of what became a dozen operations throughout western Kandahar. The Americans would provide the helicopters, air support, and medevac, and conventional forces would form an outer perimeter as Riga and Raziq's men entered the villages. Riga and about a dozen of his men saddled up the next day to accompany Raziq and four hundred of his border police into one village after another. Helped by tips from local residents, on the first day they found over one hundred improvised explosive devices (IEDs). They captured about thirty Taliban in the first day. Riga found them to be younger and more poorly armed than the fighters he had seen in earlier years. "They had one or two magazines and little ammo, and no heavy machine guns," he said. The IED was now the weapon of choice.

In one day, Raziq had cleared a notorious insurgent stronghold and identified a spot for the conventional forces to set up a patrol base. He walked the conventional officers to the spot and then he and Riga moved on. Riga and his operations officer, Mike Sullivan, found that Raziq was a savvy tactician. His men were adept at spotting the lethal buried mines. They also had contacts in the districts, and the intelligence gathered allowed them to operate quickly. Both American officers said they saw no evidence of any human rights abuses in their operations with Raziq; nor did Sullivan hear of any when he debriefed the other operators who had been in the field with him. Riga pushed back against the allegations of Raziq as a bloodthirsty Afghan. "He is an incredibly brave, phenomenal combat leader," Riga said. "I found him to be shockingly empathetic toward the enemy." He recalled Raziq telling a captured fighter, "You are my brother. You need to come back to our side. I will give you the opportunity to come over so the NDS [Afghan intelligence] does not have to take you away."

The fight in the Arghandab was not over. The next month, in October, the conventional battalion commander ordered the bombing of two nearby villages, Tarok Kolache and Khosrow Sofla, after seeing insurgents in what he said were deserted towns. The two villages had become factories for making homemade explosive powder, which was manufactured from fertilizer ingredients and then spread out to dry inside abandoned qalats. The villages were razed to the ground. Most of the civilians had left the villages beforehand. Some may have been under pressure to leave from the Taliban, which wanted to use the villages for their own purposes; others may have left in anticipation of a US offensive. In any case, it remained unclear whether any villagers had been killed; those who returned were furious to find their homes and pomegranate orchards gone. When Terry arrived, he inherited the public relations disaster. He ordered the local mosque to be quickly rebuilt along with a massive tree-planting campaign to replace destroyed orchards.[4]

Riga's readiness to ride out alongside the Afghans earned him the respect of many of them. As his tour drew to a close, Afghans mounted a campaign for him to stay. Elders and officials from every district in Kandahar wrote letters or attached their thumbprints to the letters of others, and Ahmed Wali Karzai sent the appeal to President Karzai. They wanted Riga and his men to stay. "We had some incredible momentum going at that point," Sullivan commented. "It gets personal." Petraeus explained to the Afghans that the next battalion would be just as good, but Riga reported that this rebuff felt like a "kick in the gut to the leadership of the south." He added, "Such trust can't be built overnight." Before Riga left, Kandahar's mujahideen council, veterans of the anti-Soviet war, feted him with a banquet, and a popular Kabul singer performed a farewell concert in his honor.

By the time Riga left in April 2011, Arghandab was largely pacified, but Zhari, Panjwayi, and Maiwand were not. They straddled Highway One, the sole paved "ring road" linking Afghanistan, in this case Helmand Province, into Kandahar City. These districts would be Terry's focus. The conventional brigade based in Zhari would also work in Panjwayi; Terry requested special operations teams in both of those districts, and he especially looked to them to turn around Maiwand, where he had few troops.

MAIWAND

Captain Dan Hayes and his team, Operational Detachment Alpha (ODA) 3314, were ordered to Maiwand to look for a suitable site to embed. Maiwand was a desolate place marked in history by the 1880 Battle of Maiwand, an ignominious blow to the British during the Second Anglo-Afghan War. The economic rhythm revolved around the poppy crop, grown in fields irrigated by American-supplied pumps, followed by hashish. Once the opium tar is harvested, usually in May, the young men pick up their guns and the fighting begins.

The team moved into the Maiwand district center (akin to a county seat), a place called Hutal, and began daily patrols into every corner of the district in a ceaseless search for a village that wanted help defending itself. The conventional battalion assigned to Maiwand tended to hug the Highway One corridor, attempting to keep it open and free of bombs and ambushes. As the special operators left the gate of their Hutal base each day, they passed by the old British fort, a reminder of previous failures and their possible fate.

Unsurprisingly, Hayes found the going slow in this Taliban stronghold. He found no welcome south of Highway One, a rich agricultural belt along the Helmand River known to be a Taliban safe haven and transit zone. Its Ishaqzai tribe was cut out of the opium trade and did not have a role in the district's Noorzai-dominated government, which was linked to the Karzais by marriage. To the west of Hutal was the area where Tunnel's rogue band had done its killing; it was unclear whether anyone there would give the Americans another chance. So ODA 3314 began to scout villages north of Highway One.

Scott Miller's staff had discovered a possible source of help. A local defense group called the Gomai militia had operated in the Soviet era, and its leader in Maiwand, Hero Jabbar, was not only still alive but a member of parliament. He agreed to come to Maiwand to try to rally the population and ask old leaders of the militia to come forward. He sketched a map for the Americans showing the villages around Hutal that had contributed to the Gomai militia, which the team called the Hutal hub. Jabbar also introduced them to his friend Fazil Ahmad Barak, an engineer who had helped to build irrigation canals and other infrastructure in Kandahar and Helmand. His old blueprints and expertise were invaluable in planning restorative and new development projects.

Hayes finally settled on Ezabad, a flyblown village just north of the district center. The elder of the town had a foot in each camp of the war, one son a doctor and the other a Talib. The elder agreed to support the arrival of the team and arranged for the special operators to live in a nearby *qalat*, as the mud-walled compounds where Afghans live are called. The high walls built of mud and straw were surprisingly sturdy. The walls enclosed one or more homes, a garden, a yard for animals, and a shed for crops or animals. Qalats sometimes shared adjoining walls when family members or neighbors built their homes next door. Outside the walls were defecation areas, as the soldiers quickly realized.

Ezabad was only a few kilometers off Highway One, but it was a world away. Over several days, the team ferried their impressive collection of armored vehicles from Hutal to the qalat—their new home. Each team was supplied with vehicles with varying levels of protection and mobility. The heaviest were the massive RG-33s, which were the safest but, weighing in at 50,000 pounds, the least able to traverse steep hills, narrow passes, or the deep moondust of Maiwand. Next in their inventory was the Military All-Terrain Vehicle, which, like the RGs, had a V-shaped hull to deflect the blasts of buried bombs. The manufacturer had designed a special operations variant with improved suspension, a gunner's turret, and a larger windshield for better visibility, but even this lighter vehicle clocked in at 27,500 pounds because of its hefty armor. The teams tended to rely on their Humvees for navigating the dirt roads and wadis (dry riverbeds) of rural Afghanistan, even though they were flat-bottomed and made of lighter steel. The operators' new favorite in the Afghan war was their lightest vehicle of all, Kawasaki dune buggies mounted with the special operations variants of either the M249 or M240 machine gun. The teams favored mobility over armor, but they always wanted as much firepower as they could carry.

On the road to Ezabad, the team's convoy of vehicles careened and spun their wheels as they climbed and rolled through the hilly terrain, sinking up to their axles in fine powdery dirt. Up they climbed to circle a lone hilltop lookout, and then went down to Ezabad, bordered on the east by a wadi. That small canyon was the superhighway of the insurgents, who often came into the village and slipped away again without being detected.

The truth was that the team had no idea how many Taliban lived right in Ezabad. Their most valuable asset would be the four signals intelligence teams, which were coveted by the special operators and parceled out to those living in the toughest territory. These units, called Special Operations Teams–Alpha, or SOT-As, were part of the special operations support staff, uniformed military intelligence officers and noncoms rather than special operators per se. Trained in technical intelligence collection, analysis, and languages, they took shifts listening around the clock to the communications intercepts or "ICOM chatter" on the airwaves. They relayed breaking threat information in real time from a team's operations center or on patrol and were essential in helping the teams build a picture of who the insurgents were and where they were. It was a safe bet that quite a few of the young men riding through Ezabad in twos on motorcycles were insurgents. They would have to get to know them all.

Across the wadi, the village of Eshqabad was even less welcoming, and farther north, another, called Moshak, was totally dominated by the Taliban. The village lived in the shadow of Gormabak Pass just to the north, where the Taliban convened a shadow court that dispensed rulings that were subsequently enforced at the point of a gun.

As soon as they "embedded," Hayes and his team visited every qalat in Ezabad and the adjacent village of Nasu Kalay, asking each head of household to attend meetings where they could discuss the local problems and needs. At the same time, they worked to convert their mud-walled compound into a home. They rented two adjoining qalats and created a common yard, filled with gravel, to serve as a mechanics bay for their extensive collection of vehicles. At first the team members had lived out of a kicker box, a cardboard and plastic box kicked from planes, and burned their feces in an oil barrel. A row of sleeping containers and a shower trailer were then brought in, and three plywood "B" huts were built for their "op cen," or operations center, which included a dining hall, a TV room, and additional lodging for the interpreters, intelligence and other support personnel. When their squad of 1-16 infantry arrived, the troops moved into Quonset tents erected across from the mechanics yard. Two additional tents served as the all-important gym—one weight room and one cardio room, the latter including treadmills, elliptical trainers, and stationary bikes. Containers of canned food and dry goods were hauled in through the moondust canyon, and netting strung in between the metal boxes created shade for outdoor shuras. Meetings requiring more privacy were held in the mud-walled shura room that was part of the original qalat building.

From the outside, the qalat looked like any other qalat, except for the antennas sprouting up over the high walls. Camo netting on the rooftop obscured a lookout post and machine-gun nest. The qalat next door would serve as a classroom for the local police volunteers. A mud-walled watchtower outside was manned by hired Afghan security guards. The Ezabad outpost was finished, with just enough creature comforts to make the long tour bearable.

The qalat attracted insurgent attacks right away. The Taliban launched mortars from tubes from north of the village, and AK-47 potshots regularly peppered the qalat. The team knew that the best defense is offense and began aggressively patrolling day and night. The biggest danger was hitting buried bombs, most often fashioned from mines left over from the Soviet era or homemade from ammonium nitrate. Often the explosives were strung together—one to stop a vehicle, then clusters of smaller bombs to hit the troops as they dismounted the vehicle.

The team's hopes for a quick rapport with Ezabad ran aground when the elder who had invited Hayes in was kidnapped and taken north to the Taliban court in Gormabak, where he was threatened with death if he continued to cooperate with the special operators. Somewhat surprisingly, he returned, but he hunkered down at home and declined further invitations to meet. Hayes was crestfallen, but after several meetings the team decided to stay put in Ezabad and seek new allies. Hayes and his team held shuras to assess village needs and determine what projects might benefit the town, and they kept up an aggressive meeting schedule with the Maiwand police chief. They also met with the district subgovernor whenever he ventured out to Maiwand from his home in Kandahar. Hayes worked hard to convince the governor, Obaidullah Barwari, who was staying in Kandahar City, to spend more time in Maiwand despite the security risk. He believed that if they were to make headway with the population, something had to happen—something that would show people that they stood to gain if they took a risk. The special forces captain had the right personality for the incessant and patient lobbying. A slender and winning young man with a slight Asian tilt to his eyes, he could pass for an Afghan when dressed in a *shalwar kameez.*

Hayes and his team rotated back to Fort Bragg and were replaced by another team, but they returned a few months later. Reeder, who was now the special forces commander at Bragg, had decided that the 3rd Special Forces Group would come back for an extra-long tour in order to accommodate the 7th Special Forces Group's move from Fort Bragg to the Florida panhandle. This was not a popular decision with the families. The team was hopeful that they would partner with an Afghan commando company—but it was not to be. They were heartbroken. Not long after their return, Hayes's team sergeant quit due to personal, family-related problems. The team sergeant was typically the lynchpin of a special forces team, and it was an unsettling event, since few operators ever quit and certainly not on deployment. Losing a team sergeant—the father figure—can upend the ten more junior sergeants on the team. An experienced, no-nonsense master sergeant arrived soon, however, and immediately restored order. He used the F-word like all-purpose seasoning to flavor every sentence, but he was no drama and all business.

Hayes could also rely on his newly minted but superb chief warrant officer, Eli. The chief warrant officer's duties had evolved over recent years to focus more on intelligence gathering and assessments than in the past, but he was also supposed to serve as the team's deputy commanding officer and future planner. Eli was a short, muscular soldier with a quick wit and outgoing personality—and a fluent linguist. He led by doing and could outrun, outpress, and outthink any member of the team except his intelligence sergeant, a quiet giant named Brant. Brant was the longest-serving team member to date. He had come straight into special forces in 2003 after graduating college in Indiana and had gone through the medic training. He had previously deployed to Paktia and Kapisa and had helped to train Afghan commandos before the team moved to Maiwand.

Brant helped buck up the team. He had immersed himself in the details of the district as well as in the fundamental logic of the place;

his thorough and thoughtful SITREPs (situation reports) were read and shared widely among the various units in Kandahar. They would have to learn to play chess, because there would be no easy wins here. "They are all fence-sitters here," he said, noting that the Taliban provided useful services, such as transporting opium tar balls once the farmers harvested the crop. "There is a lot of passive support for the Taliban—and massive distrust of a government they never see," he said. Brant, thirty-two, was more philosophical than some of his younger and more impatient teammates. "This is a very slow process," he said. "It may be the next team that will reap the benefit and see results of what we do." To help his teammates and the attached infantry master learn the arcane but important tribal and local history, the five pillars of Islam, and the local officials' names, he concocted a game he called the Trivia Bowl. He tried to involve the infantry in every aspect of the mission and encouraged them to engage with the people of Ezabad. Having the additional manpower of the infantry squad made a huge difference. The previous tour, they had had a very hard time managing with a team of only nine. They had no Afghan special forces either. They had picked up a squad of Afghan uniformed police to patrol with, but they were terrible. They were from the north, not Pashtuns, and would routinely steal fruit from the bazaar and sneak off to smoke hash.[5]

Hayes's team was a diverse mix of personalities, but they were all Type A individuals who thrived on competition and rough humor. Parker, the communications sergeant, had talked over his reenlistment carefully with his wife during his short stay at home. This would be his seventh combat deployment, but he loved the life. He had been in the Ranger Regiment before going to special forces selection. The medic, Jimmy, was an irascible but highly capable redhead who pored over his thick medical textbooks to ensure that he correctly diagnosed the flood of sick and injured Afghans who began coming to the compound for medical attention. His treatment did more to build a bridge to the wary and intimidated people of Ezabad than anything else the team did. The first serious injury he treated was that of a small girl who had developed a deep abscess in her upper leg. After that, the word of his careful and respectful treatment traveled far and wide. Jimmy took on a young Afghan boy as his medical assistant, teaching him hygiene, first aid, and English.

Hayes returned determined to find some way to make a break-through. The fact that the same team returned to the village helped immeasurably, since they could pick up where they left off. It sent a signal to the people of Ezabad. "The looks on their faces when we came back—it was huge," Brant said. "It's a trust thing. I saw a guy I had treated last time; he gave me a big smile." Most of the world operates as a relationship culture, rather than the transactional system common to the United States. Afghans responded on the basis of friendship and kin ties.

The team had to find some way to lessen the climate of intimida-tion. The men resumed their grueling pace of day and night patrols to create a security bubble for themselves and the village. After four men and a bomb dog were wounded when their RG-33 hit a 120-pound bomb made of homemade explosives, the team decided to abandon the vehicles for foot patrols. A "route clearance package"—units that would drive through with special mine-detecting equipment—had not worked, because after they went through, within hours new mines would be planted. The team hiked long distances around the village and also patrolled the wadi and badlands to the north.

The team members did many foot patrols, loaded with their kits, through rolling dirt terrain. They logged nineteen "TICs," or troops-in-contact incidents, as combat encounters were officially called. They knew it was important to fight through every encounter, secure the village, and complete their search. They could not always get attack helicopters to provide close air support; in one case, Parker was pinned down by rocket-propelled grenade (RPG) fire, but he held on, know-ing that Jimmy, the medic, would blast through to his location.

Hayes started an ongoing fitness contest that he named the 1,000 Pound Club as a diversion, knowing that it would keep the team in good shape for their treks and boost morale. Each team member who managed to bench press, squat, and dead lift a total of 1,000 pounds became a member of the club. Visitors to their Ezabad outpost and other units in Kandahar were invited to participate. Each week, a new spreadsheet with the latest results was posted in the TV room, which doubled as a dining room. Word of the contest spread, and resupply convoys began to time their visits to the qalat to compete in the monthly event. Soldiers would gather around when Brant made his appearance; the intelligence sergeant kept ahead of the pack, one month lifting a total of 1,393 pounds in the three events.

The nature of the threat was subtle, constant, and wearing. The shots could come at any time, forcing the team members to be on alert while simultaneously greeting villagers, kicking a soccer ball with the village kids, and trying to persuade local officials to do their jobs. It required practicing sound tactics every day, every time they swung open the wide iron gate of their qalat. One day half the team and a few infantrymen patrolled on foot to Nasu Kalay. Following procedure, they fanned out in a diamond shape, with Parker riding along in one of the Kawasaki dune buggies. On their return, a shot cracked overhead as they crossed a barren field that would soon burst forth with poppies. The farmers were annoyed that the soldiers tromped across their fields, which were latticed with hand-mounded irrigation channels, but it was the best way to avoid IEDs. The soldiers knelt on the ground to lower their profiles and scanned the horizon. There was no cover between them and the gate of their mud-walled compound. Parker sped off in the direction of the shot, radioing the intelligence intercept team to see what they heard. The soldiers then moved out double-time and reached the gate without incident. No further shots were fired, and the team surmised that the insurgent's PKM machine gun had jammed. Afghans hiding in the distant treeline sped off on their motorcycles.

These random potshots were a typical low-grade threat. What the soldiers feared most were the IEDs, the buried bombs that were hard to detect and responsible for the vast majority of deaths and serious injuries. To search for explosives, working dogs and their handlers were attached to teams in the highest threat areas: in Ezabad, Mocha and her sandy-haired handler were welcome additions on every foot patrol. Mocha walked point along with her handler, a tall, quiet young man who was aware that he remained an outsider in the team's close-knit social dynamic. The well-behaved brown female Labrador sniffed out more than her share of bombs.

Perhaps the most valued and versatile aid came from the Afghan special forces team that came to live alongside them in the adjoining compound. One of its members had an uncanny ability to spot the tiniest telltale signs of an implanted bomb—and was equally skilled at disarming the crude devices—usually a wooden clapper built to evade metal detectors. The Afghan special forces teams had recently been formed with recruits from the commandos, so they were the best soldiers Afghanistan had and the beneficiaries of six years of joint training and operations with the US special forces. Their team organization mirrored the American special forces: each team had an officer and noncom leader, two intelligence specialists, two medics, two engineers, two weapons specialists, two communicators, plus two additional members to handle psyops and cultural/religious engagement.

The Afghan special forces team that came to Ezabad next door to Hayes and his men was led by Captain Azizullah, a grave black-haired young man from Nangahar. He was articulate and projected a calm assurance when speaking with both the villagers and the local officials. He would urge them to stand up and take responsibility for protecting their families and improving their lives—the kind of speech that might have alienated Afghans if delivered by an American, but was effective coming from this sincere, confident young man. Azizullah addressed the elders in a respectful but firm tone, and both they and local officials came to trust him. His team became a familiar presence as it alternated with another team on three-month tours in Maiwand.

Hayes's patient courting of the district governor, Barwari, persuaded him to come to Ezabad for his first-ever visit. Soon he began to visit unprompted. Unlike many other district governors appointed by Kabul, Barwari was from Maiwand—and he was educated. But he had not passed the formal exam required for a permanent appointment, so he could be replaced at any time. Barwari seemed to be well-liked, and he was less corrupt than many local officials, but there was a fundamental impediment to bringing the government closer to the people of Maiwand: most of the population relied on the illegal opium business for their livelihoods. The provincial government had mounted an aggressive campaign to eradicate the poppy trade, but viable alternatives were scarce. Growing and harvesting opium poppies yielded a farmer $8,400 in profit per acre, while growing wheat would result in a net loss of $130, thanks in large part to the effect of USAID's distribution of wheat seeds, which had depressed the price of wheat.[6] The opium traffickers made it easy: they would front farmers money to plant poppies each spring and then buy the balls of opium tar they harvested.

Weeks and then months passed. Ezabad and the surrounding villages remained reluctant to court the Taliban's wrath by forming their own local defense groups. Still, the team poured its energies into village stability operations. After many shuras with the male residents, the team decided to build a road, start a school, and open a clinic. If life in the village improved and travel to Hutal became easier, better security might follow. Engineer Fazil Ahmad Barak hired a crew to grade and then gravel the moondust road to the town, and Jimmy began an outpatient clinic with the help of the Afghan special forces medics. A temporary school was started, and Hayes managed to finagle a teacher on loan from Kandahar while beginning the laborious process of petitioning the Ministry of Education for a permanent school.

The extended family at the Ezabad outpost also included a new innovation called Cultural Support Teams, composed of two servicewomen who had volunteered and trained to join the special operators in the field. The original rationale for this program was to provide women to search Afghan females during raids, but the program evolved into an effort to build bridges to the female population and better understand the needs of the villages. The American women tried their best to connect with the women of Ezabad and offer them something of value. Just entering the conservative Pashtuns' humble homes, however, was a delicate cultural crossing. For example, during a visit to one home on the outskirts of Ezabad, a woman dubbed "the egg lady" (because she sold eggs from her house) reluctantly chatted with the uniformed women as she sat on the dirt floor turning a metal churn, which was wrapped in a frayed green sweater to keep it cool.

She had a smile on her face, but her eyes, lined with heavy kohl, were wondering and wary. One of the American women inquired after her health and her children and offered some first aid advice based on their last chat, but the woman's reserve did not thaw. The gap was an enormous one to bridge: the Afghan mother could not comprehend why these foreign women had no children of their own and had ventured so far from their own homes. As the American women collected their rifles and got up to leave, the woman, still polite, asked them not to return. The Afghan American interpreter, also a female, explained as they left that the Afghan woman was terrified that the Taliban would think she was collaborating with the Americans and would come to kill her and her family.

About six months into its second tour, the team's dogged persistence finally paid off. After many hundreds of meetings, Hayes had gathered five older Afghans who would become his Afghan Local Police commanders. They looked like characters out of J. R. R. Tolkien's *Lord of the Rings* trilogy, with craggy faces and long, wispy beards. Soda Khan was a dour, white-haired elder who decided to return from Kandahar to help rally the villagers. Out of Hero Jabbar's former Gomai militia came Jan Mohammed (no relation to Karzai's mentor, Jan Mohammad Khan of Uruzgan), a one-eyed former commander with a twinkly smile and teeth stained from constant smoking. He immediately enlisted his sons and volunteered to man the first outpost on the north side of Ezabad. Soda Khan was not such a hands-on leader, but he appeared at every meeting, gliding into the seat next to the district governor or appearing at his side when he made his rounds. He was no doubt seeking some type of windfall, but in the meantime, Hayes was happy to use his tribal stature as a legitimizing force to galvanize the timid villagers.

Ezabad residents endorsed the idea of local police in a shura, but they would not volunteer their own sons, so the five commanders' recruits came mostly from the Hutal hub villages around Highway One and the district center. Some came from farther afield, including neighboring Helmand, where Jan Mohammed had a house. Some recruits were elderly and some very young. Rob, the weapons sergeant, oversaw the recruits, their training, and their pay. He snapped their photos and ran them through the biometric database to try to ascertain where they had come from and to ensure they had no record as a criminal or insurgent. One of the first recruits to go through the course held up a car to shake down the occupants. A few days later he was shot dead on orders from the Taliban shadow court. The incident had a salutary effect on the next class of recruits.

Some of the Afghan recruits knew how to handle an AK-47; others were totally raw. The special forces weapons sergeants and other team members patiently corrected the neophytes' hunched-over posture as they tried to brace their thin bodies against the weapons' recoil. The only way to get better, as with most skills, was to practice. One technique the sergeants used to teach the green recruits how to shoot was to seat them cross-legged at a slight angle to the target, so the body formed a natural cradle to brace the gun against the shoulder. The recruits sat in rows, watching as those in front took turns firing at paper targets stapled to boards. When they finished, the instructors beckoned them to the paper targets to examine their shot groups. The three-week program of instruction was a modified version of the standard bread-and-butter infantry training that special forces gave all over the world. They taught basic squad movements (overwatch, bounding overwatch, breaking contact, and the like) and basic marksmanship. Other instructional blocks covered human rights, the rule of law, and police and checkpoint procedures.

Much of the target practice was at close range, twenty-five meters. The role of the villagers was to defend, not to go on offensive raids. Any suspects they detained were to be immediately turned over to the Afghan district chief of police or his officers. Those blue-gray uniformed police were never deployed outside of district centers, and as of 2010, about half of that force still lacked training. In the rush to provide a police force, they had been recruited and sent to work without even the three weeks of training that Hayes's recruits were receiving. This created immediate tension as the district police chief watched the new force receive instruction from America's elite forces.

The skills of the police recruits gradually improved, and new recruits slowly materialized. Hayes spent a lot of time sitting in meetings but saying little. His entire method was to let the Afghans take the lead, so he only provided input before or after meetings. He sat on the sidelines and let Captain Azizullah sit at the meeting table with Barwari, the elders, and the other local officials. Hayes knew his most important role was behind the scenes; it was vital that Afghans interact directly in the formal meetings. Many conventional forces, and even civilian diplomats, did not heed that basic rule of advising, choosing instead to sit at the main table and often dominate the discussion. Hayes had developed an excellent relationship with the conventional battalion in Maiwand as well as with the brigade commander in Zhari. He used his easy and irreverent humor to build rapport, and he offered suggestions frequently without being pushy. He played a role well above his rank—and no one bristled.

One day after a shura at the district center, Jan Mohammed and the other local police commanders gathered around Hayes to share the latest news: they had just received the first pay for their recruits from the district police chief. Hayes was astounded. He had expected that it would take months and endless bureaucratic hassles for the Afghan government to take charge of the payroll, but the money spigot had turned on shortly after the office of the Ministry of the Interior (MOI) in Kabul processed their biometrics, ID cards, and MOI contracts. The first payday was not perfect—some commanders had received too much or too little based on their number of recruits—but it was a welcome first step, a sign that the Afghan government was embracing the local police concept and might just be able to make it work.

Hayes felt that the district government was also coming along. Barwari, the governor, was known to make money on the side, but he was relatively popular because he never tried to solicit bribes from the poor. Hayes had read intelligence assessments from the hydra-headed coalition forces recommending his removal on corruption grounds, but Hayes thought removing him would be a mistake. Barwari was reaching out to more and more communities, and he had begun to stay in Maiwand, only returning to his family in Kandahar City on weekends.[7]

One incident in Ezabad led to a breakthrough as the team's long tour drew to a close. Jan Mohammed's checkpoint was attacked one night and some of his police were wounded in exchange of fire. He was livid. Believing the shooter had come from Ezabad, he rampaged through the village seeking the perpetrators, firing at those he believed responsible. The next day, the elders appeared at the team's gate, demanding the departure of Jan Mohammed and his men. An elder named Daoud offered to generate a police force from Ezabad residents. They would rather have their own sons out at the checkpoints, he said.[8]

Thus the American and Afghan special forces teams trained the first class of eleven Ezabad defenders. Hayes did not intend to let Jan Mohammed go, however, since he was a very reliable anti-Taliban leader who was respected in the district. Hayes also suspected that the new Ezabad leader might partly be motivated by the prospect of skimming off some of the money or other benefits that he could access by being an ALP commander. Daoud, a short man with deeply sunburned skin and white hair, said his family had lived there for two hundred years. When asked in an interview how many men he thought he would need to secure the village when the special operators moved on, Daoud answered, "None." Asked to explain, he said, "Ten days after the Americans leave, they [the Taliban] will take over Maiwand. We got along with those people before, and we will again."

Daoud did not want the Taliban to take over again—they had shot and wounded his brother, and he did not agree with their strict Islamist rule. He was not fatalistic so much as practical. "If a central government is established, I am willing to work for it. In the time of the king the laws were obeyed, and the maliks took care of the problems. If there is no government, we will need to adapt," he said, adding, "We are good at quick adaptation." His brother Mahmoud chimed in. "We have to live here. That means we have to have an understanding," he said.

As they prepared to hand off Ezabad to the incoming team, the special operators took satisfaction from the projects that had come to fruition. The school was a wild success. Even the poorest Afghans were eager for their children to be educated, knowing that it was the path to a different future. The school in the qalat was bursting at the seams with boys of all ages—girls attending school was still a bridge too far in this most conservative Pashtun bastion. The teacher, who had come from Kandahar, was assisted by the educated adult son of one of the ALP commanders. The road to the district center was now humming with traffic, although the new gravel road led to speeding, and at least one crash that took the lives of two of the ALP children who worked in the qalat as kitchen helpers. Abdullah Niazi, the gifted Category 3 interpreter who worked with the team, waved the papers triumphantly as he concluded the laborious process of obtaining thumbprints from every Ezabad head of household to complete the formal application for a ministry-funded school with schoolteachers.

All the men were exhausted after a grueling eleven months in the outback, and many wives were ready for their husbands to leave the force. The team had been deployed for nineteen of the past twenty-four months. Dan Hayes and his wife were hoping to start a family, and Parker's first child had been conceived during their brief six months at home. He had not yet seen her. Rob, the weapons sergeant, had only seen his daughter for six weeks of her young life. "She thinks I'm a computer," he said. "She walks over and points to it and says 'Daddy.'" Jimmy, the medic, joked about ordering his three young children to stand at 'parade rest' in the kitchen at home, but he could not wait to see them. As he shaved his tattooed arms, Parker speculated that their last few days would be uneventful. "I think fighting season is winding down. The Taliban are focused on getting their crops in." Although the insurgents still held most of Maiwand, Hayes believed they had created an inkspot that would spread, if tended properly. Time would tell if their hard labor had produced a lasting foothold in one of the toughest districts.

SUMMER OF ASSASSINATIONS

There was no such glimmer of light next door in Panjwayi, however. Scott White, the company commander who oversaw the teams in western Kandahar, liked to go on the resupply convoys because it gave him a chance to see his teams and assess the threat environment firsthand. Powerpoint briefings at staff meetings could never fully convey the gritty realities. But the supply trips were risky. The road through Panjwayi was a virtual shooting gallery, with one especially ideal ambush point formed by the convergence of walls, a hedge, and a building just after the road crossed the river. The brigade commander in Zhari had built a concrete wall that was twelve miles long, with the aim of impeding insurgent movement between Zhari and Panjwayi. White was skeptical that this tactic, which had been successfully used by US units in Iraqi cities, would work here. It seemed to be pushing the enemy further into the Panjwayi area and making it more dangerous.

One day as White's convoy approached the bridge, it slowed down to pass two checkpoints, an American one and an Afghan one. He radioed the two vehicles behind him to be ready to hit the gas as soon as they were off the bridge. Their last trip through this spot had been a close call. They had come under attack by insurgents with RPGs. They passed through the ambush without taking a hit, but unfortunately, a Stryker behind them was struck, and men inside were killed. This time, the men floored the gas and sped through the chokepoint without incident. Later that day as White returned through Panjwayi from Maiwand, he stopped at the Panjwayi district center to talk to the team there. Just after he left, a car bomb went off at the gate of the district center. The Panjwayi district governor had been the intended target. The governor escaped, only to be killed in another attempt the next spring.[9]

The gauntlet successfully run that day, White rewarded his comrades with a stop at their favorite restaurant in Kandahar City for a grilled chicken dinner before they returned to their base at the airfield. Their armored RG vehicles pulled up in front of the restaurant, and White went in to order the meals while a few soldiers stood guard by the trucks. The others carried the takeout cartons of chicken and rice pilaf to the median and sat down in the grass to eat. Curious Afghan men crowded around, and bold children sat down next to the soldiers, who were digging into the cartons and pulling apart slabs of chewy *nan* bread. Only a few moments passed before the first soldier shared his meal with a doe-eyed little girl at his elbow.

It was a lively Saturday night. Colored lights festooned shop awnings as Afghans strolled the sidewalks. The city was safer in 2011 than it had been the year before, and Kandaharis had begun to go on weekend jaunts—but it was still not at peace. The violence was targeted, and it very often found its mark. Earlier that very night, the Provincial Reconstruction Team next to the governor's palace had come under attack.

The Taliban, which was taking a beating in the countryside, soon turned to a strategy of assassination. Four killings in the spring and summer of 2011 had profoundly shaken Kandahar and the Karzai power network stretching from Kandahar to Kabul. Kandahar's police chief, its mayor, the president's half-brother, and Karzai's oldest confidant and family friend, Jan Mohammad Khan—the former governor of Uruzgan—were assassinated one by one. Khan was killed by attackers, including one suicide bomber, who stormed his home in Kabul. At the funeral, the grief-stricken Karzai fell sobbing into the old Pashtun's grave. As the drumbeat of killings continued, the governor of Kandahar, never a brave soul, refused to come out of his palace. The president's half-brother Ahmed Wali Karzai had been the real power of the province, and now that he was gone a power vacuum opened up.

The only leader in Kandahar left standing was Abdul Raziq, the controversial young border policeman who became the acting provincial chief of police. It did not take long for the Taliban to target him. On January 11, 2012, Bill Carty, the special operations battalion commander who had replaced Chris Riga, visited Raziq at the police headquarters in downtown Kandahar to discuss increasing the number of recruits permitted to join the growing ALP force. An Afghan in the outer office demanded to see Raziq but was denied entry. Suddenly Carty and the US officers with him heard a loud boom. The blast shattered the windows of the one-story building and blew the door off its hinges and into the office. Carty, who was sitting next to Raziq, threw himself on top of the police chief. He was reacting instinctively, but the thought also flashed through his mind that both Raziq's predecessor and Karzai's half-brother had been killed by their bodyguards.

Was the explosion a single event—an inside attack—or the start of a sustained assault? With the help of Carty's interpreter, Dee, the two men scrambled to their feet and dashed into a side room.[10]

After a quick huddle, they decided to move into the outer office, where their body armor was stacked. The next move would be to get Raziq out of the headquarters and to a safe location. Carty pulled his pistol and led the way through the smoking debris. When the group reached the outer room, the Americans donned their bullet-proof vests. Raziq's was in his vehicle outside. Carty shoved his own vest at him. "Put this on," he said. Raziq shook his head. "No, you can't go out there without your vest," the Afghan protested.

There was no time to argue. Carty and Dee strapped the vest onto Raziq and hustled him outside into a waiting armored Afghan police vehicle. The rest of the Americans piled into their armored vehicles with a lightly wounded member of their security detail, then headed to the hospital. Carty and Dee cleared the grounds on foot, parting the crowd that was gathering in the chaos. They saw several wounded Afghan policemen who needed first aid and transport to the hospital. Once that was under way, Carty jumped in beside Raziq, and their armored convoy sped to Mundagak Palace, where security reinforcements were arriving from the Afghan army and RC-South.

Afghan officials began to come by to check on Raziq, and his cell phone started ringing as word of the attack spread. The interior minister and then President Karzai called to make sure he was all right. As the press converged on the palace to find out what had happened, Carty's tactical team arrived from Camp Brown to take him back to the base. Raziq wanted him to wait so they could eat lunch. "Why did you give me your vest?" he asked. "There are thousands of me in the US army," Carty replied. "But there is only one of you."

The special operators had been working with Raziq for years; Mahaney had considered him an effective and courageous leader in combat. Raziq had by all accounts made a lot of money from the hefty smuggling trade through his Spin Boldak border crossing, and he was reported to have overseen massive ballot-box stuffing to ensure Karzai's 2009 reelection. Yet Raziq had left his border post and stepped forward to lead the Afghan charge against the Taliban across Kandahar in 2010,, and in the past two years he had been greeted in many towns and at bazaars by hordes of well-wishers. Ambassador Eikenberry and other US officials in Kabul wanted him to be cashiered or at least sent away, but Terry and others believed the police could fold without him. The 205th Corps army commander in Kandahar was a sterling character, a modest man with a squeaky clean reputation who lived in a bombed-out barracks built in the Soviet era. But the army did not have enough forces in Kandahar to cover the populous province, and the general's retiring persona did not rally the population the way Raziq could.

The coalition military officers in Kandahar did not see many alternatives. Security had to be accomplished by warriors leading the fight. Many of the appointed governors and other civilian officials were expatriates who had returned home in a patriotic gesture, but most of them had little ability to rally Afghans or broker deals with the tribes, subtribes, clans, and factions that constituted Afghanistan's political world. Faced with the vacuum caused by the assassinations, President Karzai chose to leave the governor in place and make Raziq acting provincial police chief. He also sent Asadullah Khalid back to the south temporarily to compel the police, army, and intelligence service to work better together. Karzai's brother Qayum began to spend more time in Kandahar as well.

Afghanistan is an extremely bloody place, and wishing it weren't so would not change the facts. Disputes were often resolved at the barrel of a gun, as Terry frequently noted. Kandahar still bled, but Terry felt he had made headway, especially given that most of the conventional forces of the surge had gone to Helmand next door. He had a greater number of special operations teams than any other province, and had used them to the hilt. But hardcore Taliban areas such as Panjwayi were unyielding. These were not ratlines or transit zones; they were the Taliban's home.

Reflecting on his tour, Carty noted three factors that limited the success of special operators in parts of Kandahar. First, the teams had been asked to do "forced entry" in some places, contrary to the prescribed method of villagers inviting special operators in to help them resist the Taliban—and this was true of Panjwayi. In these cases, a high level of Taliban presence meant operators made little or no headway. Second, in some cases district residents were happy to have special operators provide security and coalition money to pave their roads and refurbish their mosques, which were popular destinations and sites of festivals, but they would not take up arms against family members who were Taliban. Carty saw this as a "paradox of security." Villagers felt more secure when special operations teams moved into their area, but they did not want to provide for their own defense; only if they saw the special operators as temporary assistance would this paradox be resolved.[11]

The third factor was the "false start," which occurred when a team relied on the wrong elders or factions to select commanders or recruits, so that those whom they chose ended up exacerbating rather than resolving security problems. This had happened in Shah Wali Kot, one of Kandahar's districts. Intertribal and interclan conflict, most often based on a property or water dispute, was a fact of daily life in Afghanistan. When the special operations forces arrived in a village or district, they had to peel back these issues to understand and then try to address them. If they did not, trouble would ensue.

The conclusion that Carty drew was that teams could not take shortcuts or be asked to produce defense forces in places where the population incentives were not in place. The teams had made headway in many districts of Kandahar, but in Taliban strongholds people remained intimidated. As he packed up to go home, Carty believed further progress in Kandahar would not come easily, but was possible—and essential to the nationwide chessboard. If insurgents controlled Kandahar, they would be halfway to victory.

CHAPTER FOUR

PAKTIKA

PAKTIKA 2010–2011

CHAMTU

ODA 3325, like most teams, desperately wanted the commando mission. Partnering with the Afghan commandos guaranteed a tour of planning and executing raids, plenty of target practice, and night operations. "Shoot, move, communicate," were the basics of the soldiering life, and the bread and butter of special forces work because they were doing it with their indigenous partners. ODA 3325 was a dive team, and its operators tended to be aggressively physical because their scuba-diving specialty involved grueling training and periodic requalification tests. The team's "personality" was also influenced heavily by its captain, Michael "Hutch" Hutchinson, and his intelligence sergeant, Greg, backed up by Dustin, the team's communications sergeant. Hutch and Greg were smart and smart alecks, and it quickly had become clear that anyone who could not hang with their pace, their humor, or their taste in music (Journey, Led Zeppelin) need not apply.

There was no arguing with the team culture, whether in the special forces, the SEALs, or any other subset of special operations forces. The club or clique dynamic would take hold and reinforce the ethos, camaraderie, and esprit de corps that is vital for cohesion in military units. It is exclusionary, competitive, and mostly beneficial. Sometimes these small cliques would go astray, if they were led by the wrong leader, or if that leader lost his way. Hutch was a cheerful product of the Midwest, set upon following his uncle into the auto industry until his mother insisted he go to college. He chose West Point, despite her dismay at his decision to join the military in the wake of 9/11.

Hutch was smart and tended to poke fun at himself and everyone around him. He was frequently in trouble at West Point, and it seemed that the long gray line might reject him if it could not break him with endless punishments and threatened demerits. Clearly, the only place that was remotely suitable for his obstreperous temperament was the special forces. He instantly bonded with his whip-smart, tow-haired intelligence sergeant, an even more irascible and condescending wit than Hutch. Their battalion commander, Bob Wilson, took a somewhat benign parental approach to the team, but the company commander was less understanding and regularly tried to ride herd on them. On one occasion after they reached Afghanistan, the company commander overruled their proposed course of action, and Hutch, hearing the news over the secure line, kicked his desk to pieces.[1]

Failing to get the commando partnering assignment, the team sought the remotest possible corner to gain the freedom of maneuver to make things happen. They wound up in Shkin, the loneliest border outpost in Paktika, right on the border with Pakistan's South Waziristan tribal area—in other words, one of the hottest Taliban and terrorist transit zones in the country. Over the years South Waziristan had played host to a collection of Al Qaeda and allied terrorist groups, such as the Islamic Movement of Uzbekistan, as well as a shifting federation of tribal militants. The major insurgent leader in South Waziristan was Mullah Nazir, and the US military dubbed his group the Commander Nazir Group. He expelled the foreigners but struck alliances with other groups, including the powerful Haqqani network in North Waziristan. Nazir, born in Paktika with family on both sides of the border, had amassed a fighting force of some 10,000. He had been captured by the Pakistanis but released in a prisoner swap; he reportedly helped the Pakistani government by turning on the Pakistani Taliban, which was aiming to topple the Islamabad regime. In any event, Nazir's focus was Afghanistan.

The special forces and the CIA had been bedded down at Shkin since early 2002, but Paktika was always what the military called an "economy of force" effort—meaning few conventional troops were sent there. Paktika was the southern lobe of a three-province area historically called Loya Paktia, and in fact it made more sense to think of Paktika, Khost, and Paktia as a region than as separate entities. The military used the shorthand P2K to refer to the area. In the map drawn up for the Afghan Local Police initiative, several districts in both Paktika and Paktia were selected for ALP development. Not a single district in Khost was designated, however, because the population was considered to be hostile and therefore unreceptive to the notion of local defense. But this logic was somewhat circular, as the approach employed in Khost had primarily been one of hunting and killing, and no effort had ever been made to recruit a local defense force. In addition to the conventional brigade, which was located at the capital of Khost near the border, a large CIA-hired Afghan force—one of the CIA's Counterterrorist Pursuit Teams, or CTPTs—focused on the cross-border threat.[2]

Hutch and Greg had done their pre-mission study of Paktika, but they were eager to get out and augment their research with a firsthand tour to meet the players. They arrived on January 19, 2010, and the team spent the first two months doing reconnaissance patrols to every corner of eastern Paktika. "You can't succeed by doing firebase diplomacy," the captain said. "You have to establish your street cred."

Their CIA colleagues at Shkin were generally aloof and arrogant, even though the father of one of the team members hailed from that organization. As the team sat in Shkin's tactical operations center one day early in their tour, writing up a report about a border op they had just conducted, a scowling black-bearded Afghan strode in and passed by them without a word. It was Aziz. They had heard a lot about him from the previous team. Aziz had been a fixture in Paktika as long as the Americans had been coming there. He had participated in Operation Anaconda in Paktia in 2002 as part of Zia Lodin's blocking force. Aziz had then joined the Afghan Militia Force until it was disbanded, and had later transitioned over, unhappily, to the Afghan Security Guard force. But Aziz was not inclined to sit around in a guard tower like some rent-a-cop. This was his country and he planned to help take it back from the Taliban.

Aziz did not greet the team that day. He knew they were the new team he'd be working with, but his experience had taught him to be wary. Each team was different, and the coalition's war plans had taken many twists and turns. Sometimes the coalition commander simply wanted to hunker down and ensure his men got out of these bad-lands alive. But the new battalion commander from the 101st Airborne Division, Lieutenant Colonel Rob Harmon, had arrived with a new approach. He gathered conventional, special operations, and civilian PRT personnel together for weekly planning meetings; it was the first time anyone had tried to lash together the scarce resources being devoted to Paktika. Hutch's team, which would go through four battalion battlespace owners on two Paktika tours, was impressed by the way Harmon orchestrated the various military and civilian entities so that each could do what it did best.

Aziz's fierce motivation was partly a function of his personality, but he was particularly driven by the searing experience of being the lone survivor of a bloody Taliban suicide attack while eating at a restaurant in the bazaar of his hometown, Orgun, with his cousin Sardar in 2006. Sardar and many other fighters were killed, and the badly wounded Aziz was flown to Kabul for medical treatment. Special operations forces came to find him in the Afghan military hospital. "Where is Aziz?" they asked one of the doctors, not recognizing him through his bandages. Once they found him, they took him to Bagram, where he was attended to promptly and received better care than he would have received in Kabul. When Aziz returned to Paktika, he rejoined the fight. He added two new patches to his tiger-striped uniform.

One patch commemorated Sardar's death; the other read: "Taliban Hunting Club."[3]

Aziz had acquired serious fighting skills over the past decade of war. When the team met him, he was babysitting the Shkin base and patrolling its perimeter. But the teams based there realized they needed Aziz for combat operations, as no one else had the detailed grasp of the terrain that he had or understood enemy tactics as well. Hutch and his sergeants recognized Aziz's tactical proficiency in the way he conducted himself, handled guns, and assessed the terrain and situation. They also observed his leadership skills and his strict discipline of his subordinates. When a truck driver who hauled supplies arrived at their outpost, Firebase Lilley, and complained that one of Aziz's guards had tried to shake him down by demanding protection money, Aziz confined the guard for six months without pay as a demonstration to all of his men. Aziz was extremely strict with his group, which then numbered about thirty-five men, who were called his "Special Squad," and the team observed a certain pride and esprit de corps among them. They had adopted and enforced strict standards as part of modeling themselves as an elite unit.

Meanwhile, Hutch was pleased with the way his own team was jelling. The men had been to Afghanistan on a previous deployment, but they had since gained new members—and now, a new mission. Following pre-mission training in Wyoming to prepare for high-altitude operations in mountainous terrain, they were slated to serve two tours with only a short break, and Hutch wanted to make sure they did not suffer burnout. One of his points of friction with his company commander was the high-spirited hijinks of ODA 3325: just because they liked to have fun did not mean they were not serious professionals. Before every mission, they gathered in their team room to play their favorite songs on the computer as they were kitting up. En route to the target, they cranked more tunes over the loudspeakers in the Humvees. And as they crested the hilltop leading back to the firebase, they played the team's theme song, "Don't Stop Believin'."

Special operations teams are given a certain latitude to accomplish their commander's intent, and Hutch would not hesitate to take the initiative and innovate as he saw fit. After two months of driving around and sitting with Afghans in dozens of towns and qalats, he concluded that the basic dynamic there was strength and honor. A tribe would seek and use guns and money to protect its honor, and shame or loss of honor was the worst fate it could suffer. He would play on the tribes' desire to be strong and to protect their honor. To be effective, the team also had to establish its identity, and a reputation of strength as well as fairness. The large Waziri tribe straddled the border between Paktika and Pakistan's South Waziristan. As the name suggested, the Waziris were the dominant tribe in Waziristan, and the Waziris in Paktika had many family and business ties across the border where most of their kin lived. The team's academic studies had suggested that the Waziris were unalterably opposed to the Afghan government because of ideological differences and their geographical tie to Pakistan. But the team reached a different conclusion after spending time among the Waziri. They found the tribes to be overwhelmingly motivated by their own local status and concerns and largely indifferent to a government that provided them nothing and compelled nothing from them.[4]

The team ranged all over eastern Paktika—a region the size of Rhode Island—frequently encountering bands of Taliban. Speed and aggression were their friends; they learned that standing and fighting would usually cause the insurgents to disengage. They became known as the little band that would fight, not break contact. They relied on their Humvees and the Kawasaki dune buggies, since the narrow dirt mountain roads and winding trails were too tight and steep for the hulking RGs and even the smaller Military All-Terrain Vehicles, which, despite their name, were still not agile enough for this terrain. Adding weight through armor to protect the soldiers ultimately made them less safe, unless their job was to drive up and down paved roads. One of the team members called the Kawasakis their $12,000 "IED defeat machines," because they allowed the soldiers to travel off-road and avoid the buried bombs entirely. They enabled them to escape—and therefore defeat—what had become an endless cycle of US manufacturers building bigger and bigger vehicles while the insurgents simply rigged ever bigger bombs. Physics favored the insurgents, who could pack ever greater amounts of homemade explosive powder into jugs or culverts. The dune buggies allowed the team to fight like the Taliban, but faster: they could handle almost any terrain, take unexpected routes, and pursue and overtake their attackers. The team regularly ridiculed the top-heavy, grotesquely expensive American way of war. They had been trained to think and act like guerrillas, and that meant improvising on shoestring budgets. Hutch was radical about overspending in general—he came to believe that the typical behavior of Americans actually lessened their stature in Afghan eyes. Americans constantly offered handouts with no strings attached and allowed themselves to be ripped off—and every Afghan knew it.

From their base in Shkin, the team decided to focus on the most populated valley corridor, which ran up to Orgun, where the battalion was based, through the towns of Rabat and Surobi. They chose Rabat as the place to begin their version of village stability operations. Rabat sat beside the Spedar Pass, which was a critical chokepoint for vehicle traffic traveling from Pakistan through Shkin on the border to the populated central valley and main city of Orgun and on to the provincial capital of Sharana and the intersection with Highway One. The Spedar Pass was dominated by a group of Taliban insurgents who extracted money at checkpoints through the pass and exercised control of the water resources in the area, which was a constant source of friction among Rabat's five subtribes. The group was led by an Afghan named Chamtu who had a fearsome reputation; the team heard tales of murder, torture, and rape from Afghans who lived in the valley.

The team carefully laid the groundwork for a showdown in Rabat. Hutch, who had grown up in Chicago, proved to be instinctively streetwise in Afghan-style politics. The younger men of Rabat were tired of Chamtu's predations and frustrated that their elders were so thoroughly intimidated. But they could not overrule their elders alone. After an April 28 firefight in Spedar Pass, when Hutch and his team killed eight of the twenty insurgents who attacked them, he decided it was time to call for a shura. He requested that the Rabat elders come to Shkin for a powwow. He had already enlisted the attendance of the Bermel district governor and had discussed the script with him and the Shkin shura leader. These two began the meeting by berating the Rabat elders for not keeping the pass open and secure. Their truck drivers were regularly shaken down and sometimes attacked. As the Rabat elders began to make excuses, the Shkin shura members interrupted them with more complaints. The pressure began to build. Then Commander Aziz asked each elder to declare which side he was on, the government's or the insurgents', and began to separate the elders into two groups based on their response. The ultimatum forced the elders to side with the government.[5]

Aziz then invited the district governor into a side room and showed him a document. It had been Aziz's idea to prepare a written agreement for the Rabat elders to sign with their thumbprints. By signing, they would be committing their five subtribes to forming a local defense group to defend the pass. In return, the government would support them. The governor agreed to the idea, and he and Aziz returned to request the elders' signatures. The elders asked for a fortified observation post to be built on the pass to help protect their men, and the team agreed. Chamtu came to Rabat two days later to berate the elders and demand that they renege, but they told him they had had no alternative.

The team was on the hunt for Chamtu, hoping to take him down. A few weeks later, on June 8, they were in Surobi at the district center when they came under mortar fire from the mountain range to the west. Three passes leading out of that range served as ratlines for the Taliban, who enjoyed sanctuary in the sparsely populated district beyond, which connected in the south to Pakistan. The team members jumped into their Humvees and headed due west to the closest ratline. At its mouth sat the little village of Nawi Kalay. Their plan was to gather the elders and try to persuade them to give them some information as to the insurgents' whereabouts. It would be difficult. Many of those villages along the mountain range found it easier to submit to Taliban domination than to fight it. In addition, they had less economic incentive to deal with the Americans than the poorer tribes on the east side of the valley did. Quite a few of their sons worked in Dubai and sent home money. Their silk *shalwar kameezes* testified to their comfortable, if rural, circumstances. Hutch also had the SOT-A intelligence team attached to them monitoring the radio traffic as they sped along.

As they entered Nawi Kalay, the group came to an open area. Fifty meters off the road, near the tree line, they saw Afghans taking down mortar tubes, probably the very ones that had shot at them. The team reacted instinctively. They wheeled to the left and attacked. The sergeant in the lead Humvee led the charge into the midst of about two dozen Taliban fighters, who began running in every direction. Hutch did not need to issue orders; the team just went on automatic pilot. Every infantryman had practiced the maneuver thousands, probably tens of thousands, of times. As they closed in, the soldiers jumped off their trucks to chase down fleeing insurgents.

A few of the Taliban stood and fought. Caught at close quarters, one soldier drew his Yarborough knife, an item that every Green Beret receives upon graduating from the qualification course. The knife was named to honor William P. Yarborough, the Special Warfare Center commander who persuaded John F. Kennedy, an ardent special forces supporter, to authorize the beret as their official headgear, over army opposition. The headgear was to symbolize their special skills as well as the higher ethical standards Yarborough believed they should uphold to carry out their credo, "To free the oppressed." The knife is usually a ceremonial item, used to cut open rations or fix gear, but in this case the soldier put it to its intended use: hand-to-hand combat. Training in close quarters battle tactics is standard in the special operations forces, as is "combatives" training, when a fight goes to ground. It is a mix of martial arts, grappling, and all-out ultimate fighting.

Very rarely had the men been in such close-range fighting, but they reacted with a practiced fury that overwhelmed their enemy. Hutch's gun truck ran over one of the insurgents, literally mowing him down. In the middle of the firefight, a car drove down the road and was hit by a round. A ten-year-old boy riding in the car was killed.

After the fighting stopped, Greg took photos to aid identification of the fighters. They confirmed that one was the insurgent leader Chamtu. Many of his premier fighters were dead as well. They also found RPGs, cell phones, code books, and a motorcycle rigged with a bomb for a suicide driver. Greg, the intelligence sergeant, was ecstatic at the treasure trove, which would help him and the team's intelligence analysts track down the group's affiliates in three districts, its support network, and its contacts in Pakistan. In all, eleven enemy had been killed.

They loaded the corpses into their trucks. There was nowhere to put them but inside, under their feet. When they got back to the Surobi district center, however, the Afghan police there were too afraid to take control of the bodies. They refused, certain that there would be reprisals. Finally the operators persuaded the district governor to take custody of the dead Taliban and arrange for their burial. Hutch also explained what had had happened to the boy who was killed in the car. No outcry from the villagers or the district governor ensued, and Hutch surmised that the Afghans understood that the father had been in error to drive into the middle of a firefight with his son. In their subsequent shura with the Surobi elders, Hutch gave detailed instructions for what civilians could do to avoid harm if a battle was occurring in their vicinity. He promised his team would always seek to engage insurgents outside of the populated areas.

The next day, in the Orgun bazaar, Aziz issued a public challenge to Abdul Aziz Abbasin, the Taliban shadow governor for Orgun District and the number-two Taliban leader in the province. "Come fight me," he said on a handheld speaker. "I will fight you anywhere." The following day, a gas station attendant arrived with the reply: Abdul Aziz Abbasin will fight you in Pirkowti tomorrow morning. Pirkowti was the Taliban stronghold.

Challenge issued, challenge accepted. As in an old-fashioned duel, further terms were offered. Hutch relayed the message that if the insurgents didn't use IEDs, they would not call in air support. He was confident they could win with only infantry. The team reached Pirkowti thirty minutes before dawn. In addition to their ODA, they had Aziz and his platoon, psyops, which was now called Military Information Support Operations, or MISO—a terrible acronym that spawned bad jokes about Japanese food—and the signals intelligence guys, about fifty men in all. They passed through Pirkowti itself without incident and proceeded eastward toward the next village, Shaykhan, where Abbasin reportedly lived, or at least bedded down. They took a hard right into an uninhabited area between the two villages, and as they came around a bend they encountered a flaming "jingle truck"—one of the fancifully painted and decorated trucks that hauled goods throughout Afghanistan and Pakistan, named for the bells that adorned the railing above the cab. As soon as he saw the fire leaping upward, Hutch braced himself. This is really going to happen, he thought. A split second later the barrage began, with rounds from two 82 millimeter recoilless rifles coming from the ridge-line across the road. These were the standard big guns of the Taliban, their heaviest stand-off weapons. The site was well chosen: the team was caught in a kill zone with minimal cover. The men could not drive through, guns blazing, as they normally would, because the burning truck was blocking the road. RPG fire began to come from the wadi below them on one side of the road and the mountains that rose up directly from the road on the other side. They fired back against the unseen enemy. It was about 8:30 a.m. Greg, the intelligence sergeant, clambered up the sheer mountainside, seeking an angle from which he could throw a grenade into the crevice where the Taliban were hiding. The greenery growing out of the wadi was waving with the Taliban movements.

A MISO soldier named Buck was shot. Hutch sent the medic to check on him. Buck, who had been manning the .50-caliber machine gun on the exposed back of one of the Humvees, was hurt pretty badly. He had been hit in the neck, and the bullet had traveled down his shoulder to lodge in his ribs. Hutch yelled: "What's going on?" He wanted to push ahead, if possible. They had not yet run out of ammo, but they were getting low. Matt was on the .50-cal on the back of Master Sergeant Cameron Ua's truck. Ua was their new team sergeant, a veteran of 1st Special Forces Group and a very calm, steady presence. He formed the perfect balance to the hyperactive and highly verbal duo of Hutch and Greg. Ua asked Matt for an ammo check, and Matt reported that he had started the day with 12,000 rounds, of which he had expended 8,000.

Then one of the attached intelligence sergeants was lightly wounded. A bullet ricocheted off an ammo can into his chest, hitting a side plate. With two down, Hutch knew they would need to call for medevac and more ammo. He hated to leave the fight, but they pulled back through Pirkowti to a big green space with a small mud hut nearby. The team checked their ammo. They were down to 10 to 40 percent of their total per truck, so they cross-loaded what was left while the call for medevac went out. At 9:15 the medevac bird came in, about forty-five minutes after the battle began. The team had preplanned an ammo resupply back at Orgun base. Ua and Jeff had packed the cans, and the packet was sitting there ready to be sling-loaded under a helicopter. But there were no gunships available. Hutch swore. The maintenance platoon at Orgun offered to drive ammo to Pirkowti in an RG-31. But there was no way that vehicle could climb into and out of the steep walls of the wadi and then navigate the narrow canyon into Pirkowti.

Hutch did not have much time to make a decision. They heard the insurgents talking on the radio; they were already flooding into the wadis to block the exit from the valley. As it was, the team would have to blow through there hard to make it out without further casualties. Dustin was Hutch's driver; he had been a motocross racer in Oklahoma and he knew how to drive as well as fix vehicles. He'd applied directly to the special forces through the "X-Ray" direct accession program, formally known as Initial Accession, or IA. He had been assigned to the "Schoolhouse"—that is, the US Army John F. Kennedy Special Warfare Center and School at Fort Bragg, and found himself on a bus out to Camp Mackall. Dustin had the air of a laid-back California hippie, and he was a true sun worshipper. No sooner did the team arrive at one of their camps than he would strip down to his Ranger panties, as their black nylon workout shorts were called, and stretch out on a rooftop or a folding camp chair to soak up some rays. But Dustin's appearance and manner belied his mechanical and technical skill and an inquisitive, contrarian nature. There were no yes men among the sergeants. Hutch gave the order to go, and Dustin floored it. A recoilless rifle round narrowly missed them, landing five meters away. The next one shot out their satellite antenna. Greg was driving his truck, crazily, with two Afghan trucks bringing up the rear. An RPG hit his right rear, blowing out his back tire. He kept driving on the rim. The poor working dog cowered in the back, under the feet of her handler. Working dogs often suffered post-traumatic stress disorder (PTSD), and this small black lab was no exception. She had been through a lot already.

The insurgents' tactics were practiced. Another trap was sprung as the team left the wadi and rejoined the road. The insurgents were used to shooting at the trucks from the wadis on either side of the road. The larger mine-resistant armored vehicles were sitting ducks and had a hard time returning fire effectively. The insurgents were so close that the tall trucks could not depress the barrels of their automated guns low enough to reach such a close-in target. The latest innovation, called CROWS (for "Common Remotely Operated Weapon System"), allowed a gunner to locate and fire on targets using a joystick, video and thermal cameras, while staying safely cocooned inside his armored vehicle. The experience was something like playing a video game on a roller coaster. But the Humvees had an advantage in this situation because they were closer to the ground. Their .50-cal guns were just about level with the heads of the insurgents when they popped up from the wadi edge to fire at the team through the foliage. The team later heard intercepts of the Taliban talking about how many they had lost in that wadi and concluding that they had crept up too close.

The team pushed the Humvees as hard as they would go. They hit forty miles an hour, driving through the ambush, then jostled violently down into the wadi and over the rocky bed until they exited the valley. The team and their Afghan comrades rolled into Orgun as bystanders turned around to gawk. Their trucks were limping, full of bullet holes, windows shot out. The RPG was still sticking out of Greg's wheel rim. Aziz took the opportunity to taunt Abbasin. "We went to meet you and you did not show yourself," he said, issuing another challenge with his megaphone. When the returning fighters entered their base camp at Orgun, the "Rakkasans" of the 187th Infantry Regiment, part of the 101st Airborne Division, came over, offering to help fix their vehicles and refit their ammo. "It was like having a pit crew," Hutch said of the warm welcome their infantry brethren gave them.

The team and Aziz went back to Pirkowti the next day to show the flag and see if Abbasin would give battle, but he did not. They did not want their departure the day before to be interpreted as unwill- . ingness to fight. Hutch and his team were learning the finer points of the "Kabuki" theater of Afghan warfare. There is a show of force, and then someone loses face. Rarely are the battles fought to the last man. It is combat for position and psychological dominance. The special operations team and their Afghan allies had shown themselves to be the undaunted ones, and this narrative stuck. They picked up chatter to the effect of "if you see the Humvees, run away."

The effects of Chamtu's death and word of the Pirkowti showdown were dramatic. When the team and Aziz's fighters returned to Rabat, they were greeted like heroes. Men lined up to join the local defense group and began helping to construct the fort. In addition, the young men of Rabat built a smaller observation post on the biggest mountain in the pass. When they were done, they raised the Afghan flag above both. The symbol of Taliban on motorcycles had now been replaced by a locally manned outpost flying the national flag.

As word of the recent battles and observation post construction spread, sentiments changed. Hutch and his team along with Aziz and his men brokered similar agreements with the elders in Orgun. Then they went to Surobi for a shura with the district governor and the elders there. That day, seventeen elders signed an agreement to raise a self-defense force, and dozens more signed in the coming days. The team had perfected its formula. It had shown itself willing to fight, hand to hand and face to face, and had prevailed. The psychological impact encouraged others to stand with them. The Rabat agreement was reached via a series of side deals; the power brokers of each subtribe had to be engaged away from the rest, not at the shura. Once they had agreed to come forward publicly, their assent would pull the other, more reluctant tribes along. This was how Afghan decision-making occurred. The real decisions did not occur in the shura; the shura or jirga was the place where decisions already reached behind closed doors were ratified, positions aired, and terms of the deal recited. It was politics in action.

In a place as intimidated as Paktika, villagers were not going to come forward unless they were convinced the new leaders stood a chance of winning. The climate of fear had to be dispelled by demonstrating a willingness to fight fire with fire; this is what Hutch meant by saying firebase diplomacy alone would not work. They had to establish their warrior credentials before people would begin to have hope. The pervasive belief had been that the Taliban would inevitably come back to rule the province; a new dynamic had to be set in motion for the people to believe they could shape their own fate.

The team's success quickly outstripped its ability to provide quick reaction forces for all of the mushrooming local defense groups from the base at Shkin on the border. After an elder in Surobi was kidnapped and executed, Hutch realized he should have enlisted the help of the 1-187 infantry company at Orgun as a 911 responder. From the team's base in Shkin it was a two-hour drive to Surobi. It was not so much deaths as the lack of support that mattered to the Afghans; having someone come to back them up showed that they had allies and thus superior strength and standing vis à vis the insurgents. Hutch had been in enough firefights to know this; it was all about standing with those who stood up. He would have to construct a better support network, using the conventional forces, his team, and the Afghan partners to shore up Surobi's fledgling defense force.

The team managed to reach an agreement with the elders in Pirkowti, with the district governor's help, but the elders in this insurgent-dominated area buckled under the pressure, finding legal loopholes in their agreement that allowed them to continue business as usual. The team would have to take on Pirkowti again in its next tour.

CATASTROPHIC SUCCESS

The members of ODA 3325 went home to North Carolina for a short hiatus in late 2010 before returning in 2011 to pick up where they had left off. The command had finally learned how critical it was to send the teams back to the very same places they had been before, as they had with the team in Maiwand. Aziz greeted the team warmly, and the various ALP commanders were ecstatic to see them again. Although Pirkowti remained solidly in enemy hands, the team's plan had survived and flourished in the central corridor of eastern Paktika running from Shkin to Orgun. The observation posts were like a magic talisman. Once they were established, the Taliban, in the great majority of cases, effectively conceded the area.

Hutch had heard insurgent talk on the radio many times: "Why haven't you attacked yet? You have over fifty men." "They built OPs, we can't do anything." Villages along the route clamored for observation posts to be built. Hutch and his team obliged where it made sense to do so—that is, when the area was strategic and not within range of an existing OP. In the end the team built fourteen posts, manned with local Afghan police. The structures were simple affairs made of the same Hesco barriers that the Americans used to ring their bases. Someone had likely made a mint on the simple design: canvas was stretched over a collapsible metal frame that formed a box; the men popped the box open and filled it with dirt or sand to create a five- to ten-foot-thick barrier, depending on the size. It was impenetrable to the insurgents' firepower; the only way to inflict casualties was by indirect mortar or artillery fire or by overrunning the post. The roof was a simple plywood sheet overlaid with sandbags. Concertina wire was then strung around the top of the Hescos as an outer perimeter. The Afghans could fill the barriers by hand, though the work was more quickly done by a Bobcat, if an engineer battalion was around to loan the team the machinery.

ODA 3325 had adopted its own unorthodox approach to building local police forces. They had departed from the village stability operations model in that they did not embed in a single community but instead worked to raise village defense groups all along their corridor and beyond. They had determined that embedding with one tribe or subtribe would only inflame tensions among the other tribes of Paktika and limit their reach. They were experiencing catastrophic success with their approach, and they needed to manage it carefully to ensure it did not go off the rails. Instead of "one tribe at a time," the formula advocated by an early proponent of tribal engagement in Afghanistan, Major Jim Gant, Hutch and his team wound up winning over twenty-five subtribes with a population of more than 100,000 in a 1,200-square-kilometer area. In this way, they achieved more than local, tactical impact.[6]

To mentor Paktika's burgeoning local police force, which now numbered 550 in all, the team split into two and sometimes three units. They maintained a split team in Shkin and one in Orgun. The team scouted various locations as Hutch debated where they should expand next. The border was too hot to expect locals to risk their necks: conventional troops at Forward Operating Base (FOB) Tillman and Combat Outpost (COP) Margah right on the border were getting hammered daily by artillery from Pakistan. The frequency of this cross-border fire quadrupled over the course of 2011 as US-Pakistan relations deteriorated. Using a map that covered the wall of his office at Orgun, the battalion commander pointed out a dozen locations where the fire was coming from. These "points of origin" had been definitively located by radar, thermal, or video detection. They were all within sight of, if not directly emanating from, Pakistan Army or Frontier Corps outposts.[7]

Hutch decided to keep his focus on the most populated area of the province and expand his current corridor of security west from Orgun to link it with Sharana, the provincial capital. Greg took a few team members to Sar Howza, outside Sharana, to lay the groundwork for expansion of the Afghan Local Police. In Sar Howza, the conventional battalion commander was eager to get involved, so Greg was happy to give him and his company commander the lead in expanding the local police initiative there. This would ease the burden on the team, which was already geographically stretched to its limit. The tempo of activity was also beginning to wear on the men.

Greg and Hutch improvised by relying on partners, whether conventional forces or Aziz and his men. Greg and the team would provide oversight and mentoring, while the training would be conducted by Commander Aziz's men. The team had no hesitation about outsourcing the training: all of the special operations teams who had worked with Aziz judged his men to be the most tactically proficient of any force in Afghanistan—more so than the regular army and even the commandos. The reason was continuity: for a decade Commander Aziz had been their leader, and most of his men had been part of the original Afghan Militia Force recruited by special operations teams and had partnered with them through every rotation since 2002.

The combined effort would expand the security zone through the last rugged mountain range separating Orgun from Sharana, a pass that was jokingly called the Gates of Mordor from Tolkien's *Lord of the Rings* by the unlucky soldiers who had to drive resupply convoys through this guerrilla-infested zone. The Taliban had planted the mother of bombs here, so large and powerful that it had flipped one of the mammoth 52,000-pound RG-33 armored vehicles end over end. Since the soldiers inside were all strapped into their five-point harnesses, no one was killed. But two of them had not been riding with their feet on the foot straps hanging above the floor. Instead they were resting their feet on the floor, and the gigantic blast had broken their legs. A gaping twenty-foot crater at the scene of the attack served as a reminder to all who passed.

The road from Shkin to Orgun became passable thanks to the defense pacts between the tribes and the district governors and the constant vigilance of the local police standing guard in their checkpoints. Hutch then launched his team into development and governance activity in earnest. He believed that paving roads was the development initiative that would pay the greatest dividends. The road was the economic lifeline of the population, so Hutch first sought to pave the entire stretch and make other infrastructure improvements. This would help Afghans get their crops to market and improve commerce, which in turn would stimulate the businesses of shopkeepers and others.

Hutch railed at new restrictions on their contracting authority that had been imposed after contracting abuses received widespread attention. The problem was real, but the fix was wrong. The team had a better grasp of which contractors were reliable and what work should cost than a distant contracting officer in Kabul, who inevitably went to an Afghan company with ties in the capital, which allowed several layers of middlemen to take their slices of the pie, greatly inflating the final price. The team, the US officials in Kabul, and the Afghan contractors in Orgun wrangled over the final stretch of unpaved road for months.

Afghans were also keen to expand cell-phone coverage in eastern Paktika, so Hutch's team got involved in pushing for this. The towers that did exist were turned off at night by the cell-phone companies at the Taliban's demand. The Taliban knew that one of the principal ways they were tracked was through their cell phones. The companies were not about to risk their investment when the government provided no help to rebuild dynamited towers.

The effect of the road improvements and increased security was dramatic: Shkin became self-sustaining once it was connected to the rest of Paktika, and Orgun in particular. Orgun's bazaar grew from 5 shops to 1,500. The complaints that used to revolve around shootouts in the bazaar suddenly were about sewage and lack of parking. Motels sprouted along the highway, and the number of gas stations grew from one to seven. So many jingle trucks plied the route that traffic jams even occurred. The towns with OPs did not fight each other, and in fact began to serve as quick-response forces for those who were attacked. In a watershed moment, a Tajik OP came to the aid of a Kharoti OP and evacuated the post's wounded to the hospital in Orgun. It reaffirmed Hutch's view that the Tajik minority and the welter of Pashtuns—Kharotis and Waziris, with their two main subsets of Ahmadzai and Utmanzi—could, with the right incentives, start to see themselves as Afghans. The self-interest of each tribe along the highway was now aligned, and they had a vested interest in maintaining their newfound security.

Although Hutch's sergeants would much rather be out hunting bad guys, they set to the tasks they were given. One sergeant was assigned to help draw up a city management plan for Orgun, and another worked with the civilian agricultural experts at Orgun's base to understand what the most effective programs were. The civilian district support team included Mary Kettman, a veteran USAID official who had spent years in conflict-ridden corners of Africa—including Sudan, Kenya, and Somalia. She had arrived in Paktika in September 2009 and would extend her tour to stay for two and a half years, making her the American on the ground in Paktika with the longest tenure by far. "We started to make a lot of progress, so I wanted to stay on," she said. One evening, Hutch and a sergeant came to her tent to ask if they could use her Internet access, as theirs was down. She realized as she overheard their discussions that Hutch was serious about stability operations, not just bagging Taliban trophies. Of course, he was also interested in the latter, and his team was quite proud of having rolled up five of the high-value targets on the JPEL (Joint Prioritized Effects List) that the special mission units had hunted.[8]

Kettman was impressed that Hutch even knew what her part of USAID—the Office of Transition Initiatives (OTI)—was. For their part, the team members came to see Kettman as an impressively intrepid civilian who could hold her own with them. Hutch joked that she had originally seen the team members as wild-eyed killers, but had wound up being as enthusiastic as they were after a successful mission. Outwardly an odd match, the peace-loving development expert and the rowdy team forged an effective partnership and even friendship over their two years in Paktika.

When Hutch's team organized its first big shura with the provincial governor, the chief of police, and all the district governors to formally kick off its ALP/VSO effort, Kettman realized that the initiative, if it worked, would facilitate her entry into many communities that she had not been able to work in before. She arranged to send her Afghan partners into a village right after the team conducted a mission. USAID is a hydra-headed organization with many divisions and projects; the one Kettman represented, the OTI, focused on small-scale, grassroots projects that would have an immediate impact in rural areas or conflict zones. OTI was the most expeditionary of all the civilian agencies; it prided itself on recruiting adventuresome souls who were ready to work in war zones or other disasters. OTI was unique in that it maintained control of its program design and could overhaul programs that were not working; most other USAID programs were entirely outsourced to implementing partners. In the case of Paktika, Kettman used Development Alternatives, Inc., which hired Afghans to enter the communities and do the work, but she trained them and kept oversight of all of it.

OTI projects were funded through small grants of no more than $50,000 each. This was far more than the Commander's Emergency Response Program (CERP) money the team could readily authorize, so the team would usually start off funding whatever small project the elders agreed upon, and OTI would follow on with more sustained programs. Some grants went to improve roads, but many were used to train farmers in more productive agricultural techniques; to construct *gabians*—simple wire-mesh baskets of rocks that slowed erosion and reduced flooding; and to clean *karezes* of trash and debris so water would flow to more communities. Shkin was the easiest place to start, since a relationship had already been forged with Waziris there who supported the government. OTI helped to pave the road to the border and also trained local farmers in beekeeping and orchard techniques. Work farther north, in Bermel, was stopped after a bomb killed construction workers. Kettman then focused on Rabat, Surobi, and, with three different governors, Orgun for the rest of her tenure. She was even able to do some work in Pirkowti after the initial agreement was signed with the elders, with farmers from the area going to Orgun and Khost for training. She held seminars in conflict mediation also, which the feuding Utmanzai and Ahmadzai Waziris attended. Although Pirkowti remained problematic, she believed these seeds might later bear some fruit.

Kettman was convinced that training and education were the way to make a lasting difference, as the adage about teaching a man to fish implied. A literate local official armed with good management and accounting techniques could turn around unpopular perceptions of the Afghan government. But the American military and civilian incentive structure, internally, revolved around expenditure of authorized dollars. If program monies were not spent, that was considered a demerit. Eastern Paktika received $2.89 million in development funding in 2010, and West Paktika ten times that. Hutch argued that for $5 million he could amply fund development, security, and governance in eastern Paktika. This was a far smaller sum than the $1 billion it took to maintain an American brigade there annually. And, he noted, the United States paid $400 million to lease the base at Shkin each year.

TO PIRKOWTI AGAIN

The virtuous circle of security and commerce resulted in an increasingly peaceful Paktika as the team's tour progressed. This set of circumstances left the sergeants crestfallen—try as they might, they could not get into a firefight. Then one day in October 2011 they picked up chatter that Abdul Aziz Abbasin—the Taliban shadow governor—was back in Pirkowti. He was on the United Nations blacklist and had recently been added to the asset forfeiture list of the US Treasury Department, but those sanctions had not touched him. The arm of the Haqqani network in Paktika, he was responsible for ambushing and killing many US soldiers and ran a training camp that still turned out Taliban fighters.

The team dropped everything and went into mission planning mode. Abbasin had eluded them before, but the team was determined to get him this time. Aziz and his lieutenant strode into the operations center to discuss the mission to Pirkowti that would kick off that night. Hutch and Greg engaged in extended negotiations throughout the night with their counterparts in Task Force 310—the special mission unit charged with hunting high-value targets in the region—and the CIA. The task force wanted to wait for more signals intelligence to confirm the target's location and identity. The CIA's Counterterrorist Pursuit Team, which was located in an adjacent camp, decided to send a small contingent along. The Afghans in the CTPT drove trucks and wore different uniforms from others in the alphabet soup of the

Afghan security forces. Their chain of command ran through the intelligence hierarchy.[9]

At 3:30 a.m., the team rolled out of the Orgun gate, stopping to
pick up Aziz and his men, whose base adjoined the American one. The
US team was loaded into three Humvees, and the Afghans were in an
assortment of Humvees and trucks. They drove under night observation devices (NODs) toward Pirkowti until day broke, the sun rising
just as they climbed down the banks of the wadi and began the jos-
tling, splashing drive up the riverbed. Their target was actually beyond
Pirkowti, at Shaykhan, the town where they had been ambushed by
Abbasin's forces the year before. The line of vehicles, Cameron's in
the lead, pulled out of the wadi and quickened its pace as it entered
Pirkowti, then sped through and made the sharp right turn down into
Shaykhan.

The surveillance aircraft overhead was supposed to be jamming
communications, but for some reason Hutch was picking up insurgent
traffic. He did not need to wait for translation to be relayed. "Run,
run," the insurgents said. "They are coming." Someone had tipped
off Abbasin, and he and his men were fleeing Shaykhan. "Step on it,"
Hutch relayed, urging his men forward into the town. They pulled
into their predetermined spots, one Humvee parking on a high street
to oversee the town's rolling landscape, and then sprinted through the
street, ducking into the target houses. Oddly, a helicopter had been
spotted overhead as they arrived—a sure tipoff that Americans were
on the way. The team never found out whose bird it was.

Commander Aziz led his men into homes they had targeted where
Abbasin and his men were known to sleep. They searched them thoroughly. Then Aziz called for the elders to gather the young men in
the village for an impromptu shura. They came out reluctantly, but
without resistance, and sat on their haunches, Afghan style, in front
of a building on the main street. Aziz reminded them of the agreement they had signed the year before, to defend their village against
the Taliban. He said they had breached the agreement repeatedly and
had lost their honor by behaving in this fashion. Hutch stood by but
did not speak. This dialogue was more effectively conducted among

Afghans. Aziz's men spotted two young Afghans they said had ties to the insurgent leader and recommended they be taken for questioning by the NDS, the Afghan intelligence service. Two dwarves joined the gathering, and Aziz and Dustin began chatting with them playfully, attempting to lighten the mood. The sun was well up, and Hutch was ready to go. They had failed to bag their prey once again.

The convoy loaded up but was briefly delayed by a caravan of brightly clothed Kuchi herders who were making their way into town on several camels and horses, their children and belongings piled high on donkeys' backs. Women and dogs on foot rounded out the slow-moving parade. They had stayed clear of the town until they were sure it would not become a battle zone. Hutch had planned a stealthy raid this day, but his standard practice, when issuing challenges to the Taliban, was to let villagers know beforehand. The team would challenge the insurgents to show themselves outside of town at such and such an hour to do battle. If the insurgents failed to show, they lost face before their kinsmen. And if they showed, they would be outgunned in short order. The villagers were glad to have the advance warning to stay off the roads, and it minimized the risk of civilian casualties.

Hutch was dead set on bringing Pirkowti around before the end of the team's tour. Before he went on leave, he suggested that the team propose a combined operation to the conventional battalion commander at Orgun. The latter agreed, but his commander then retasked him to ferry their armored vehicles out of FOB Tillman on the border to refit them with heavier armor. The scheme exposed the truck drivers to attack along the narrow ambush-prone road. In the end the battalion expended an entire month in the final stretch of its tour pulling out ninety vehicles for refitting, suffering several wounded in the process. The team went ahead without the battalion to Pirkowti, again with Aziz. They hit an IED in the wadi, but no one was injured. They came up empty-handed again; they did not capture Abbasin, and the villagers were not inclined to help. The team was frustrated. It would take more time and more maneuvering to bring Pirkowti around.

While ODA 3325's energy and acuity—and the decision to send the team back to eastern Paktika—were major factors contributing to the quantum leap in security, stability, and renewed economic activity that the region experienced between 2010 and the end of 2011, the team was quick to say that the improvements would not have been possible without the Afghan partner force led by Commander Aziz. He and his men played key roles in brokering deals and bringing the various district governors and elders into the fold. The province had been cowering under Taliban intimidation, and none of the appointed leaders or army or police commanders had demonstrated any leadership in the effort to change matters. But they did follow Aziz.

However, a different version of Aziz was circulating. Stories from Pirkowti and other Utmanzai Waziris were shared with United Nations officials, who wrote a report that was sent to the coalition. The ISAF headquarters investigated the allegations against Aziz, which included acts of murder, abuse, and pedophilia in 2009, but found no corroborating evidence. Then the UN report was given to a Kabul-based freelance reporter, Julius Cavendish. Hutch was with Aziz when the reporter called to ask him to respond to the allegations. Aziz hotly denied the charges. He was incensed by the first question he said Cavendish asked him: "Are you a Muslim?" Aziz felt the reporter was prying into matters that were none of his affair. The article was published in *Time* magazine in October 2011, and Aziz became the target of renewed questions and inquiries.[10]

When Hamid Karzai asked his aides about Aziz, he received favorable reports. The deputy NDS director, who was from Paktika, made positive comments. Mohibullah Samim, the governor of Paktika, and his chief of police, Dawlat Khan, also told the president of the helpful role Aziz had been playing. These high-level Pashtuns brushed aside the article's implication that Aziz, a Tajik who had been born and raised in Orgun, had a vendetta against Pashtuns. The village elders had endorsed the commanders that Aziz had nominated. The force now included 625 Pashtuns and 66 Tajiks. The provincial council chief, a Pashtun, decided that more needed to be done to rebut the claims, and he urged village elders and district leaders to go to Kabul and seek an audience with Karzai to convey their view that without Aziz, eastern Paktika would not have moved forward. If he was removed, the relative peace and security might quickly unravel.[11]

The police chief told Aziz that Karzai wanted to meet him face to face. Aziz told Hutch he was going to Kabul in a taxi, unarmed. "Are you crazy?" Hutch said. But Aziz would not listen. The president wanted to meet him, and he wanted to clear his name. He drove to the presidential palace and met Karzai. The president heard him out, and, according to Aziz, began crying. Karzai also received a delegation from Paktika, which convinced him that this Afghan had been slandered. The Utmanzai Waziris, particularly those from Pirkowti, had an incentive to spread stories: Aziz was the most formidable enemy in Paktika of anyone linked to the Taliban, the Haqqanis, or the Commander Nazir Group.

The matter was put to rest, at least from an Afghan standpoint, when the Afghan officials and elders publicly rallied around Aziz. Jess Patterson, the US State Department head of the provincial reconstruction team based in Sharana, knew that the provincial governor and police chief both strongly supported Aziz. She believed he had been effective in bringing security to the province, but she did not know whether the specific allegations were true or false. "I'm sure he is no angel," she said, but added that "the accusation that he was on some kind of anti-Pashtun crusade has no credibility." Most of his force was Pashtun, as were the governor, the police chief, and the head of the provincial council, who were all from different subtribes (Andari, Zadran, and Kharoti, respectively). ODA 3325 had been in combat with Aziz countless times, but Hutch and Greg said they had never seen him execute anyone in cold blood. Any incidents that took place in 2009 would have occurred before the team arrived, but Hutch and Greg said that some of the alleged crimes were linked to combat operations in which Aziz had not even participated.

Aziz, who felt his honor was gravely injured, wondered why the reporter had not come to interview him in person. "I am ready to meet him at any time," he said. "Why would he say these things?" Aziz said he had not pulled Chamtu from a mosque and killed him;

he had never been in a heliborne operation; and he was in the hospital at Bagram recovering from injuries on one of the dates when the reporter alleged he had flown to a qalat, burned it down, and killed two women and children. The special forces had been with him on all of his operations. "If they don't believe me, ask the teams," Aziz said. What he viewed as a smear campaign seemed like it would never end: "The Taliban are now saying that this is what happens to those who are allies of the United States."[12]

Hutch and his team had succeeded by unorthodox methods, and Aziz was undoubtedly a departure from the model. He had not come to the team through the village elders, but through his long association with special operators. He had been embraced by the local elders and officials, however. Nonetheless, Aziz's situation was precarious from a practical standpoint because he held no formal position within the Afghan security forces apparatus. He was not a member of the Afghan Local Police or of the Afghan Uniformed Police. He was paid out of US Afghan Security Forces Funds in an arrangement that was due to expire as the security forces came under the Afghan government's purview. He had been made the trusted agent or paymaster of the Afghan Local Police by the provincial chief of police, and he was clearly functioning as the primary trainer, quick reaction force, and intermediary between the provincial and district police. To regularize the role of Aziz and his Special Squad, the special operations company commander suggested in the spring of 2012 that his group be named the Village Response Unit and that the Afghan Ministry of the Interior pick up his salary. The provincial police chief, Dawlat Khan, did not want to lose Aziz as his ally and asked him to become his deputy. Aziz wanted to remain in Orgun, however, rather than move to Sharana, the provincial capital. He was willing to do whatever Khan asked, but he wanted to do it from his home city. He also did not want to lose his tie to the special forces. "I work for them," he said. "I work with them."[13]

CHAPTER FIVE

ON THE BORDER

KUNAR 2010–2011

ODA 3316

If Paktika held the dubious honor of being the most ignored province in Afghanistan's insurgent belt, Kunar probably ranked as the province that received the most attention throughout the war. The war's most heroic and horrific fighting occurred in this mountainous region, where six of seven Medal of Honor recipients fought with extraordinary bravery. Korengal, Wanat, and Ganjgal top the blood-drenched roll call of fearsome battles in Afghanistan, much as Khe Sanh, Hue, and Tet do for the Vietnam War. Unfortunately, however, the blood, sweat, and tears expended in Kunar had not translated into anything approximating victory by 2009.

A look at a map explains why Kunar was such a battleground: the narrow, mountainous province borders Pakistan, most of its population a scant fifteen kilometers away. In northern Kunar, the Hindu Kush rises up in a dense, formidable massif that forms a perfect, natural sanctuary for insurgents and terrorists. For years the military threw both conventional and special operations forces into ill-designed raids, each time expecting a different result from the bloody nose they received before. Steve Townsend, an incisive and sharp-tongued officer who fought several tours in the east, was scathing in his criticism. On a piece of paper he sketched the location of the US bases built at the bottom of the Korengal and Pech valleys, where they were sitting ducks for enemy fire from the surrounding mountains. "If you had proposed that at Benning [in Officer Candidate School], you would get an F," he said flatly.[1]

By 2010 the military had begun to pull out of these remote, beleaguered bases and was ready to try something new. A population-focused strategy needed to be applied. Special operations leaders believed that civil defense just might work to secure the populated southern half of Kunar, where Afghan farmers and merchants presumably had a concrete stake in the prospect of peace. From Asadabad south, the mountains are gentler. The Kunar River forms a broad, fertile floodplain where 80 percent of the province's population lives. The special ops commander for the east, Lieutenant Colonel Bob Wilson, thought that Afghans there might be willing to defend their lush agricultural valley, which stretched from Asadabad south to Jalalabad, the capital of Nangahar Province. By creating this bulwark in the valley, the insurgents would be bottled up in the sparsely inhabited mountains of the Hindu Kush, unable to attack Asadabad or Jalalabad, the two major cities of the east. Securing these two cities would help ensure Kabul and the Afghan government's survival.

Kunar was the cornerstone of the region the military referred to as N2K, for Nangahar, Nuristan, and Kunar. It had historically been the route through which guerrillas had threatened the government. The first mujahideen to fight the 1979–1989 Soviet occupation rose up in Kunar, and when the Soviets decided to withdraw, it was among the first to fall. Kunar was both buffer and bellwether for Nangahar to the south. Nangahar was heavily populated and well traveled, with its Khyber Pass crossing from Jalalabad into Pakistan serving as the main east-west link to Kabul and the principal commercial artery. Smuggling abounded, but by and large there was enough business to go around. Nuristan, to the north of Kunar, was sparsely populated by the ethnically and linguistically distinct Nuristanis. Al Qaeda and foreign terrorists regularly trickled in and out of its billy-goat terrain, but Wilson believed their southern Kunar strategy could effectively wall off the badness in Nuristan.

Some outreach to the people of Kunar had already been started by a special forces major named Jim Gant, who had befriended a tribal chief whom he nicknamed Sitting Bull and regarded him as something of a father figure. He wrote about his experiences in a paper entitled "One Tribe at a Time," which Admiral Olson and General Petraeus both read.[2] Gant was known throughout the district as "Major Jim," and his relationships provided a springboard for the formal Afghan Local Police program in the province.

Operational Detachment Alpha 3316 arrived for a ten-month tour in 2011 with orders to expand the local defense initiative along the Kunar River Valley. The team was led by Matt, an angelic-looking, blond-haired, blue-eyed captain from the base at Combat Outpost (COP) Penich on the east side of the Kunar River. The highway was frequently mined, so one of the first steps the CJSOTF-A command took was to bulldoze a landing strip next to the base for its recently acquired M-28 Polish-made planes to land. Team members quickly learned that they were in the crosshairs of the Taliban: their base was mortared four or five times a week from the surrounding mountains. When the M-28 came with visitors or supplies, the loader scanned the horizon from a bubble window in the back as they descended, ready to alert the pilot if he saw movement in the mountains or the flash or smoke of an RPG. The loadmaster would drop the back hatch for quick unloading while the Air Force special ops pilot stayed in the cockpit, ready to take off.

Whenever a flight was inbound, the team would roll out of Penich and barrel down the road to meet it, two dune buggies taking up positions toward the mountains, guns at the ready and gunsights trained on the ridgelines. One day the handoff at Penich's gravel airstrip was especially hurried given the number of passengers coming and going: about a dozen French commandos had come to learn about the local police program so they could apply it in their area near Kabul. A sergeant hoisted gear and shooed new arrivals into his idling Toyota Hilux pickup. For a decade the Hilux had been the runabout vehicle of choice. Although the trucks were unarmored, special operators frequently used them to drive in towns because they blended in and caused much less disruption than the wide, tall, heavy military vehicles. Being unobtrusive was often the safest way to travel. Miller's command had interceded when Toyota decided to shut down the Hilux production line, and the company decided to keep it open. The operators purchased the double-cab model in white for the Afghan Local Police to use as patrol cars, with a green, red, and black logo painted on the doors.[3]

From the lookout tower on the eastern wall of COP Penich, the broad plain that stretched east to the mountainous border with Pakistan looked unbroken, but in fact it was laced with wadis that led right up to the perimeter of the small base. The insurgents could and did sneak up the wadis to fire on Penich, so the first thing Matt did was post a rotating guard of the 1-16 infantry squad that had been assigned to him. A conventional infantry company was based on the west half of the tiny Penich outpost, but it would depart later in the year as the coalition began to consolidate and draw down its forces. While 1-16 pulled guard duty, Matt also integrated them into all of his team's operations. The unit had been sent to help special operations forces with very little notice and even less training, but the platoon leader, Lieutenant Jake Peterson, turned out to be a natural with Afghans; he made friends easily while keeping a weathered eye open to security threats. The young infantrymen were delighted to have a chance to hang out with the special operations forces. They were all permitted—nay, encouraged—to grow beards, which Afghan men regarded as a symbol of male adulthood. Any American who appeared youthful and did not have a beard could be open to ridicule or sexual advances. The teams that made the infantrymen feel part of their mission were repaid with all-out effort and potential future recruits.

Upon his arrival, Matt faced an immediate problem. The leading elder from the nearest village to the south had agreed to form a contingent of Afghan Local Police, and for his boldness the Taliban had crept down the valley and beheaded him. They laid his severed head on a doorstep in another village to dampen any enthusiasm there for joining the movement. Trying to counteract the intimidation, the team made the rounds to visit surrounding villages and ask new leaders to come forward.[4]

Although the Afghan Local Police were intended to be purely defensive forces, the special operators could not afford to gain a reputation for passivity. Matt's team, like other teams who were very nearly alone in the Afghan countryside, made regular forays into the insurgent-infested areas to the east in an exercise they called "creating white space." Sometimes they waited until the Afghan commandos were available to conduct a combat operation with the special operations team with whom they were partnered. But the commandos were in high demand, so the teams often conducted their own patrols to flush out guerrillas and ensure that both the tentative villagers, sitting on the fence, and the insurgents knew the team had more than enough firepower to win any battle. One such battle took place shortly after the beheading incident. The team had determined that the insurgents had come from a camp near a village called Maya, which was right on the Pakistani border. It turned out to be a major guerrilla camp, training, and rest area. Less than ten kilometers away from Penich, Maya sat at the apex of a V where a valley adjoined another valley that ran to the Kunar River just to the north. Insurgents in Maya could easily attack either their district or the one to the north, Sarkani, and retreat back to their lair on the same day. Studying the geography, the team knew that something would have to be done about the camp in Maya if the main Kunar River Valley was to be secured.

The men decided to push eastward to the edge of the mountains. Two Humvees descended into the mazelike wadi and Matt's Humvee, packing a minigun mounted on the roof turret, traveled on the valley floor. As they drove east, Matt found himself too far from the Humvees down in the wadi. He turned to drive back to a spot where he could provide overwatch for the other two vehicles, and suddenly a wave of Taliban popped up out of a crevice and began firing AK-47s and RPGs.

Matt wheeled again and his gunner let loose with the lethal blast of an M134 minigun, an incongruous name for a weapon that fired 4,000 7.62 mm rounds a minute. The Taliban retreated, although not before several fell dead or wounded. Matt raced back to the rest of the team, which also came under attack just as he arrived. An RPG hit the rear of the trailing Humvee, and then one of the weapons sergeants was wounded. The wadi had narrowed, so the men were unable to turn around. They stood and fought off the attackers. One of the medics attended to the injured weapons sergeant, who was evacuated home. Matt was furious with himself for getting tangled up in the terrain, but the fact was that few had traveled where they had gone. They would come to know that terrain well. The firefight put the Taliban on notice that the newcomers would come out to fight and stay to fight. The team picked up radio chatter in which the insurgents called the mini-gun "the breath of Allah," a phrase that delighted Matt and which he and his teammates often repeated.[5]

Matt was blessed with a solid team sergeant, Jay Schrader, who was on his last combat assignment after twenty-five years of service. At age forty-six, he was the same age as the father of his youngest sergeant. Schrader had the even temper of a soldier who had seen it all. He had been coming to Afghanistan since 2003, and the team had been through a trying rotation the year before in Kakhrez, Kandahar, where they had to untangle a very complex tribal, familial, and insurgent human battlefield. Working with indigenous tribes was difficult, dangerous, and maddening, but ultimately rewarding—when it worked. Schrader appreciated the extra help from the 1-16 infantry, but it also represented an additional oversight task, as he had to make sure the discipline among the younger soldiers did not break down. The team was being pressured to split into two as soon as possible so they could expand the local police force. Schrader would move north a few kilometers to head the new site. The idea was to establish a new site with new recruits at least three months before their planned departure in January 2012, so that the incoming team would inherit a relatively mature operation. Split-team operations created a significant additional managerial and logistical burden, not to mention an increased security risk. Most importantly, no one on the team wanted to risk the unraveling of a local police force that was going well but still learning to look after itself. Their Afghan charges were not yet being supported with fuel, ammo, and pay from the local chief of police. The team wanted to make sure they were building something that could last and would not go off the rails.[6]

The team applied the textbook methods of the Afghan Local Police methodology and enjoyed rapid success in recruiting, training, and fielding the force. Because of the district's strategic location, the police allotment was 400 rather than 300, and the force was almost full with 393 trainees. The team profited from two key advantages. First, there were relatively few tribal frictions, because most of the population in this area came from the Mohmand tribe. The other leg up, in addition to a homogeneous population, was the commander, a thirty-five-year-old man named Nur Mohammed, who had stepped forward to become the Afghan Local Police leader with the blessing of the Khas Kunar district elders. Nur was an industrious Afghan with a steady temperament and good management skills. He was low-key rather than a swashbuckler like Commander Aziz, but he was respected by his men and the townspeople, and he quickly proved to be an adept administrator and an effective recruiter.

The Afghan Local Police adopted a way of operating in Khas Kunar that was different from their counterparts in Paktika: instead of building many observation posts, the police lived at home and conducted roving patrols and snap checkpoints in the valley. They built one main outpost east of the main populated area under the shadow of a huge but nearly vacant Border Police post, high atop a hill, and a few more small ones as they expanded up and down the valley. There was virtually no activity or assistance from the Border Police; even the location of the post, ten kilometers from the border, suggested that they were not serious about their assigned duty.

Matt tried to balance assisting the nascent police force with guarding against dependency. He also tried to prod the reluctant district police chief to support Nur and his men. Nur, for his part, understood that they were all supposed to work together. When a suicide bomber blew himself up by a national police truck at the far side of the bridge across the Kunar River, Nur and his men raced to pick up the wounded and secure the site. The Afghan Local Police also received some backup from the Afghan commandos, who came to Kunar on several occasions to spend a week with them on their training or "yellow" cycle. During Ramadan, the commandos joined Nur and his men at their main outpost for an *iftar* dinner to break their daily fast. As they waited for the sun to set, the commandos and police-men played with a baby monkey the commandos had brought home from one of their mountain operations. The monkey scrambled up the posts and jumped on the laughing men, biting at their clothes and hats. Other men set up cots in the open-air interior of the fort and spread large tablecloths on the ground to serve as both seats and table. They distributed the nan bread and bowls of food. The 1-16 platoon sergeant had been a chef at one time, and he helped the Afghans man the drum-barrel barbecue while Nur and Matt and others chatted. Another team member stood watch on the ramparts of the outpost, scanning the horizon with binoculars as the rose-colored sun set over purple velvet mountains. All the Americans refrained from eating or drinking anything, even water, out of respect for the Muslims' fast. As the sun disappeared in a flaming finale, the Afghans gathered at one edge of the compound to kneel and pray. When they were finished they urged all their guests to be seated on the cloth. In keeping with Afghan custom, Nur and his men refused to eat until their guests had their fill.

The members of ODA 3316 were buoyed by the success they were having with Nur and his men, compared to the frustrations they had experienced in Kandahar on their previous tour. They were out living the team life away from the headquarters and senior officers. But making the program work as intended required looking after a lot of minutiae. When the Ministry of the Interior team arrived to process the newly minted police, the officials suddenly demanded to see their contracts, not just their government ID cards. Then they said the con-tracts needed to be in a new format. Seve, the normally genial senior medic, and Ricky, the weapons sergeant, were beside themselves that after weeks of effort to prepare for this milestone that would turn on the Afghan pay spigot, the ministry suddenly presented them with a new requirement. Nur Mohammed, dressed in a sharply pressed white *shalwar kameez*, patiently worked out a solution with the ministry team. The contracts were transferred to the new forms, and eventually all his men filed through the tent at the edge of the base to have their retinas scanned and their fingerprints taken.

Nur was philosophical about the glitches. They were minor annoyances compared to the benefit he believed Kunar would realize from the program. He had had no difficulty raising recruits for the force. One old man had answered the door of his home with an old Enfield rifle in his hand. "I'll gladly give you my sons," he had said. Nur personally knew all of the recruits, since he had lived in the valley his entire life. His men all knew who belonged and who didn't, which was not the case with most of the Afghans in the national police and army stationed in Kunar. "Many of the Afghan army and police are not from here, so we have a much better idea of who is causing trouble," Nur said.[7]

The trouble, he added, emanated from the east. "They come down the valley from Pakistan," he said. When asked if he considered the people on the other side of the border the enemy, he said, "No, no. They are us." Asked to explain, he said, "They are Mohmand too. It is the Pakistani government that is the enemy."

FIGHTING UPHILL

The success of the team in Kunar was tempered by reality: the conventional forces kept tasking the Afghan commandos to help with their own priorities farther north. This left the team and the nascent Afghan Local Police without a remedy to the threat closer to their doorstep: the ever-present shadow of the border, and the numerous ratlines leading right to them. Special operators had cheered when General Petraeus had declared their Village Stability Operations and Afghan Local Police program a top priority for the overall campaign. He issued a FRAGO (fragmentary order) directing the conventional battlespace owners to prioritize requests for transportation, gunships, and surveillance assets to support VSO/ALP. But despite that order, in practice the conventional units' combat operations always seemed to trump the special operators' requests, especially in the east. The gravitational pull of combat for the military was inexorable. After the remote outposts in northern Kunar and Nuristan were closed, the conventional commanders began to run frequent "disruption operations" to keep insurgents from consolidating their hold in these areas—or chase a few Al Qaeda–affiliated targets that might slip into Nuristan for a while.

The special operations battalion commander for the east, Bob Wilson, was a genial and easygoing man, but this exasperated him no end. Continual disruption operations meant there were likely no assets available to support the special operators' priorities. It also meant the Afghan commandos and the special operations team assigned to them were in constant demand. The conventional commanders wanted the commandos on all the operations, since they were the best-trained Afghan force. The time commitment amounted to about six weeks in all, when training time, mission planning, and recovery were factored in. In addition, the commandos often took casualties, since they were the sharp end of the spear.

Every four to six weeks, Wilson was asked to send his team and commandos to Nuristan, with a population of only 120,000. His assessment of the seven operations for which he was requested to supply commandos and his team was scathing. "These operations achieved nothing permanent. They did not extend the government's reach," he said. This focus on enemy-centric operations in lightly populated areas was contrary to the campaign plan. Wilson reminded his conventional counterparts that Village Stability Operations were supposed to be a priority, but they viewed their priority as disruption operations.[8]

Wilson also argued that the overreliance on the Afghan commandos was keeping US conventional forces from bringing their Afghan army partners to a higher level of battle-readiness. The conventional forces were not prepared to partner and mentor as intensively with their own Afghan partners as special operators routinely did. Usually

American conventional forces sent 3 or more of their own troops on an operation for every 1 Afghan partner soldier. By contrast, the special operations teams—12 to 16 men—would go into battle alongside a 120-man Afghan commando force. In the case of Afghan Local Police, one team oversaw an average of 300 police. As the special operators routinely partnered in ratios of 1:12 or higher, the conventional command set a goal of moving from 3:1 to 1:1 partnering ratios. This was not a formula for moving Afghans quickly to the forefront.[9]

Wilson did his best to represent the special operations' perspective from his tiny headquarters in the middle of the sprawling Bagram base of 40,000 souls. But he was a lieutenant colonel pushing against a two-star command led by a division and a general who had never been to Afghanistan. Wilson's subordinate company commander, Major Eddie Jimenez, based at Jalalabad Airport, lived an even unhappier life. Jimenez shared the Jalalabad base with the conventional brigade commander responsible for N2K, a colonel who apparently disdained the junior officer. Jimenez and his company sergeant major, Pat Rotsaert, were for their part astounded by the weak concepts of operation drawn up by the brigade staff. In those operations, troops—often their commandos—were dropped on low ground and forced to fight uphill to enemy positions. Jimenez cemented the animosity when he went over the colonel's head to object to a planned mission in a hornet's nest called Watapur. Jimenez objected because his men would be on the firing line. They had already come to the rescue of soldiers dropped into a hot landing zone in Nuristan and pinned in a six-hour firefight. The general agreed, to the fury of the colonel.[10]

OPERATION SAYAQA

Just before winter set in, Jimenez's company was granted permission to run a commando operation to support the local police and stability operations in lower Kunar. They were going after the insurgent camp in Maya village at last. The conventional forces agreed to supply the needed air support and surveillance assets in early October 2011. Matt and his team were ecstatic. The intelligence reporting was ample and consistent: insurgents used this village on the Pakistani border as a major way station to stage attacks in two districts and beyond.[11]

The commandos and the special operations team partnered with it, ODA 3313, submitted their "concept of operations," or CONOP, which described the purpose of the mission, the detailed plans for conducting it, and the types of support that would be required. The team received the green light to launch. The major issue was where the helicopters would land. This was tricky because the Afghan and Pakistani governments did not agree on the exact location of the border, which had never been formally demarcated. To make sure they were landing on the Afghan side of the border, the team studied two sets of images. Then the soldiers hit the shooting range, which was about fifty yards from their dining room and gym at Camp Dyer, on their patch of the Jalalabad base, for some last-minute nighttime target practice, as they always did before missions. They drove to the flight line and boarded the two Chinooks that would ferry them in. As they approached the landing site, insurgents fired rocket-propelled grenades, and the pilots decided to abort rather than risk losing the birds. The commandos and the team returned to Camp Dyer. They would let the area cool off for a bit, and make another try after the insurgents' attention had turned elsewhere.

In late November, the mission was reapproved. The commandos and their special operations team brushed off their plan, updated it, and rehearsed it. It was officially called Operation Sayaqa. *Sayaqa* was Dari for "lightning," which was the motto of the 1st Afghan Commando battalion, or *kandak*. This was the original Afghan commando battalion and therefore the most experienced one. It was based in Kabul, but the company that was on active rotation lived at a forward base in the barracks beside the team at Camp Dyer.[12]

Once again, the team and the aviators surveyed the possible landing sites. The pilots pushed for a site close to the village, but the team selected a site that was a bit flatter and with fewer obstacles to navigate in the nighttime insertion. Given the steep terrain, it was still going to be a two-wheeled landing. The Chinooks would touch down on their back wheels, keeping their noses in the air, and open their rear hatches for the commandos and teams to offload, before taking off again.

On the day of the mission, November 25, the weather threatened to scrub the launch, but it lifted by nightfall. At 8:30 p.m. they loaded into the ramshackle base trucks. Eddie Jimenez and his sergeant major, Rotsaert, accompanied the team and the commandos to the airstrip to see them off, as they always did. After the birds lifted off, Jimenez returned to the operations center at Camp Dyer to monitor the mission. He would spend the night in the bare-bones center, watching the video feed and listening to the satellite radio communications. Jimenez's bedroom was across the hall, in a room that doubled as his office and private conference room. Their boss, Bob Wilson, would also be watching from his base at Bagram, along with those on watch duty at the CJSOTF down the street at Camp Vance.

It was cold, about 30 degrees, and there was very little moonlight, as the moon had not yet risen. The half-hour flight due north of Jalalabad to the staging base at FOB Joyce, just south of Asadabad, passed without incident. The two Chinooks made several trips to ferry all the commandos and the team first to the base and then on to their destination, Helicopter Landing Zone (HLZ) Khoda, deep in the mountains. Hovering like a giant mechanical insect, rotors chopping the thin air, the first Chinook tilted back and delicately touched its tail wheels down. The Americans and Afghans released their harness belts and jumped out of the rear hatch as it yawned open. The team's chief warrant officer, Mike, was the first to unload with his portion of the team. They fanned out to secure the landing zone for the rest.

Mike was the ground commander for the operation. There were fifteen Americans in all: ten members of his special forces team plus a Special Operations Team–Alpha (SOT-A) signals intelligence specialist, an Air Force combat controller, two navy Explosive Ordinance Disposal experts, plus an army combat cameraman. Two or three Americans were distributed among each of the four thirty-man Afghan commando platoons, as was the team's usual practice. Those in the second group disembarked, hoisted their packs and weapons, and set off at a quick clip so that the troops would not be all bunched up on the landing zone. They went forward about 150 meters and began conducting searches of the woods and manmade structures to clear the area.

Mike's plan was for the entire force to stay together and move around the bowl from west to east and then enter Maya. They had landed about a kilometer and a half from the border, southwest of Maya. They were at roughly the same altitude as the village, but the undulating terrain meant that they would need to go down and climb again to reach it. The mountains right behind Maya, on the border, rose straight up about 2,000 meters in sheer cliffs.

Mike sent the first group down into a hollow to clear a cluster of buildings, and then moved off the landing zone to make way for the two final drops. They all started moving around the bowl. As he reached the ridgeline, Mike heard machine-gun fire. The troops clearing the small village below were being shot at. Mike peeked up over the knoll, and the fire suddenly shifted to his location. He called the battalion on the radio and told the assistant operations officer, "Hey, we are sitting here near the Pakistani border taking fire. There's fire coming from the Pakistani border. You need to make sure the border coordinations were done." The major agreed to contact the conventional two-star command, Regional Command–East, which was the entity responsible for making sure the Pakistanis were informed of impending operations.

The accuracy of the machine-gun fire led Mike to believe that the shooters were wearing night vision goggles. The team, per procedure, was wearing infrared strobe lights that helped their own aircraft avoid hitting them. He instructed the team members to turn them off.

A few moments later a barrage of 60 mm mortars landed about twenty-five meters from Mike, who immediately called the battalion back to let them know the team was now receiving mortar fire. He requested permission to fire on the targets that were shooting at them.

The Chinooks had already lifted off, but the men on the ground were not alone. Their overhead support consisted of a lumbering but heavily armed AC-130, two AH-64 Apache helicopter gunships, and two F-15E fighters on station higher up, in addition to an MC-12 King Air plane loaded with additional intelligence and surveillance sensors. Mike did not have a direct line of sight to the origin of the fires, but the AC-130 crew told him they saw the fire coming from the mountaintop behind Maya. It was too dark and too far for the men on the ground to see the location with their NODs, but the air crew described the structure on the mountain that was firing in their direction. A fort, which had not existed a month before, was surrounded by men with guns who were visible through the plane's thermal and infrared sights.

The combat controller suggested to Mike that they request a show of force from the F-15E Strike Eagle. Mike agreed and told him to call the jets. Less than a minute later, the F-15E swooped down with a deafening roar, screaming through the narrow valley between the team and the mountaintop that was firing on them. "I think anybody would know what this means," Mike said. "It is US forces there and please stop firing." The "or else" was hardly implicit. Yet, much to his surprise, a few minutes after this bone-rattling display of superpower might, another mortar landed right between Mike's group and the one behind him. The team's positions had been bracketed, and the next mortar would almost certainly hit them. Mike had the SATCOM line open to the battalion, which heard the huge explosion through the phone. Mike then requested permission to fire, which Lieutenant Colonel Wilson approved immediately.

Mike had requested the F-15E show of force as an extra step, one not required by standard procedure. But now, knowing that he did not have a minute to spare, he quickly relayed Wilson's approval to the combat controller, who in turn radioed the AC-130 with the request to target the location that had fired the mortars. Recalling that critical juncture, Mike said later, "If [the fire] had continued we would have definitely taken multiple casualties. It would have been a mass casualty exercise after that."

The AC-130 came in for the kill, firing its fearsome side-mounted 105 mm cannon at the mountaintop structure that was the source of the attack. About that time the Apaches returned; they had flown back to Asadabad to refuel about twenty-five minutes earlier. The

Apaches began scouring the valley and identified more targets, along with the AC-130, which reported a lot of people running around the mountaintop.

The first strike did not end the firing. Mike and his team soon realized that the fire was coming from more than one location, as two more mortar rounds landed about twenty-five meters away from the lead group. These team members and commandos happened to be inside clearing a building, preventing certain injury or death, given the proximity of the fire. Twenty-five meters is considered "danger close" for an exploding mortar. The AC-130 immediately identified the second mortar location and moved in to shoot at the target. Enemy fire then ceased for the time being, and the battlefield fell silent.

By that time, the full force had reached the edge of the bowl. Mike was concerned that his lead element would not be safe crossing the exposed area leading into Maya village. He called the battalion and told the operations officer that even though they faced no imminent threat, he wanted to destroy the target that had previously fired on his men to ensure he would take no casualties. Wilson approved, and the second location was engaged again. It was about 1 a.m.

To reduce the risk to the commandos, Mike had also ordered that they not use white lights in their searches and that they throw away their chem lights—gel-filled plastic tubes that glowed green when cracked, a cheaper tool for identifying friendly forces than the strobes. As usual, the commandos had tied chem lights to their vests.

At 1:44 a.m. the AC-130 crew radioed that they spotted people moving around the target on the mountain top. "Do you want to engage?" they asked. Mike called the battalion; the reply was no, cease all fire unless you are getting directly shot at. "Come up on the Iridium [satellite phone]," Mike was told.

He called the battalion back on the handheld satellite phone. This phone was less iffy than the SATCOM 130 system, which also required them to stop and unfold a spiderweb antenna. But it was also a direct line between the team and the battalion for sensitive communications, since the other command centers monitoring the operation could not hear this conversation. Wilson told Mike that the team had been engaging Pakistani forces. Mike's principal concern throughout the battle had been making sure he was following procedure to guarantee the safety of his men and that of the civilians in the village. He had not had the time to think much about who was shooting at him. The machine guns had been firing indiscriminately into the village. He had initially assumed they were under fire from the Taliban, because none of their maps showed Pakistani outposts in that area. He had heard from the team at Penich about being regularly mortared, and there were reports that the Taliban in the area had a DShK machine gun. Still, he was not overly surprised by this news. Both the machine-gun fire and the mortar fire were more precise than the Taliban's normally was.

Given this new information, Wilson told Mike that if anything else happened, Mike would have to paint him a precise picture before he would be able to approve any subsequent fire. There was discussion of an emergency exfiltration to get the troops out, but it was decided that they would stay and clear the area at daybreak. It would be better at this point to continue the mission and do a thorough search to see what turned up.

At about 4:44 a.m., the team started receiving recoilless rifle rounds, fired from a location on the mountains above Maya that was about two and a half kilometers north of the structures that had already been targeted. The Apaches were also fired on by RPGs as they searched an area to the west of the village, in a place where the team and the commandos had caught a high-value target (HVT) some weeks before. In neither case was the fire effective, but Mike reported it to the battalion to keep them informed. Whoever was firing at them, or around them, had not been deterred by the fireworks of the previous hours.

Mike gathered his men and the commandos into a strong point location, a building on the edge of Maya, to wait for daybreak. From this defensible location they would search the entire village. Starting at 7 a.m. he began to send out recon teams to search different locations one area at a time. The MC-12 plane overhead carrying full-motion video, thermal, and other sensor gear relayed what was going on up on the mountaintop, one kilometer away and two kilometers straight up. Mike could see smoke rising from the two smoldering ruins, but that was all. The air crew reported that the Pakistani soldiers had placed their weapons on the ground and moved away to the back side of the ridgeline so their movements would not be interpreted as threatening.

Officers back at the battalion operations center requested that he call again on the Iridium, at which point he was told the Pakistanis would be flying in on two helicopters, armed UH-60s, to investigate what had happened. They demanded that the two Apaches be pulled back from the border to the Kunar River. Mike was uneasy, thinking that his troops might be shot at, but he ordered everyone inside. The Pakistani choppers came in and landed on the back side of the mountain. They stayed about twenty minutes, loading up their dead and wounded. Twenty-four had been killed, and thirteen were wounded.

Mike was glad they had been allowed to stay, because of what they learned and found that morning in Maya. His team and the commandos conducted a thorough search while he and the commando commander talked to the elders. "They were quite relieved that we were there," Mike said. The elders wanted someone to see what they had been living through. One of the elders told him, "This happens all the time." For the last six months, the villagers told him, when they ventured out to get water, tend their goats, or work in their gardens, they would be shot at from the mountains above. One elder said his daughter had died of gunshot wounds the previous month, and they had gone to complain to the governor in Khas Kunar, to no avail. The elder alleged that the Pakistani border guards fired on them to allow the Taliban to come into their villages and stash their weapons there. The Taliban had even raped two girls in the valley. The warrant officer surveyed the village and found a bullet-pocked house with a mortar round in its roof.

Meanwhile, the team and the commandos had unearthed an astonishing array of weapons and munitions from multiple caches around the village. They found AK-47s, PKM machine guns, RPGs and launchers, Pakistani uniforms, and the 7.62 ammunition for the Pakistani G-3 rifles. The quantity of ammunition was mindboggling.

There were more than 15,000 rounds in all, including 2,000 DShK rounds; 9,000 PKM rounds; 3,000 Pakistani rifle rounds; and mortars.[13] The operation's haul had more than confirmed Maya's status as a major insurgent hub. Mike felt sorry for the elders. They had not wanted the Taliban to make use of their village, but they had no means of resisting and no one had come to help them.

It was afternoon by the time the team finished the site exploitation in Maya and was ready to exfil. When Mike radioed in, he was told they would have to hump out three kilometers further than planned to a more distant pickup spot. "You're kidding," Mike said. The men were exhausted from the past twenty-four hours, the high-altitude march in full kit, the attack, and then the detailed search of the village. Now they would have to hike twice as far as they had expected, through a wadi deep in enemy territory that was vulnerable to attack from the high ground, to get a ride out.

It was just a foretaste of the holy hell that their operation was about to unleash.

There were three basic elements to the drama that followed: the investigation, the Pakistani reaction, and the American response. In addition, out of public view, there were significant repercussions within the military chain of command and an ensuing impact on military operations in Afghanistan. Operation Sayaqa's operation was in many respects a watershed moment for the war and everyone engaged in it.

An official investigation was opened by Central Command, the four-star military headquarters in Tampa, Florida, that oversaw operations throughout the Middle East and South Asia. In the weeks of grilling and endless meetings that followed, Mike was mollified by his own conscience and his own command's support. As he went over every detail of the operation, the decisions he made, and the actions he took, Mike concluded: "I would not have done one thing different. If that situation were to happen again I would do the exact same thing."[14]

Central Command's four-star commander, General James Mattis, came to Afghanistan to celebrate Christmas with the troops just as the investigation concluded. Mattis ordered his staff to find Mike. He knew this young soldier had been at the center of the storm, and he wanted to bring his four-star power to bear directly. He had waited until the investigation was completed, since any overture before that would have been a violation. Mattis was as Spartan a warrior as America had, stern, learned, and intensely caring. He was a bachelor, and the military profession was his life. "I looked for things you did wrong, and I could not find any," Mattis told Mike in their meeting. The general praised him for his "tactical patience" in ordering a show of force by the F-15E before returning lethal fire, even though his troops were in imminent danger and he was fully authorized to respond immediately.

Mike was immensely grateful that the general had personally validated the choices he had made in the battle; he would never forget that. But he was disappointed at the public reaction, or, more precisely, the news media's coverage of the event, which shaped the general public's understanding of what had happened. "For the team, it was disheartening that the American media turned on us so quickly without knowing the facts," he said. "And even afterward when everything had come out and the investigation has completely cleared us, there has been no [recognition that] hey, these guys did do the right thing." The massive campaign launched by the Pakistani government to shape public opinion was met by a very weak American reply, which led many to conclude that the Americans had been the aggressors. That interpretation of events was well entrenched by the time the official investigation concluded. When the investigating officer briefed the Pentagon press corps, he faced a barrage of accusatory questions implying that the United States had been in the wrong and had cut out Pakistan in the course of the inquiry, when it was Pakistan that shot first and had declined to participate in the US investigation. Pakistan's official response to the US official report was to claim that its soldiers had shot in the opposite direction at what they believed were militants, and that those posted on the border routinely engaged in what Pakistan called "speculative fire."[15]

Mike wished that more of the intelligence could have been declassified. "It would shed a lot of light on the [Pakistani] thought processes," he said. Throughout the war, Pakistan had played both sides of the fence, supporting insurgents when its interests dictated, while taking massive amounts of American money. Mike's team had been caught up in this central contradiction of the United States' tolerance for what might be called enemy behavior. The United States, for its part, possessed evidence of Pakistan's direct complicity in the death of US soldiers—not just near-deaths—and constant firing on US troops along the border. But the United States chose to look the other way.

Mike did not like it, but he also knew his place within the chain of command. He had joined the service in 2000, had entered the special forces in 2002, and was a newly minted chief warrant officer as of 2010. He and the warrant officer on their sister team in Maiwand had graduated from the course at the same time. Mike loved his job and hoped he'd have another four or five years on the job, but he acknowledged, "I'm not sure if my wife loves the job." For this extra-long deployment, she had moved home to their native Wisconsin, where both sets of parents lived and were available to help her with their baby boy and five-year-old daughter.

The basic fact that got twisted from the very beginning was that the Pakistanis had fired first, on US and Afghan forces. The battle is now enshrined in public memory as a US attack on Pakistan, when it was the opposite. Pakistan leaped immediately into the public fray with the charge that it had been attacked. Then it tried to feign total ignorance of who had been shooting from its side. Then came the extraordinary claim that Pakistan's military thought that it was under attack from guerrillas, which did not stand up to the slightest scrutiny. Mike's men may not have known for certain who was firing at them that night, and he was within his right to call for a return of fire no matter who they were. But there could have been no doubt in anyone's mind that Americans were there on the ground. Although they had landed under cover of night, the sound of their aircraft was a dead giveaway as to their identity. The Chinooks that carried them in could be heard from five or six miles away, and only coalition forces had them, or, for that matter, Apache gunships, AC-130s, or F-15Es—certainly neither the Taliban nor the Afghan government had these things. The

Pakistanis repeatedly fired on the American troops—continuing to do so after the show of force—leaving little doubt that this was a concerted attack. But the American government chose not to clarify the basic "who shot first" facts owing to concerns over the diplomatic fallout.

The confusion that had occurred that night was not on the ground, where Mike's team was fighting. It occurred among those responsible for transmitting advance notice of operations to the Pakistanis. This coordination was most certainly botched, but it is uncertain whether the sharing of that information would have forestalled or halted the Pakistani actions that night. The team had passed its mission concept of operations up the chain of command as required, and it had been approved. It had been sent to the Regional Command–East, the conventional two-star command in charge of sending the relevant information to the border coordination centers that had been established with the Pakistani government. In this case, the coordination center was located at the main conventional base near Asadabad, FOB Joyce. The normal protocol was for the US coordination officer there to share basic information with the Pakistani military liaison officer who was assigned there. A handful of these centers existed on the Afghan side of the border, established by mutual agreement. The Americans had also pressed for coordination centers on the Pakistan side of the border but had been rebuffed by Pakistan.

The border coordination centers served two purposes. One was to relay general information ahead of operations so that the Pakistanis would not be caught totally unawares. The other purpose was to sort out incidents once they occurred. The US military did not relay the specific coordinates of missions in advance, in order to protect them from deliberate or inadvertent compromise. This practice was justified by a long trail of previous incidents in which intended targets had vanished after intelligence was shared with the Pakistanis. Mike's team had been party to just such an incident the previous month. They and the commandos had gone on a mission to Lalpur, a district in Nangahar along the Pakistani border, where there was a reported insurgent training camp. The Pakistanis had been informed of the pending operation twenty-four hours earlier. When Mike and his team arrived, the villagers told them that forty insurgents had left the village just hours before. The team found the second-largest cache of their tour there after Maya. Providing advance notice not only jeopardized the mission, Mike noted, but his men's lives. "People don't understand that it puts us in a lot of danger," he said.

After Operation Sayaqa was launched, when the team came under fire, Wilson had called Regional Command–East to verify that there were no Pakistani border posts in the area of the engagement. The command had replied that there were no posts marked on its map and authorized Mike's request for fire. Wilson only found out as the events unfolded that Regional Command–East had not passed the concept of operations the team had prepared, with the slide of information releasable to the Pakistani military, to the border coordination center, so nothing had been shared with Pakistan. Wilson had sent a back-channel copy of the slide to Joyce, but it had not been briefed to the Pakistanis.

When the team came under fire the second time during Operation Sayaqa, Wilson had tried to determine definitively whether Pakistani forces were involved. The situation became even more snarled at that point, however, because the US officer at the coordination center incorrectly loaded a map overlay into his computer, possibly because he was a reservist unfamiliar with the relatively new "command post of the future" software. That error led him to identify the wrong location to the Pakistani liaison officer, a spot fourteen kilometers north of the scene of the fighting. The Pakistani had confirmed that there were no Pakistani forces at that erroneous location, which heightened the confusion.

Wilson became dismayed, as the investigation unfolded, that the RC-East command did not clarify its own actions with regard to the CONOP and the border coordination. The official investigation's final report was clear on this point, however.[16] Wilson's battalion had briefed the operation in a video teleconference, and the border coordination center at Joyce had asked RC-East's border cell for more information but received no response. A tap dance was beginning that would go on for weeks and consume hundreds and hundreds of hours. Wilson's decisions and the actions of Mike and his men that night were straightforward and entirely justifiable, as the investigation later confirmed. The men were under fire, pinned down, and in imminent danger of being wounded or killed. It did not matter who was shooting at them or why. The rules of engagement were clear. US forces under attack had the right to defend themselves.

What happened next was not just a product of the November 25–26 incident. It was part of a toxic climate of mistrust and bitterness that had reached epic proportions, driven by a series of events. Pakistan had been chafing under the greatly increased pace of US drone strikes that occurred during the Obama administration, often at politically inopportune times. The news media's publication of diplomatic cables via Wikileaks had revealed just how deeply the United States mistrusted Pakistan. A CIA contractor had shot two Pakistanis in Lahore, and the raid six months earlier by SEAL Team Six deep into Pakistani territory to kill Osama bin Laden—with no advance notice—had deeply humiliated the Pakistani military. The escalating rhetoric over the course of the year was matched by a quadrupling of fire from Pakistan's side of the border. The Pakistani government was itching for a fight, and Operation Sayaqa provided just the pretext it needed.

CHAPTER SIX

THE BURDENS OF COMMAND

KABUL NOVEMBER 2011–JANUARY 2012

"WHO IS GOING TO TAKE THE BLAME?"

General John Allen, the four-star commander of ISAF, was in Pakistan the night of Operation Sayaqa. He was pleased with how well his meeting had gone that day with Pakistan's military chief, General Ashfaq Parvez Kayani. US-Pakistani relations had been all but frozen since the Osama bin Laden raid, and yet the Pakistani general had embraced him at the end of their meeting and invited him to a retreat in the Pakistani countryside. The two men had even discussed how they might together "squeeze" the Haqqani insurgent network in North Waziristan—the insurgent faction most closely linked to Al Qaeda and responsible for a recent spate of bombings and US troop deaths. Such action by Pakistan would represent a fundamental shift. Its intelligence service had maintained close ties to the Haqqanis since the Soviet era, when the CIA had helped fund their anti-Soviet operations. Allen said nothing of the impending Operation Sayaqa—in fact, his staff had not informed him of it. He learned of it in the middle of the night when his aide awakened him with the news that twenty-four Pakistanis had been killed by US forces. He was ashen. "It was gone. All gone," Allen said of his efforts to coax some cooperation from the Pakistanis.[1]

A few hours later, Allen arrived at his headquarters, where his top aides were huddled around a press release drafted by his senior public affairs officer, Rear Admiral Hal Pittman. Brigadier General Chris Haas, who had come back to Afghanistan in July as the CFSOCC-A special ops commander, was in the cramped conference room, along with the British deputy commanding general, Lieutenant General Adrian Bradshaw. Haas knew the press release would be carefully crafted, but he was a little mystified by the direction the meeting was taking.[2]

After Pittman presented his draft press release, Allen ordered him to delete the statement that Pakistan had fired on US troops and that no US ground forces had crossed the border. Apparently nothing would be said about Pakistani actions during the operation. Finally Bradshaw spoke up. "Aren't we going to say anything about the Pakistani role?" he asked. Allen's answer was swift and unequivocal: "We are going to be contrite. We are going to apologize. We are not going to talk about Pakistan."

Haas's chief of operations, Colonel Heinz Dinter, sat next to Haas, getting angrier by the minute. The special operations team was still on the ground in Maya, but Allen did not inquire as to their condition or whether they had taken casualties when attacked. He ordered exfiltration of the team farther away from the border even though it would increase their time on the ground and the chance that they would once again come under attack. The massive cache of weaponry the team had unearthed did not seem to have fazed Allen either. He was solely concerned with damage control, which Dinter viewed as placating the Pakistanis. "It was clear that his whole focus was strat comm [strategic communications]," Dinter said later. "Apologize, admit guilt. You owe it to the guys to get the facts first."

The press release that Pittman issued a short while later was brief: it quoted Allen promising a thorough investigation and offering condolences to the families of Pakistan's security forces, and it concluded with a pledge to improve security cooperation. It stuck in Dinter's craw.[3]

Allen was placing a great deal of hope in the power of personal diplomacy to think he could sway the Pakistanis into turning on their longtime Haqqani clients. For decades Pakistan had relied heavily on armed proxies to attack its enemies and shore up its own defenses, primarily to prevent encirclement by its large and powerful neighbor India, which it regarded with fear and loathing bordering on paranoia. But his immediate goal was damage control. He offered the soft-pedaled press release in an attempt to mollify the Pakistanis. Instead, after months of simmering anger, they pounced.

The implosion of US-Pakistan relations was swift. Claiming it had suffered an unprovoked attack, Pakistan finally played the cards it knew would hurt most: it closed its borders to all US military traffic and expelled CIA and military personnel from its Shamsi Airfield. Most of the special operators who had been advising Pakistani forces in a low-profile training mission had already been expelled earlier in the year, but unlike the training mission—which was a long-term effort that would ultimately benefit Pakistan—these two steps would hurt the United States far more than they would hurt Pakistan. Most supplies for US troops in Afghanistan were shipped through Pakistan, so shutting the border would threaten the viability of the entire Afghanistan mission—both ongoing operations and the massive exfiltration about to begin. The expulsion of personnel from Shamsi also narrowed options for launching drone attacks on the border area, limiting the launching pads to bases in Afghanistan. The closure of transportation routes was the most critical: Central Command had diversified its supply routes, but with the drawdown due to begin in the summer of 2012, the Pakistanis knew they had their erstwhile ally over a barrel. It was impossible to move tens of thousands of massive vehicles and other pieces of equipment, containers, and machinery out through the dodgy, mountainous routes of the north. Pakistan would inflict as much agony as possible and hold out for a formal apology, which it would then play to the world as an admission of wrongdoing.

The US investigation initiated by Central Command was limited to reviewing US actions. Brigadier General Stephen Clark came to Kabul and spent two weeks interviewing all who had been involved and reviewing surveillance footage of the operation and intelligence intercepts. The investigation was concluded and the recommendations briefed publicly in late December.[4]

The report made several recommendations to improve coordination, but it found no fault with the actions of the special operations forces. Given this, Haas was dumbfounded when Allen subsequently asked him, "Who is going to take the blame for this?" Haas replied evenly: "I'm the general in charge of the troops involved, so if you want to hold someone responsible, I am the one." Allen formed a "tiger team" from his own staff to scour the details of the investigation once again. Lieutenant General Curtis Scaparrotti, commander of ISAF Joint Command, was appalled at the attempt to find a scapegoat and intervened on Haas's behalf. "We are not going to do this," he said. Sacrificing an officer to placate the Pakistanis in an attempt to repair relations, reopen the border, and put CIA personnel back into Shamsi would have been a travesty. In the end, Allen had a counseling letter placed in Haas's personnel file—not a career-ender but an unwarranted demerit. Haas hid his anger with a forced joke. "I think I'll frame it and put it on my wall," he said.

So this is what it felt like to be without top cover. Since he had arrived, Haas had bent over backward to support Allen's campaign plan with special operations forces in whatever way requested. Haas felt the burdens of command keenly and knew the onus was on special operators to prove they could be good partners to the conventional forces. They had deservedly earned a bad rap early in both the Iraq and Afghanistan wars as the guys who came in the night, caused civilian casualties, and messed up relations with the government and the locals. "We are one of the tools in his arsenal," Haas said. He thought he had established a good relationship with Allen, which was vital. Now that all special operations forces finally had a general—Haas—at the big table, it was imperative to get along. He delivered his updates at Allen's daily briefing, and each Friday he attended what Allen called his "SOF Tribes" meeting together with the other two SOF commanders—the US officer in charge of the special mission task force and a British or Australian officer who traded command of the coalition SOF. Allen called this his "SOF Tribes" meeting because none of them knew what the others were doing, so he had to hear from all three.[5]

The effect on morale was noticeable. Allen's reinvestigation soured many of Haas's staff on Allen; they saw him as a "political" officer who had groveled before the Pakistanis and was ready to throw his own troops under the bus. Dinter was furious. He felt that Allen preferred to conduct diplomacy rather than war and was launching investigations to cover his own rear end. "Thirty-one investigations!" Dinter bellowed in the privacy of his own office. "The endless investigations are wearing the force out."

For his part, Allen felt that from the day he had assumed command from Petraeus in July, his tenure had been marked by a series of what he called "meteors" that struck without warning and threatened to derail the war effort. A sustained attack on his own headquarters; a massive car bombing on a large US base; assassinations of key Afghan leaders; the burning of Korans at a US base, which sparked days of violent riots; Marines urinating on corpses; and the Sayaqa incident—he seemed to lurch from one crisis to the next. The precious two years of the "surge" were passing and with them the chance to show the world that the momentum of the Taliban had been blunted.

Decisions taken by Allen after Sayaqa did not just have psychological impact but concrete consequences as well. Allen might not be able to mend ties with Pakistan, but he was determined to prevent any more incidents along the long, fraught border. He declared a five-kilometer buffer zone along the border, which made any proposed operation there a "Level Two CONOP" that required notifying him and gaining approval by Scaparrotti. Given the supercharged climate of this international crisis, every subordinate commander got the implied message: no such missions would be approved. Therefore, no such proposals were submitted. The net effect was to move the border five kilometers west. No public announcement was made, but it did not take long for the insurgents to realize that the coalition was ceding ground, and they took full advantage. Pakistan, for its part, would pocket any concessions made.

The effects were most dramatic in the narrow province of Kunar. Kunar's capital and the populated Kunar River Valley lay fewer than fifteen kilometers from the Pakistani border. The new edict brought the insurgents that much closer and made the job of the Afghan security forces, including the local police, that much harder. It meant that Maya was untouchable. And, since many of the operations that the special ops commanders wanted to conduct were in the buffer zone, it meant that the Afghan commandos and Eddie Jimenez's company were essentially on ice for the rest of their tour. The buffer zone was reduced to four kilometers—the Pakistanis had wanted ten—but a number of special operations outposts located close to the border, including the ones at Dand Patan, Chamkani, and Shkin in Paktika, were shut down. CIA operatives remained because they were unaffected by US military decisions.

The stand-down came at a critical moment, when the maximum gains of the surge ideally would be felt and the momentum could shift in the Afghan government's favor. Had the United States and its allies made any appreciable difference since the adoption in 2009 of a counterinsurgency approach? Judging the progress of wars, especially insurgencies, is difficult; they are like ocean tides that rise and fall, obscuring the underlying movement. The most obvious fact was that American political support for the war was ebbing, and the US president was resolutely committed to handing off combat operations by 2014. The US military believed it had made progress in rousting the Taliban and quelling the violence in the south. But it was difficult to know what would happen when US troops went home. Would Afghan security forces be ready to carry the ball, and did their people believe they would? The psychological state of the Afghans was perhaps the most important question of all, since a lack of confidence would sap the country's will to fight.

Continued US assistance would be critical to both Afghans' confidence and their ability to keep fighting, but the US-Afghan relationship had become a loveless marriage. Both sides were to blame. Even veteran Ambassador Ryan Crocker, who came out of retirement in the summer of 2011 to replace Eikenberry as ambassador in Kabul, quickly grew frustrated with Karzai, whom he had known since he had arrived in Kabul in 2001 to reopen the US embassy. Crocker was also annoyed by White House micromanagement, and even more at the administration's decision to order troops out more quickly than the military thought wise. Crocker's primary task was to negotiate a strategic partnership agreement that would pave the way for long-term security and economic assistance to help Afghanistan keep the Taliban and Al Qaeda from regaining their former sway.[6]

Karzai had become increasingly adamant in asserting Afghan sovereignty and exasperated at continued civilian casualties. He was determined to halt unilateral night operations, which were primarily conducted by special mission units in search of high-value targets. Haas's troops were always partnered with Afghan special operators, and ISAF coalition special operators were partnered with Afghan special police or intelligence forces. Foreseeing the end of unilateral operations, the special mission units had followed suit, creating their own Afghan partner unit, which initially was primarily a "face" they put through the door once they reached their target. Karzai made clear that he would settle for nothing less than Afghan approval of every mission launched.

In addition to night operations, the other neuralgic issue was the control of detainees. Karzai wanted Afghanistan to assume full control of Parwan, the main detention facility, and all detainees. There were two problems. One was the US concern that detainees would be released for lack of evidence or as a result of the weak justice system. The other issue was that international conventions forbade the handing over of detainees if there was reason to believe they would be tortured. United Nations, Red Cross, and coalition reporting all indicated that prisoners, especially those in the custody of the Afghan intelligence service, were being abused.

The United States dragged its feet in acceding to Karzai's demands regarding night raids. Under the congressional authorization for the use of military force that was approved in the wake of the 9/11 attacks, the US administration had asserted the right to capture or kill any Al Qaeda operatives or affiliates anywhere in the world. There were in fact very few sightings of Al Qaeda in Afghanistan—fewer than one hundred had been the standing testimony of US commanders for years—but the US command believed that its special mission units were keeping the Taliban off balance by rolling up thousands of field commanders and key nodes of its network. These were not high-value targets, but they did constitute the majority of those being captured in Afghanistan. Any time these raids caused civilian casualties, General Allen would be summoned to the presidential palace in Kabul for a tongue-lashing from Karzai. On one such occasion, Crocker protested the harsh language and reminded the president that Allen was a four-star general. American officials intimated that Pakistani intelligence and Iran were influencing two particularly antagonistic Karzai aides, his chief of staff and his spokesman. Crocker was able to keep a number of crises from escalating (such as the assassination of former Afghan president Burhanuddin Rabbani in September 2011, which threatened to sunder the Tajik-Pashtun governing coalition), and he finally did ink the partnership agreement in May 2012.

GROWING PAINS

This was the troubled bilateral context in which special operations forces were trying to make their part of the campaign work. A lot rested on their success or failure: they were being asked to change the dynamic of the war with the Afghan Local Police and to train and mentor the most proficient arm of the Afghan military and police—its special operations forces and special police units. Moreover, there was talk of turning over the entire post-2014 endgame to special operations forces.

Haas felt his teams were making progress on the two lines of the special operations effort: the Afghan Local Police initiative had expanded steadily since its inception in August 2010, and the Afghan special operations forces were growing and getting better. As of November

2011, there were 8,405 Afghan Local Police guardians in 70 sites spread out over 51 districts that had been vetted, trained, and validated by the Ministry of the Interior. It was easy enough to track the numbers, but understanding each little microcosm took enormous effort.[7]

To gauge how individual sites were doing, Haas visited different provinces weekly. So did his trusted longtime comrade Colonel Mark Schwartz, who had replaced Don Bolduc as the CJSOTF-A commander. Schwartz had been with Haas in 2002 in Operation Anaconda, and his colleagues still remembered his heroic effort to stop the friendly fire from killing their Afghan militia force. Heinz Dinter, Haas's blunt and sarcastic operations officer, described Schwartz climbing on top of a tank and banging on it with his helmet to get it to stop firing. Between the three of them they had shared many experiences, and, importantly for this job, they had the full screen version of the Afghan movie playing in their heads. It kept them from overestimating any single event as a Technicolor breakthrough or the crisis to end all crises. Schooled to take the long view, they would do what they could to nudge the country along.[8]

Schwartz was cautiously optimistic about the local police program. "I've seen it struggling and flourishing," he said. "Generally, it is following the mandate." The best areas tended to be the homogeneous ones; the problems tended to occur in very mixed tribal or ethnic locations. Occasionally, the Afghan government had imposed its will, as occurred in Baghlan when the NDS intelligence service insisted that former insurgents be included in the police. Schwartz ticked off some gains in surprising places. Three Marine special ops teams had moved into perennially troubled northern Helmand in May, and by fall elders had come forward to ask for an Afghan Local Police force to be formed. Marine special operators had also won converts in the once-dicey Margab River Valley in the west, where unimpeded travel was now possible, and raised seventy police recruits in Dare Bum. The foothold in northern Kandahar was expanding. But teams had been pulled from a few areas that proved inhospitable. In one case, the Taliban had beheaded three elders for collaboration. In another, the local police had struck a deal with the Taliban to allow them safe passage. Before reaching decisions to withdraw, the teams were generally allowed time to try to work through problems.[9]

Rather than rely on anecdotal impressions, the command tasked a team of RAND analysts to produce a rigorous, quarterly assessment of whether the program was producing the desired effects. The analysts drew on three main sources of data: polls they commissioned; the "significant activity" database of hostile acts, as reported by coalition forces in the vicinity of the sites; and the voluminous situation reports that the special operations teams filed. The hostile-activity reporting showed that between six and twelve months after an Afghan Local Police force had been formed, the violence in an area, after an initial spike, tended to decline compared to similar areas in which no local police existed. Over 70 percent of those polled expressed support for the Afghan Local Police in their area. The most recent poll in the fall of 2011, however, showed a worrying increase in the number of Afghans who said they had been asked for a bribe at ALP checkpoints; still, at 27 percent, the incidence was lower than that reported for other security forces and officials.[10]

Haas was concerned about the need to mentor district chiefs of police more intensively, since the teams reported mixed support from district chiefs. They were the vital link for the police to receive pay, supplies, and support, if this was to become a genuinely Afghan program that would be sustainable when the special operations teams were no longer available to hold their hands. Haas began thinking about whether teams should move from villages to the district centers in a "hub and spoke" approach to encourage district chiefs to support their local police. The vast majority of his sixty-five teams were devoted to this initiative, so he wanted to be sure he was getting the best possible return on that investment.

Any changes made the early proponents of the initiative nervous. They feared that pulling out of the villages could cause the teams to lose touch and allow bad influences to take over. Some change was inevitable, if only because each commander had his own style and made course adjustments as he saw fit. Haas was not one to sit in hours-long video teleconferences, for example, so he did not carry over that practice from Miller. Some felt Haas was less committed to the Village Stability Operations half of the VSO/ALP program. A certain pressure to focus on numbers was created by the weekly spreadsheet that tracked how many Afghan police were on the ALP payroll in each site, but Haas repeatedly told teams not to act hastily. "You do not want to be looking over your shoulder when you leave," he counseled.[11]

The anxiety of those on the sidelines was also due to the fact that Haas did not advertise his changes of course. His style in general was more insular than Miller's. He did not create a big tent or rely on outside advisers, as had become common at military commands over the past decade. He preferred to trust his closest colleagues and his own gut. In addition to Schwartz and Dinter, Haas's inner circle consisted of his deputy commander, John Evans, a rising star aviator from the 160th "Nightstalkers" Special Operations Aviation Regiment, and his frank chief of staff, Navy SEAL Captain Wes Spence. Haas's door, schedule, and flank were closely guarded by his aide-de-camp and by his command sergeant major, Jeff Stigall, whose brother had occupied the very same position as Miller's senior enlisted adviser. Haas had an extraordinary grasp of Afghanistan's Machiavellian politics. One of his staff officers commented, with some amazement, "Haas will rub his bald head for a while and then predict exactly what [a senior Afghan official] is going to do." He added, "He's like Tony Soprano—if Soprano were a good guy."[12]

Stylistic differences aside, Haas supported the continued expansion of the local police initiative, but he believed that training, advising, and mentoring the Afghan special operations forces was an equally important part of the campaign. The latter were regarded as the most proficient Afghan fighting forces, an achievement that was directly attributable to the intensive mentoring approach that US special operators typically used. Building competent indigenous forces was part of their tried and true formula. Most of the US special operations work in seventy-plus countries in Asia, Latin America, and Africa in any given year involved advising and assisting those governments' forces.

The Afghan special operations forces consisted of 5,500 troops as of late 2011, including nine commando *kandaks*, or battalions, and a brigade-level headquarters. In the past year they had begun to select and field special forces teams as well. The chief of the Afghan army staff, General Sher Mohammed Karimi, was an enthusiastic champion of Afghan special forces; as a military exchange student, he had graduated from the Special Forces Qualification Course at Fort Bragg and the Ranger School at Fort Benning forty years before. He posted the chart of the expanding organization on his office wall for visitors to see. The plan at that time envisioned a force of 8,500, with two brigades of commandos and special operators; a Kabul-based mobile strike force equipped with light armored personnel carriers; and an air wing of Mi-17 Russian-made helicopters. The Afghan Partner Unit, called Kteh Khas in Dari, was a nascent counterterrorism unit. Rangers were traditionally direct action specialists, but they took up the task of training their partner unit and built a first-class shoot house in which they practiced close-quarter battle drills and marksmanship.

This plan for "Afghanization" was the special operations forces' way home. In fact, it should have been the operators' number-one priority from the beginning had they followed their own playbook. Decade-long efforts in Colombia and the Philippines had produced proficient forces that greatly diminished threats in those countries. In Colombia, an entire special operations command had been built, with special forces, Delta, SEAL, and Air Force special operations forces all taking part. The Colombians had since graduated to training other countries' forces in Latin America and West Africa. Haas's previous post before coming back to Afghanistan was at Africa Command, where he had focused on training and advising government forces—until the Libya uprising shifted his focus to unconventional warfare to aid the overthrow of Muammar el-Qaddafi.

As commanders and policymakers began debating the future course in Afghanistan in late 2011, the question arose of whether the special operations forces should prepare to assume overall lead for the Afghanistan effort in 2013 or 2014, since the United States was heading toward a small-footprint mission largely devoted to training, advisory, and counterterrorism roles. These were all special ops missions, but the question was whether the special ops command could manage all of the moving parts—the logistics, the base functions, and the legal and administrative tasks that were currently being handled by multiple four-, three-, and two-star commands. Haas's staff did some initial planning, but he concluded that it was a bridge too far. The fact was that the special operations forces had no deployable three-star command other than the one developed to do high-value counterterrorism operations. The conventional army argued that ten years of on-the-job training had given its corps as much claim to the job, so its III Corps and XVIII Airborne Corps were lined up to do the job through 2014. Having lost that battle, US Special Operations Command chief Admiral William H. McRaven then turned his attention to what was a logical intermediate step—combining all special operations forces in Afghanistan under one operational command. He had forced SEALs, Delta Force operators, and Rangers to work together when he led the counterterrorism Task Force 535, and he was known to favor more unity and less parochialism among the "tribes." He set his sights on making Haas's successor a two-star who would lead a unified special operations command in Afghanistan.

The fact was that special operators had their hands full overseeing the expansion of the largest local defense program since Vietnam, building Afghan special operators, and tracking terrorists. Special operations forces had not operated so many dispersed firebases and outposts since the Vietnam War. The CJSOTF's recently formed 120-man Group Support Battalion (GSB) handled logistics for a 6,000-man force in 103 locations all over the country—whereas the normal ratio in conventional units was three support personnel for every fighting man. Riggers worked up to twenty hours a day assembling and loading made-to-order packages to be delivered by plane, helo, or truck. They dropped a staggering 1 million pounds a month—almost half of all the airdropped supplies in Afghanistan. The battalion cobbled together air support from three sources: the conventional force's aviation brigades, the CJSOTF-A's own contract fleet, and the Air Force Special Operations Command's Combined Joint Special Operations

Air Detachment–A (CJSOAD-A). The CJSOAD-A had a centralized command in Qatar that apportioned two MC-130Ws (as well as AC-130H gunships, which provided close air support in combat missions) and three Polish-made M-28 "Truckers," which could land on a 1,500-foot runway or kick loads from its back hatch. The contract planes included three Beechcraft 1900s, two Casa 212s, and a B-200. Most conventional air was obtained on a "mother, may I" basis, so the special operators were astounded when Major General James Terry, the regional south commander, dedicated three Blackhawks, three Apaches, and four Chinooks to support them.[13]

Although both the Afghan Local Police and the Afghan special operations forces were growing, Haas, like General Allen, was bombarded by his own set of meteors that fell into his path. Some were less damaging than others, and some represented a mortal threat to the enterprise. The first one was a scathing report published by Human Rights Watch in the fall of 2011. It was sharply critical, but short on facts. The human rights investigators were only able to visit a handful of sites, and the problems they found focused on the north, Herat, and the Khas Uruzgan District, which was known for its internal strife. The report dwelled on Afghanistan's history of militias and earlier programs and predicted that this latest program would degenerate into lawlessness. It recommended several safeguards that were already in place, including US and Afghan intelligence vetting of recruits, a designated coordinator in the district police office, and rule of law and ethics training.

To some degree the report was a self-inflicted wound; the command had given out very little information about the local police program and permitted even less access, in part because ISAF wanted it to be seen as an Afghan program rather than something special operators were doing. But this prevented any outsiders from evaluating what was happening in the remote countryside. When the report came out, ISAF ordered a brigadier general to investigate. He took a thorough approach, assembling a team for each region to visit sites and conduct interviews. The month-long inquiry confirmed seven allegations and partially confirmed several others; many could not be verified. "I take it seriously when there is misconduct," Schwartz said, noting that a former local policeman had been convicted of rape and an Afghan special operator had been relieved of duty.[14]

A much graver threat to the reputation and potential success of the Afghan Local Police program—one that consumed months of staff time and caused great angst at the special operations command—was the proliferation of ad hoc forces formed by US conventional units. These programs had none of the safeguards and intensive mentoring that were the hallmarks of the Afghan Local Police initiative. Most important, they were not Afghan programs. Only the Afghan Local Police program was an official Afghan government program—it was backed by a presidential decree and run through its Interior Ministry. The special operators knew—from their own hard experience—that the Afghan government opposed the coalition taking matters into its own hands. The Marines in Helmand had created a force of thousands called the Interim Security Critical Infrastructure program. In the north, the Critical Infrastructure Protection program hired Afghans as guards for fixed installations. Then ISAF authorized a new program, called Community Based Security Solutions (CBSS), that allowed conventional forces to use Commander's Emergency Response Program (CERP) money to hire local security forces. These programs were all quick, easy ways to employ young Afghan males and address the lack of Afghans to provide security. But none of them involved any local or national Afghan oversight. This was perhaps a legacy of the Iraq War, in which US units had been encouraged to throw together local forces and let them grow like Topsy with no intensive training or mentoring. They were intended to be quick fixes.

This drove the special operators crazy, since they had carefully crafted procedures to gain the approval of a shura of local elders, vet the candidates, and ensure that the Interior Ministry validated every single district where they worked. The conventional forces' programs posed two clear dangers: their loosely overseen armed guards could run amok, and their misdeeds would be a blemish on everyone, as few Afghans or foreigners had any idea which program was which. The operators were also betting that, at some point, the conventional forces would attempt to turn the whole motley lot over to them. An unvetted, untrained force of wayward Afghans from who knew where would then become their problem.

Haas's staff spent a lot of time arguing with the ISAF Joint Command, and eventually two solutions were devised. First, a FRAGO would be issued making the special operations command the "executive agent" for local defense in Afghanistan; the conventional units would be instructed to follow their procedures and best practices for raising any local defense forces. Second, the conventional force programs would end in 2012, and if and when those forces were turned over to special operators, there would be no presumption that they would be automatically hired. They would have to go through the vetting like everyone else. The task of crafting the specific details fell to Commander Alec McKenzie, a Navy SEAL who oversaw all aspects of the local police program for Haas. McKenzie was from a tribe that was famous for shooting and taking down terrorists, and the SEAL took the same "no prisoners" approach to his bureaucratic battle. He was deeply passionate about the program and its prospects for success if the forces hewed to the carefully crafted methods.[15] The second FRAGO was finally issued in January 2012, and the actual demobilization and transition of the non-ALP groups would take more than a year. It occurred most rapidly in Helmand, where three-fourths of the Marines would be leaving in the coming months, and more slowly and painfully elsewhere.

By far the biggest problem that Haas had to wrestle with—the one that posed a strategic threat to the local police program—was the Tajiks' ongoing effort to hijack the program for their own political purposes for patronage jobs and the rearming of their militias. Nothing would damage or end the program more quickly than this. Like Miller before him, Haas had spotted problems brewing in the north: the shuras were not doing real vetting, nonlocal outsiders had been permitted to join, and at least one provincial police chief was a noxious influence. The Americans finally secured his removal only to see him sent to another job.

The problem came to a head in dramatic fashion as 2011 drew to a close. Interior Minister Bismullah Khan Mohammedi (BK), a powerful Tajik figure, issued an ultimatum: he would not authorize any more Afghan Local Police in the south or east until his bidding was done in the north. The special operators had finessed this issue for the past year and half, throwing their teams and energy into the insurgent-plagued areas while putting just a few teams up in the north. Now BK insisted they immediately create Afghan Local Police forces in all the designated districts in the north, as well as some new ones. His refusal to validate any more districts in the south came at a critical time in the south, where elders in the insurgent-infested province of Zabul had come forward. If this opportunity were lost, those individuals might suffer a dire fate.

Haas met with Generals Allen and Scaparrotti and then went with the latter to confront BK, hoping he could dissuade him. The Americans showed him the joint campaign plan that he had signed on to and pointed out that those areas in the north were not under threat. BK airily dismissed the plan, saying, "That was just a snapshot in time. We see a threat outside that area now." Haas then outlined the criteria for establishing ALP forces, which BK had signed off on and now was ignoring. The Afghan was unmoved.[16]

Haas knew that BK was under tremendous pressure from his Jamiat-e Islami Party colleagues, who had watched the Afghan Local Police growing in Pashtun areas. Jamiat's many factions, including six governors of northern provinces, all wanted a piece of the action. But sending special operations teams north and taking more of the approved slots, pay, and guns for an area with no insurgent threat would siphon off much-needed resources from the south as well as fuel the ethnic divide. Haas offered a compromise: he would send a team to Parwan Province. It was near Kabul, so shoring up its defenses had a clear security rationale.

Haas faced the showdown armed with knowledge of BK's tactics, which he had grappled with at the latter's Jabal Saraj headquarters in 2001 as they prepared the assault on Kabul. US interests and those of Jamiat, the Northern Alliance party, overlapped but did not entirely coincide. The Tajik leaders ultimately wanted what was best for their faction, not the entire country. Haas tried to appeal to BK's duty as interior minister to protect the entire country.

Haas thought his concession on Parwan had broken the logjam, but weeks went by and BK refused to authorize any supplies or pay for the south. Haas tried another gambit: he asked Asadullah Khalid, the president's confidant, to see if he could sway BK directly or through Karzai. That did not work either. He then floated an alternative proposal to BK. "You have police training centers in the north and a budget: why don't you train more police there?" Still the minister would not budge.

Finally, in January 2012, in a video teleconference with BK, Haas and Scaparrotti appealed again for the minister to relent. Haas did not believe they should offer any further concessions, and he was ready to sacrifice his decade-long relationship with the minister. They had always been able to reach some compromise, but Haas felt this was a Rubicon that could not be crossed. If the program were utterly politicized, it could become a tool for the possible regeneration of a civil war. Haas said no, he would not accede to BK's demands. "I told him that there was no insurgency there, and I was not going to put teams there," Haas recounted. "I told him that the south had to survive to be part of Afghanistan."[17]

BK blew up. "Chris is no longer my friend," he shouted at the Americans. "From now on I am only going to talk to General Allen."

Haas had drawn a line in the sand, and he was ready to stand by it. In the end, after consultations up the chain of command, Haas and his staff were told to hold their noses and produce a plan for a new compromise. They were to build "accelerated ALP" forces in four districts in the north: special operations teams would be sent north to train recruits, but only for four months. Afghan officials were to complete the vetting and have all required equipment ready. In return, the draft memorandum requested that the minister approve the southern districts awaiting his validation. When he sent the memorandum forward, Allen left the reciprocal demand out, perhaps because he was dealing with the fallout from the Koran burnings and Karzai's denunciations. Haas's staff had to grit their teeth and move ahead with their end of the bargain.

Haas's ops chief, Heinz Dinter, was glum. "We are putting the program at risk by making this compromise," he said. The entire staff was distressed to see even these four districts depart from the standards. Problems emanating from the north could taint the whole program, and even worse, the concession could be used as a precedent for further diversions of effort. At the moment, the operators had no choice but to salute and move forward, trying their best to make the plan work. Haas had tried his best but was unable to influence the Tajik perspective on such an existential matter. This powerful faction in the Afghan government would ultimately have to decide whether it trusted Pashtuns enough to embrace the vision of self-defense in the south. If the leaders of Afghanistan did not buy into the core purpose of the initiative, it would falter over the long term. Moreover, it would bode ill for the country's much-needed reconciliation. Recounting the showdown and the rupture in his relationship with BK, Haas hid his emotions as usual. "The Afghans get a vote," he said gruffly.[18]

◀ Maj. Gen. Scott Miller and Command Sgt. Maj. J. R. Stigall

◐ Captain Dan Hayes and Maiwand District Afghan Local Police (ALP) commanders

JS and Afghan special perators train ALP in Maiwand ●

● Hayes and the rest of Operational Detachment Alpha (ODA) 3314 in Maiwand
● ODA 3314 on patrol in Maiwand

ptain Mike
"Hutch"
utchinson and
ommander
iz ▶

Hutch greets
ktika elders

MICHAEL T. HUTCHINSON

⬤ Aziz's men after patrol in Pirkowti

◀ Aziz's special squad and ALP defuse bomb

⬤ Greg and ODA 3325 after Pirkowti raid

● Afghan interpreter Rock, Captain Matt, and ALP Commander Nur Mohammed in Kunar Province

● Captain Brad Hansell meeting with ALP commanders in Maiwand

ALP commander
Jan Mohammed and
his sons ▶

◀ Bombed truck of
Jan Mohammed's
son

◀ Navy SEAL
Commander Mike
Hayes and Taliban
leader receiving a new
Koran and turban in
reintegration ceremony
in Uruzgan Province

⬥ Afghan commando fires a rocket-propelled grenade

⬥ SEALs and 8th Commando Kandak in clearing operation in Zabul Province

MC2 JACOB L. DILLON

MC2 JACOB L. DILLON

⬥ Aerial resupply of SEALs in Zabul

⬥ Captain Jason Russell and Master Sgt. Russ in Yahya Khel District

ALP checkpoint in Zarghun Shah District

Captain Jae Kim and Lalu, one of Aziz's men

● ODA 1411 outside their mud-walled qalat in a village called Nawi Kalay

● ODA 1326 teaches ALP class in Ghazni Province

⬆ Brandon and Marawara District ALP

⬇ Nur Mohammed and Kunar ALP

⬆ Observation Post Shiloh

⬇ Maj. Gen. Tony Thomas in graduation ceremony at the Special Police Training Center in Wardak Province

CHAPTER SEVEN

ON THE SAME TEAM... OR NOT

KANDAHAR 2012

HUGGER AND SLUGGER

ODA 7233 took the reins from Dan Hayes's team in Maiwand in 2012. Brad Hansell, the new team leader, was well suited to be a special forces officer, though the idea appalled his father, a navy admiral. Hansell had first gone off the reservation by going to Basic Underwater Demolition/SEAL (BUD/S) training. Though the SEALs had captured the public imagination, they were still a tiny, outsider club in the world of submariners and big ship brass. During the grueling tryout, Hansell had suffered a freak near-drowning accident that rendered him unable to continue. Undaunted, he decided to transfer to the US Army Special Forces Qualification Course in a program that permits sailors to "go green" and don the army's colors. Hansell loved his father, but wasn't in thrall to family traditions. He was a restless soul, a thinker, and an incessant talker. He took to the complex puzzle of Maiwand like an iron filing to a magnet.

Hansell and his team sized up the situation in Maiwand. He decided that to move forward they needed to take a step back. He knew Hayes's team had sweated over two tours to gain recruits for the local police, and that many of the recruits had not come from the immediate Ezabad area. He decided that the program would be stronger if the local police commanders relocated to the villages in which they had been born. Two of the commanders were originally from south of Highway One, and under this plan these two Afghans would go into that critical area to expand the ALP. Southern Maiwand was the most populated zone outside the district center and the major insurgent ratline running into Kandahar City. Hansell had heard that one of the largest absentee landowners in the area, Kala Khan, wanted to return and get his land back into production. If Hansell could cobble together enough Afghan manpower using the ALP commanders, the local Maiwand officials, and the national police, he believed he could make inroads into this key area, particularly with a few assists from the remaining US conventional forces—a watchtower here, a patrol there. If they were lucky, this coalition of Afghans might grow numerous and become strong enough to survive even when the Americans left. Over time, they might just win Maiwand.

Fortunately, Hansell could rely on several solid partners: three or four decent ALP commanders; an Afghan special forces team led by a superb captain, Najibullah; and the excellent Afghan American interpreter who had decided to stay on for a third year, Abdullah Niazi. In Hansell's plan, the ALP commanders would move in stages to the new areas south of Highway One and recruit volunteer police there. Hansell also wanted to wean the local policemen of some bad habits he had spotted. He took away most of their trucks, except those of the commanders, so the police would stay tethered to their assigned area rather than driving around to meet each other.

The second part of Hansell's plan was to work hard on the local officials in order to limit such corrupt practices while encouraging their self-interest in expanding security from the district center to the entire district. Maiwand's police chief, Sultan Mohammed, and its district governor, Saleh Mohammed, had recently been appointed. The new district police chief had taken to using the Afghan Local Police as part of his muscle to persuade the farmers to pay him not to eradicate their poppy crops. Hansell realized what was going on one day when his team was on patrol with an Afghan police commander in his white truck. As they approached, Hansell saw a farmer's son running across a field with what he thought was an RPG launcher. The team moved in closer and saw that the boy was running away with a pump, which he thought the police were coming to confiscate. When he talked to the farmer, Hansell found out that the district police chief was not only plowing under the poppies of those who did not pay to keep the eradication tractors off their land, but taking their pumps as well.[1]

Hansell's predecessor, Dan Hayes, had invested a great deal of time in the previous district governor, Obaidullah Barwari, who had begun to connect with more villagers and stay in the district full time. Hansell believed the new district governor was in cahoots with the new police chief, but he decided not to agitate for their removal. He believed the constant churn of local officials was counterproductive and somewhat pointless, since the incentives for corruption were systemic. The constant game of musical chairs had done little good. Hansell preferred to work on modifying officials' behavior by degrees. He could not stop the eradication campaign, which alienated the population, or stop local officials from using it to pad their pockets. But he could take steps to keep the ALP from being associated with eradication or the shakedown scheme. If they had no trucks, they could not make the payola visits. Hansell also began meeting frequently with the district police chief and governor to propose ways they could expand the security bubble that currently was confined to Highway One and the district center. Both of these local officials had been assigned embedded US mentors, but those mentors were individual officers who brought no troops, guns, or money as leverage. The Afghan officials naturally were more readily swayed by a special operations team that brought all three to bear.

While Hansell worked on the district governor, meeting with him almost daily, the district police chief became the object of Captain Najibullah's attentions. The head of the Afghan special forces team ODA 112, Najibullah was a Tajik from Laghman Province near Kabul, not a Pashtun like the Afghans in Maiwand. But he was a devout and deeply principled Muslim who abhorred the rampant corruption that had taken root in Afghan society. "My religion does not allow it. We each have to answer for our behavior, so I do what I can to help," Najibullah said, explaining his views on the subject. "Things here are bad from the top, and from here we cannot solve everything. People buy positions, and there is a system of bribery. The taker and the payer are both part of it." He ran herd on the ALP, visiting check-points at random and chasing down any guardians reported to have taken bribes. He believed a different approach was needed for the dis-trict police chief, however. Najibullah was well aware that the poorly paid police chiefs were unofficially given guidelines for the "take" they were allowed, so he decided he would quietly ask Abdul Raziq, the provincial police chief, if his new subordinate police chief in Maiwand was exceeding the permissible ceiling; if so, Raziq could call him on the carpet.[2]

Najibullah's reputation had grown over the past year, and Afghans had responded to his example of moral leadership. In the towns and mosques, he spoke from the heart, and people listened. His high, deeply lined forehead gave him the look of a solemn, sorrowful basset hound. Indeed, he was greatly pained that his countrymen were kill-ing each other. Very often his sincere appeals helped to resolve village disputes, gain ALP recruits, and persuade frightened elders to support an ALP force.

While Hansell and Najibullah focused on shaping the district offi-cials' behavior, the team whipped the ALP into shape, instilling new discipline. Hansell jokingly referred to himself as the "hugger" and his team sergeant, Chris, as the "slugger." They were a good match: Chris was caustic and skeptical, balancing Hansell's energetic opti-mism, which was not naïveté so much as a determination to find a way through the thicket of Afghan complexities.

"We should have been doing this years ago," the sunburned team sergeant said as his sergeants strapped on their kits for a foot patrol outside the qalat walls. Like many other veteran special operations sergeants, Chris believed that Village Stability Operations and the

Afghan Local Police initiative was the right approach to Afghanistan's rural insurgency, but that it had been adopted too late to make a difference. He doubted the special operators would be given enough time to ensure that the program was firmly implanted with Afghan ownership before the teams were reduced or pulled out altogether. That did not mean he was going to sit on his heels; he would drive his sergeants every day to move the ball down the field. His sergeant major, Brian Rarey, had put him in charge of the team ahead of his promotion, knowing that the insouciant sergeant would be relentless. His hooch was decorated with a Georgia Bulldogs flag, and the T-shirt he wore inside the qalat was emblazoned with the word "infidel." Chris was determined to make a difference in the little time they had, but he also saw this as a live training mission to make his men better.[3]

True to his nature, Chris found the existence of a Taliban-controlled village—Eshqabad—right across the wadi from their outpost to be intolerable. He viewed it as both an unacceptable security risk and an affront to his warrior nature. The previous team had engaged in endless negotiations with the village elder, who played both sides of the fence and filibustered successfully to avoid taking a stand: he would tell the Americans in private what they wanted to hear—that he was all in favor of raising a local defense force—but no sooner had they departed than he rushed to placate the Taliban and assure them he would do no such thing. The slugger had his own brutally effective negotiating style. One day the team visited the elder, and Chris cornered him into walking with them to the site he had suggested as an ALP checkpoint. Once there, he put the Afghan on the spot and asked him to announce to the villagers who had gathered around that the first checkpoint would be built there. Next, Chris requested that he convene a meeting of the villagers and invite them to volunteer family members for police training. The villagers complied, but the day after the shura, the sons who had been volunteered left for Kandahar City. Undeterred, Chris went ahead and built the checkpoint as agreed. He then turned to Jan Mohammed, the stalwart, squint-eyed ALP commander, who stationed his son and his local police squad there.

In addition to addressing the security threat in Eshqabad, Chris was determined to see what the team could do for the village of Moshak farther north, which remained firmly in the Taliban's grip. The team arranged a medical and humanitarian mission to the town, which was so poor that little children ran around with no clothes on. They brought a truckload of food, medicine, and clothing and distributed it. The next day, the Taliban roared into town and forced the villagers to bring out all of the donated goods and put them in a pile, which they then set on fire. The message was clear: don't let the foreigners in, or you will pay for it. The team was not ready to give up, however; they decided to try stealthier means. One of the ALP commanders, Abdullah Hakim, was fanatically committed to the anti-Taliban fight. Two of his sons had been beheaded by the Taliban, so neutrality was not an option for him. He told the team he would go in under cover and attempt to find allies in the town and some useful intelligence. Hansell worried about the risk, knowing that Hakim would be killed if he was caught, but Hakim insisted. "He will do literally anything we ask," Hansell said in amazement. Hakim was old and weathered, but he had the heart of a lion. A farmer stepped on a mine next to his field, and Hakim came to his rescue. He put a tourniquet on the man's severed leg, as he had been taught in the ALP's first aid class, and then carried him on his back to the team medic's shed. With men like Hakim, Jan Mohammed, and Najibullah, Hansell believed Maiwand had a fighting chance.

Moshak proved impervious to their efforts, however, so Hakim and another ALP commander moved south of Highway One in the first of several sequential moves that Hansell had planned. Hakim used his own home as his base, sandbagging its walls, and began recruiting new trainees. To prepare for the subsequent move farther south into the Taliban no-man's-land, Hansell wanted some cover for his lightly armed Afghan police. He asked the US battalion commander to build a small observation post and persuaded the local Afghan army commander to man it with a few soldiers. Even though the conventional battalion commander was shutting his main base in preparation for the conventional forces' departure, he was willing to lend Hansell a hand.

The next move south would be key. The plan was for Jan Mohammed to move into the house he owned in Pir Zadeh, halfway into the Taliban zone. Securing that area would lay the groundwork for the major landowner, Kala Khan, to move back into the zone, where he would use his influence to support the recruitment of local police among his fellow Ishaqzai tribesmen. "We share the same cemetery," Jan Mohammed said, explaining how close their connection was in Afghan terms. Kala Khan had an economic incentive to support the move: he wanted to resume cultivation of his land and get his products to market. Kala Khan was considered by some military intelligence analysts to be too close to the Taliban to trust, but Hansell believed the road to success in Maiwand ran through Kala Khan, and that his return would bring recruits and momentum to an area long dominated by the Taliban. Kala Khan cut a somewhat mysterious figure. He dressed in the traditional long shirt and a silvery turban, but he always, indoors and out, wore black Ray Ban sunglasses. Hansell was willing to bet that bringing Kala Khan, one of the dominant Ishaqzai figures, into the circle and increasing security for the Ishaqzai population would make them feel less shut out by the majority tribe whose members held the top district jobs and controlled the opium trade.[4]

By addressing their concerns one by one, Hansell also persuaded the district officials that they would benefit from a larger security bubble, just as he had won the agreement of the ALP commanders to move south. Hansell could talk and plot for hours on end, and Afghans readily took to the energetic extrovert. He would meet Jan Mohammed or the other commanders at their houses, where they would spread a blanket or carpet outside and drink chai as they debated their next moves. Such confabs seemed tedious to his action-oriented sergeants, but Hansell would just stretch out his long frame on the Afghan bolsters and keep up his end of the dialogue. Meanwhile, his team and the local police kept watch or patrolled the nearby field or the alleys between the qalats. Hakim needed no cajoling. He reached out to his contacts in the south and began to collect intelligence on massive troves of arms and homemade bombs the team and the ALP would later seize.

In this most vital aspect of his job—building bridges and reaching agreements with Afghans—Hansell knew he was extraordinarily lucky to have an interpreter of the caliber of Abdullah Niazi. Very few teams, companies, battalions, or even brigades had Category 3 interpreters, the rating the US military gave to its most fluent and highly skilled translators. Niazi's value and role extended far beyond his linguistic skills. He was intuitive and empathetic, and he could read people in both cultures. Niazi had the skills of a diplomat and was personally attached to the mission. Some interpreters worked for the money, and many Afghan nationals hoped to gain an American visa, but Niazi could return to his business in San Francisco any time he wished. He was there to help his native country regain its footing. He did not want to see the Taliban return to power, and he was distressed by both the violence and the corruption. Niazi tried his best to serve as a bridge between the blunt American culture and the polite Afghan one; many soldiers had caused offense with crude, ignorant, or bullying behavior, often without even realizing it. Many of them had no idea how deftly Niazi smoothed over such affronts with his own warm, humorous touch.[5]

Hansell did listen closely to "Abdullah Khan," as he called him out of respect and endearment. Niazi, though, was soon exhausted by Hansell's pace and penchant for nighttime meetings. He would sigh and brew a new pot of tea to keep himself going. Hansell worked virtually around the clock, napping for an hour or two on the couch in the operations center. Like many operators, he availed himself of the steady supply of energy drinks in the team's cooler. Sugar-free pomegranate Pit Bull was his favorite. To lay the groundwork for their move south, Hansell and the team made forays there in the dead of night to meet secretly with sources and potential allies who could not be seen with them in daylight. Other times they would bring the Afghans into the shura room in the qalat.

Abdullah Niazi believed that Hansell was on solid ground in building his strategy around the one-eyed Jan Mohammed, who he believed had the character, leadership, and standing in Maiwand to be an enduring pillar of the ALP. The old Afghan had committed himself and his sons to the fight, was respected as a warrior from the Soviet era, and had deep roots in Maiwand. His craggy face was softened by a grandfatherly gleam in his eye. He had cast his lot with the Americans to support the government, and he had the backbone to persevere in the face of adversity. One day in the spring, Jan Mohammed and his son were crossing the wadi from Eshqabad. The son's truck was in the lead and hit an IED. The bomb blasted through the floor, killing the driver and tearing off the son's arm as he sat in the passenger side of the cab. The entire front of the white Toyota was twisted like a pretzel, its engine block damaged beyond repair. Miraculously, the son survived. Jan Mohammed was outraged at the injury to his son, but he was not about to abandon the checkpoint or cede the battle for Maiwand.

An even greater threat to Hansell's forward momentum than the attack on Jan Mohammed occurred just a few weeks later. Early on the morning of March 11, Hansell received word that a mass shooting had occurred in Panjwayi District next door—at the exact spot where a special operations team was based. Hansell was ordered to halt all operations and keep his team inside the compound while his superior officers looked into what had happened and what it might mean for them. It turned out to be far, far worse than any of them could have imagined. In the middle of the night, Staff Sergeant Robert Bales, the head of the conventional infantry squad that was attached to the special operations team to provide security at Camp Belambay, had walked out of the camp's compound and gone berserk. He systematically went into homes in two villages where he shot and killed sixteen Afghans, including children, and then piled up some of the bodies and set them on fire. It would later come to light that Bales had been drinking as well as taking drugs. There were rumors of marital problems and a missed promotion, but it was not immediately apparent what had triggered such senseless savagery.

Hansell, following the instructions he had been given, immediately instituted a lockdown. His men were forbidden to communicate with anyone. The conventional infantrymen attached to his team were from the same platoon as Bales, including the platoon leader, who was frantic to find out what had happened to Bales. Hansell felt strongly that he needed to be out communicating with Maiwand officials and the population, but the orders from Kabul were unequivocal: no one was to leave their bases. The only thing he was permitted to say was that a shooting had occurred by a lone gunman and that the matter was being investigated.[6]

Afghan national and provincial leaders moved swiftly to pacify hundreds of outraged villagers who gathered at the gate of the Panjwayi base and district center. The elders put the burned bodies of children into trucks and brought them to the growing crowd. American helicopters ferried the president's brother, Qayum Karzai, as well as the governor and other top officials, to the district to meet with them and calm the crowd. The Afghan leaders suggested that the American commanders stay out of sight as they worked to defuse the situation.

Meanwhile, in Maiwand, Hansell asked Captain Najibullah to take his special forces team out on patrol to talk to people in the district center and surrounding villages. Najibullah went without hesitation. Hansell then turned his attention to the members of Bales's platoon who were there in the qalat with his team. He called a meeting in the plywood operations center. The young men shuffled in, hushed and downcast. Hansell told them that a chaplain would be available to talk to them individually. He emphasized again that no one was to say anything about the matter—not on the phone, not on the Internet. As an extra precaution, he told them, he had suspended the Internet hookup on the communal computer in the dining hut. The soldiers shifted uncomfortably, avoiding each other's eyes. No one said anything, and Hansell dismissed them. They had felt like outsiders before, and now they felt like pariahs.

General Haas, the special operations commander in Kabul, had issued the orders because evidence-gathering and due process were critical issues from the moment the killings were discovered: any investigation could be easily tainted if it was not handled by the book. Haas expected one of the senior military commands to take over; he only had one young military lawyer on his staff, and his command did not have general court-martial convening authority. But no one did.

In the days and weeks of meetings and video teleconferences that followed, Haas's lawyer, a major from Florida, found herself bombarded by demands from other commands and pressured to make facts public quickly. Haas told her he would support whatever she needed to protect the integrity of the investigation. The other commands' judge advocates were advising their commanders to stay clear of the controversy so they would not be tainted or burdened by the tough choices that would have to be made. Haas was chagrined, but at this point he was not surprised. He regarded the pressure being placed on his young lawyer as unlawful command influence. Of his stalwart young major, he said, simply, "she is my hero."[7]

Thanks in good part to her effort, the procedures were followed to ensure due process despite the remote, war-torn location of the crime. Investigators made it to Belambay to gather evidence, witnesses were identified and deposed, and Bales was sent back in chains to his home base of Fort Lewis, in Washington, which was set as the venue for the trial. At a preliminary legal hearing at Fort Lewis, tearful survivors recounted the grisly details of the systematic shooting over a video link. The massacre was the My Lai moment of the Afghan war. The military prosecutor asked for the death penalty, but Bales pled guilty to avoid that sentence.

US commanders credited Afghan officials' actions with containing the fallout from the massacre. Raziq, the police chief, gave the surviving family members free, permanent housing in a building he owned near the police headquarters. The US military paid millions of dollars in compensation. At first the families refused the payments. At the meeting where they eventually accepted the money, one of the Afghan men emphasized that their acceptance of the payment did not constitute forgiveness. A young girl who was badly wounded was flown to California for extensive medical care. It had been quickly agreed that the team at Belambay should be moved elsewhere; after such a catastrophic event, there would be little to gain and much to risk from their continued presence. Another team would remain at the district center. The special operations battalion commander for Kandahar, Lieutenant Colonel Richard Navarro, went to Belambay with his company commander and sergeants major the morning after the massacre. It became clear that Bales had been drinking with other squad members in violation of General Order Number One Bravo, which applied to all servicemen and women in Afghanistan, as well as taking steroids and other drugs. Navarro found no evidence that the special operations team leader had been complicit, and the team sergeant had been at Kandahar Airfield recovering from an IED attack.[8] This egregious crime fed Haas's growing concern, however, that the US military was suffering a breakdown in discipline after a decade of war. For those troops posted at the remote special operations bases, an extra measure of maturity and discipline was required to cope with the dearth of recreation and support services, the heightened threat, and a heavy workload.

The massacre had the potential to derail special operators' efforts throughout Kandahar Province, but Hansell was shocked that he encountered little fallout from a terrible act of violence committed by an American just fifteen kilometers away. The most potent effect may have been not on Afghans in Maiwand but on Americans at home in the United States, adding yet another reason for them to recoil from the war. On the first patrol with Hansell and his soldiers after the lockdown order was lifted, Jan Mohammed, his ever-present cigarette dangling from his lips, asked a simple, succinct question about Bales: "If he was crazy, why was he in the army?"[9]

"WE'RE NOT GOING SOUTH, ARE WE?"

The massacre did not derail the ODA 7233's plan, but the decisions of the conventional force command in Kandahar did. Hansell and the team were poised to move Jan Mohammed south and begin their intensive recruitment in the critical Taliban stronghold along the river. But Regional Command–South had other ideas. The deputy commander for operations, Brigadier General Marty Schweitzer, wanted the team to move instead into the eastern edge of Maiwand to stop the flow of Taliban into Zhari. Four successive brigades had tried to beat back the Taliban in that area, and Schweitzer's 82nd Airborne was now trying to rack up this district in the win column before it was time to go home.

Hansell's chain of command supported what he wanted to do. The southern part of Maiwand along the river was a major ratline from Helmand into Kandahar City; securing it could represent a critical breakthrough for the entire province. He had moved his pieces into place and was now ready for his decisive move south. The team had seven weeks remaining in its tour. If successful, this undertaking would be the culmination of three years of hard work by the special operations teams there. Hansell had seen how southern Maiwand fit into the bigger picture, then crafted a plan and lined up the allies to get there. Like his counterparts in Paktika and Kunar, he had found a way to pacify a larger area than a single village by combining a series of tactical moves. The key was not conducting repeated combat operations or building forts, but bringing successively more Afghans together around a plan they supported. Hansell grasped that his role was to be a facilitator: to put the Afghans in positions in which *they* would be able to protect things they valued, with enough support and numbers to enable them to survive. A security bubble created in that fashion would take root, expand, become more solid, and perhaps endure. The district police chief had fully embraced Hansell's proposed move south, but the chief had no interest in going to the unpopulated eastern edge of Maiwand.

Brigadier General Schweitzer was focused on Zhari, however: he saw a situation there that needed resolving, and he saw the team in Maiwand as an asset he could use. Zhari, a recently created and tribally fragmented district, remained a violent place despite years of effort. A quickie attempt by US conventional forces to build local police there had gone awry, and Schweitzer wanted the special operators' help in fixing it. A special operations team had originally been placed in Zhari, but it departed after experiencing conflicts with the brigade commander, who did not want the team to meet with the district officials without him being in attendance. The signs that the Afghan Local Police in Zhari had gone off the rails began to mount. Hansell began receiving reports that the Zhari local police were driving around

Maiwand in their trucks and extorting bribes. One ALP member was caught planting a bomb. The conventional brigade had adopted an ill-advised policy of paying the police a reward, on top of their pay, for turning in IEDs, which was contrary to the rules prescribed for local police. Then one of the conventional unit's soldiers had been killed by an Afghan dressed in a police uniform, part of the rising number of so-called "insider attacks." The last straw came when two Zhari local police dragged a detainee behind their vehicle, killing him.[10]

Schweitzer wanted Hansell's team to move east immediately to train and mentor the Zhari local police, as well as to recruit new local police in eastern Maiwand to shore up the effort in Zhari. There were many problems with this proposal. First, the team had not done any of the usual patrolling, village assessment, and local meetings that were essential first steps before entering a new area. It would not be a quick matter to fix the Zhari police force, which had ballooned overnight with none of the careful procedures that the special operators followed. Only eleven of the four hundred police even had official government IDs. They would need to re-vet the force to weed out the bad apples. The command's desire to see quick production of additional police only compounded the risk. Finally, taking on this task would divert Hansell and his team from completing the culminating step of their own plan for Maiwand.

Schweitzer had no authority to issue orders to Hansell or any other special operations team. This fact always galled the conventional commanders. The special operators had tried over the years to placate them while maintaining autonomy. But this was an acute example of the type of conflicts that arose: there was one team and two different ideas of what it should do with the last seven weeks of its tour. Brigadier General Haas proposed a compromise to Brigadier General Schweitzer. The team could do both missions by splitting in half and dividing the remaining available positions allotted for Afghan Local Police in Maiwand between the two locations. That would allow the team to conduct its planned push south while also working in the eastern edge of the province.

Schweitzer rejected the proposal. He wanted all of the remaining slots for Maiwand devoted to the eastern edge and the special operations team's entire focus on his priority. "Are we agreed?" he replied to Haas. "If not, I can raise this with Huggins."[11]

It was a thinly veiled power play, one that occurred all too frequently despite senior officials' rhetoric about the good working relationships that special operations and conventional forces had forged in the past decade. Schweitzer was threatening to take the issue to his two-star boss, Major General Jim Huggins, the commander of Regional Command–South—who also did not have any authority over special operations forces. But Huggins did outrank Haas, and Haas would be expected to accede to his request.

Schweitzer's frontal challenge had its intended effect: Haas decided not to create a national command-wide argument over the location and mission of one twelve-man team that he would, in all likelihood, lose. The three-star commander tended to support the two-star commanders, and Haas would have to ask Allen to overrule them both. Hansell was crushed. He had a vision, he had taken the initiative, and he truly believed he and his team could fundamentally alter the situation in Maiwand with this carefully staged expansion of ALP. But he received an email from his battalion commander, Navarro, that left no further room for debate. Hansell gave the order for half of the team to move to the eastern part of Maiwand. Their new home would be tents at Deqobad, a tiny combat outpost that had been nearly vacated by the conventional forces.

Chris, the team sergeant, was angry. Conducting split-team operations in insurgent territory was not to be undertaken in a casual manner. Half of the team and half its infantry squad moved into Combat Outpost Deqobad. Hansell inspected their new home, a truly desolate scene reminiscent of the last days of Vietnam. A few forlorn conventional soldiers manned machine guns in three sandbagged, camouflage-covered lookout towers at three corners of the nearly vacant base. Two Stryker armored vehicles and a tank were parked under netting. They did not patrol outside the gate, because no one would be left to guard the base. So the young men just hunkered down, pulled their shift, and watched through binoculars.[12]

About fifty meters outside the base to the south, the brown Arghandab River marked the border with Panjwayi. A rat-a-tat of gunfire broke out one afternoon across the river in early August. This was not unusual; gunfire was often heard when the special operations team left the compound, which was barely visible through the trees. About ten attacks a day occurred in this area, called the Horn of Panjwayi. Hansell had ordered a PGSS (Persistent Ground Surveillance System), whose cameras, mounted on aerostatic balloons, allowed the team to watch the insurgents digging holes, planting bombs, and preparing ambushes.

Hansell quickly sized up how bad things were. Not only had the remaining conventional soldiers at Deqobad failed to do any patrolling to create a security bubble, they drew their weapons on any Afghans who did come to their gate—a tactic that would certainly not win them any friends in the area. The young men were totally bunkered in. Even the landowner, who had not been paid by those who built the base, was turned away at gunpoint.

Hansell, his split team, and their trusty Afghan special forces team partners immediately began patrolling the area to establish their presence and understand who was who. On their second patrol into the village just outside the outpost's gate, Hansell's men and Najibullah's team returned to see an elder they had visited the day before. They entered his qalat and found that the doorway was booby-trapped. "Why didn't you tell us?" Hansell asked, incredulous. "You and your children could've been killed at any moment."

The hapless man replied, "They threatened to kill us if we told you." He had chosen to risk killing himself or his family rather than trust an American to help him. As Hansell and the others continued their tour north of the village, Hansell shook his head at the effort the conventional forces had expended to build a row of tiny outposts that were little more than watchtowers—a Potemkin creation to give the appearance of American control when nothing could be further from the truth. The troops were almost gone, and the only regular activity was a mine-sweeping patrol that ran up and down the road once every day or so.

In the mosque of one of the villages, Najibullah spoke to the villagers who had gathered there at his request. "We've come to help," he said. "What are your problems here?" They told him that the Taliban had also rounded them up, but had never asked what they needed. Najibullah appealed to the villagers as good Muslims to help bring peace to their land. He left feeling that he might be able to gain some recruits; the villagers seemed amazed at being treated so respectfully. Najibullah heard that the Afghan army commander at the nearby base had not been seen since arriving two months before. Najibullah went to the base, introduced himself to the commander, and asked that he send ten of his troops out on patrol with them. The commander agreed, but did not offer to come along.

Hansell and Najibullah's men set out to patrol the next day, August 6, heading west from the Deqobad outpost toward a nearby police outpost. Hansell had asked the reluctant district police chief to send some of his men down there to man the post. As they approached, Hansell's men split into two groups, leaving their medic, Dan, at the "V" so he could respond, if needed, in either direction. They walked along a streambed, a standard way of avoiding IEDs. Hansell wished he had prevailed on the district chief to send his crack mine detector; the Afghan could spot a command wire or signs of a buried jug like a tenderfoot.

As the first group of Afghan and American soldiers reached the police post, they began to scale the sides of the riverbank. Suddenly, one of the Afghans spotted a mound of dirt that looked like a buried IED. The Americans radioed for the explosive ordnance disposal technician attached to the team to come to their location. As they waited, one of the Afghan special forces soldiers took a step back from the mound. His body was blown upward and landed a few feet away, bleeding profusely. Then Louis, one of Hansell's attached conventional infantrymen, stepped on another mine. He was leaning forward, and the blast caught his entire body. The force of the bomb broke one leg, mangled the other, and ripped off his arm. Louis's best friend in the squad, who was manning the radio, froze in shock for what seemed like an eternity. Then he snapped out of it and grabbed the radio, shouting for Dan, who had heard the first blast and was already on the run. There was no telling how many mines had been planted in that field by the streambed.

Dan arrived at the ghastly scene, threw down his bag, and began tearing bandages and gauze out of it. He soon ran out. He wrapped Louis's exposed leg bone and stuffed gauze around the wound to stop the bleeding and try to save the rest of the leg. The soldier's head wound had been cauterized by the blast. There was not much that Dan could do for his genitals. Before Dan arrived on the scene, one of the soldiers had already applied a tourniquet, as every soldier was trained to do, to the other leg, where the foot had been blown off. Over the past decade, the operators' tourniquets had been refined repeatedly so that they were light, quickly applied, and effective. The apparatus they used was a simple adjustable loop of webbing material with Velcro on one side that was fastened around the damaged limb. A six-inch-long black plastic stick attached to one side could cut off the circulation and stem the blood loss with a few quick turns.

As Dan worked feverishly, the communications sergeant called for a medevac helicopter, which arrived about thirty minutes later. The two wounded soldiers were loaded aboard and flown to the military hospital at Kandahar Airfield. Louis was outbound a few hours later for Brooke Medical Center in San Antonio, Texas, via Germany. The young Afghan soldier was still alive, but he had been gravely wounded. Both men were triple amputees struggling for life, and if they did survive their lives would be irrevocably altered. That night, Najibullah requested leave from his company commander to go to see his soldier at the earliest possible date. It was Ramadan, and Najibullah stayed up late every night to talk with his men after their sundown meal. They sat outside their tent in the Deqobad's gravel yard by a fire pit they had made. Normally, they would listen to music or sing, but no one felt like singing.

Back at Ezabad, Chris, the team sergeant, was furious at the news of the wounded soldiers. Furious, but not surprised. He knew that hasty plans resulted in mortal risk. The one bright spot was the stellar performance of his medic, Dan, under an extreme test of his skills. Keeping two multiple amputees alive so far from any base was a feat in itself. Chris knew this firsthand, as he had been a medic before becoming team sergeant. Dan was talented, and Chris praised him in the typical tough-guy way. He teased him by calling him "Handsome Dan"; the young man was indeed movie-star handsome, a Josh Hartnett lookalike. But he was modest and serious, unaffected by his own good looks. He had not chosen to be a medic, but once he began the training he had taken to it, and now he planned to pursue it as a career when he left the service. He had kept his head in the chaos and taken every step to stabilize the gravely injured men. The initial care usually determined the chances of survival.

A few days later, the team received a video greeting from the wounded Afghan soldier that had been sent by one of the company's sergeants who had visited him in the hospital. The young man, conscious and propped up in his bed, offered a wan greeting to his fellow soldiers with his bandaged arm. Hansell immediately went to find Najibullah to share the video with him. Two weeks later, however, they received the news that after receiving multiple surgeries, Louis had passed away in San Antonio.

The grievous injuries at Deqobad, affected morale, which was already low. Half of the team remained at Ezabad to oversee the ALP operations in central Maiwand; these operators captured some massive caches in southern Maiwand, but they were forbidden to recruit ALP there. Hansell's half of the team recruited men for the ALP at Deqobad and trained police in Zhari at the base a few kilometers to the north, a dual tasking that was stressful and exhausting for a handful of men operating in an unfamiliar, hostile area. Training Zhari police in eastern Maiwand did not sit well with the team; it was contrary to the special operators' procedure. Teams normally trained recruits near their homes so they could continue to vet them and their families and learn about any Taliban ties they might have. It was part of the continual intelligence-gathering that provided crucial insights and kept the men working with them safe.

But RC-South cared about output: the command wanted 120 more police recruits and wanted them fast. Hansell went to have dinner with the Maiwand police chief, Sultan Mohammed, to appeal for his help. Over dessert, as they sat among the lush grass and fragrant basil bushes of the district center garden, the chief promised to send his crack IED detector and a few men to help staff the police post. He called over his deputy to give him the order. Hansell knew that the chief saw an opportunity to expand his poppy-taxing scheme, and this had tipped the scales in the Afghan's decision, but Hansell had little choice but to accept the tacit bargain. His team needed help securing the area and conducting its dual mission. He and his team had relied heavily on Najibullah and his men, but Najibullah was leaving in a few days to visit his wounded soldier and take his long postponed leave. Hansell would remain haunted by that man's life-changing injury and Louis's death.

Jan Mohammed came to Ezabad one day to see Hansell, who had been spending most of his time in Deqobad. "We're not going south, are we?" the old Afghan said to him sorrowfully, more as a statement than a question. He would soldier on, just as he had after his son was wounded, but he was disappointed. Hansell did not have the heart to lie to him.

After a long military career and a decade at war, Hansell's company sergeant major, J. R. Jones, was steeled to accept the loss of men and decisions that went against the views of soldiers on the ground. It was all office politics to him, or "militics," as another senior noncommissioned officer dubbed it. But others who were less stoic had a harder time swallowing what had happened: it was heartbreaking to lose men because commanders could not come together around the right plan. Special forces tended to view themselves as the stepchildren of the army, unloved by their "big army" brothers, but that fatalism did not help solve the problems created by a dual chain of command.[13]

Jones took a long view of the special operations effort in Afghanistan: he had spent most of the past decade in that country. He was emphatically in favor of building local police, but, like Chris, he doubted that the special operators would have enough time to make a local police force succeed in Afghanistan. "We did this hamlet program first in Vietnam," Jones said. "But we are working on a compressed timeline here." He ticked off the benefits of local defense forces. "The local police know what is going on. They tell us who is who. The conventional [US] forces do not see what is going on. They do not know which ones are carrying guns or planting bombs," he said. The Afghan army could not do the job alone, he added, especially in a rural insurgency. "You can't just surround the enemy and squeeze him in a rural fight like this. If you don't have police and government, you will not win," he said. But time was the critical ingredient: the triad of competent army, police, and government could not be built overnight.

Although Jones often self-deprecatingly referred to his Mississippi origins, he spoke with authority grounded in his training and experience in war zones. Jones, Navarro, and Jones's company commander, Angel Martinez, had not only been in and out of Afghanistan for a decade. During that same decade, when they were not in Afghanistan, they had been deployed to Colombia. The two experiences offered a stark contrast. The three men had been intimately involved in what turned out to be a successful mission in Colombia that was little known outside the circle of special operators who had spent time there, patiently assisting every branch of the Colombian military and its special police units at every level all over the country. They had helped to build a proficient special operations brigade in a comprehensive and continuous program carried out with a few hundred American advisers, and they had supplied advisers to other units and commands. The US government had also sent development aid, helicopters, and counternarcotics assistance totaling about $7 billion over the decade—a large amount in terms of the US foreign assistance budget, but a pittance compared to the cost of the war in Afghanistan.

Colombia had been transformed dramatically. The once besieged government pushed the fifty-year-old insurgency out of the half of the country where they held sway, and captured or killed most of the top leaders. The remnants had recently opened peace talks with the government, heralding a possible end to that war. How was it that the

United States had succeeded so well in helping Colombia and lost its way in Afghanistan? Why had it taken eight years to adopt the right playbook in Afghanistan—just as the American public had grown exhausted with the effort? Colombia was a more developed country, but its government had been riddled with corruption, its military ill supported, and the guerrilla groups strong. One key difference was that the United States had never doubted that its central mission was to advise and assist—to help the Colombian government beat back the threat and strengthen its military and government—rather than to kill and capture. Another important difference was that success had been achieved through a succession of strong ambassadors, a unified military, and interagency effort. The efforts in Colombia had not been derailed by infighting among generals. Would it be possible, in the time left, to change the Afghanistan playbook to more closely mirror the successful formula used in Colombia?

CHAPTER EIGHT

SEALS DO FOREIGN INTERNAL DEFENSE, TOO

URUZGAN AND ZABUL 2012

SEALS TAKE CHARGE

US Army Special Forces had been in Uruzgan from the earliest days of the war, but no one had envisioned or articulated the endgame for this province, a key safe haven that insurgents used to launch attacks on Kandahar, the political center of gravity of Pashtun Afghanistan. Because of its deemed second-tier importance, it had been mostly left to the special operations teams and a handful of Dutch and Australian forces, including Australian special operators. Uruzgan was plagued by formidable terrain and by feuding among the Barakzai, Popalzai, and Ghilzai Pashtuns as well as the Hazarans. Zabul Province, next door, had been almost entirely ignored; it was a playground for insurgents who had sunk deep roots into the Ghilzai population.

SEAL Commander Mike Hayes aimed to change that state of affairs. The SEALs had been given command of a newly formed Special Operations Task Force–Southeast covering Uruzgan and Zabul provinces when the Afghan Local Police initiative kicked off in 2010. The SEALs were needed to help with this expanding foreign internal defense (FID) mission to train and advise Afghan police. SEALs had done foreign internal defense all over the world, and FID is a mission that special ops forces are assigned to carry out by military doctrine and law. This is not widely known, however, because the SEALs traditionally have emphasized direct action and special reconnaissance as their core missions, particularly in their recruiting, training, and publicity.

So, despite the fact that FID was expected of SEALs, there was plenty of grumbling all around when the SEALs were put in charge of Uruzgan and Zabul. Army special forces regarded the area as their turf and their mission. SEAL operators for the most part had joined the SEALs because they wanted to become precision raiders who conducted high-intensity, high-impact commando operations to locate, capture, or kill terrorists, hostage takers, or other evildoers. They moved into Tarin Kowt as touchy-feely recruiters of village defenders who were expected to manage a far-flung network of outposts, a managerial task for which SEAL teams were not organized, trained, or equipped. Needless to say, the first commander, J. R. Anderson, went through a lot of growing pains as his hard-charging SEAL staff learned new and mostly deskbound skills, including the lingo and hardware of army logistics and intelligence systems, since they were plugging into an army-dominated structure. Anderson was a smooth character, but he had a few run-ins with the higher command. His senior noncommissioned officer chewed nails the entire time. He had just come off a high-speed tour with SEAL Team Six, one of the United States' tier-one special mission units. His body language made no secret of the fact that he thought this assignment was a very bad fit.[1]

SEALs had successfully conducted tactical-level foreign internal defense missions around the world—training, advising, and fighting alongside other countries' forces. After clearing Iraq's waterways alongside the elite Polish GROM commandos, they had trained and fought with Iraqi counterterrorism units. They had done the same with Colombian commandos and marines, with Filipino and

Thai marines, and, more recently, with African units from Kenya to Cameroon. In their earliest years, SEALs had worked with indigenous forces in Vietnam. Their greatest recent success in this line of work had been in the Philippines, where SEALs and other special operators had deployed repeatedly to train, advise, and support Filipino forces fighting the Abu Sayyaf terrorist group in the fractious islands of Basilan and Mindanao. SEALs coached the Filipinos on conducting maritime raids with fast boats and were instrumental in tracking one of the Abu Sayyaf leaders using US surveillance drones. Ultimately, he was captured following a high-speed waterborne chase. The Americans sped alongside the Filipinos in their own zodiac boats, letting the Filipinos move in for the takedown.[2]

When Mike Hayes and SEAL Team Two moved into Uruzgan in 2012, Hayes was ready with guidance for his troops and a plan. He had an unusual background in that he had just left the White House, where he had worked for two years on the National Security Council staff. He had applied to be a White House Fellow, and then Denis McDonough, one of President Barack Obama's closest advisers, asked him to stay on for another year to work on piracy issues in the Persian Gulf as well as other sensitive special operations projects. Since 9/11 a string of smart SEALs had worked on counterterrorism issues in the White House, starting with Admiral Bill McRaven, who had drafted the counterterrorism strategy later issued by President George W. Bush. Hayes was smart and ambitious and had a head for policy and strategy. He had earned a master's degree at the John F. Kennedy School of Government at Harvard University and had become a member of the Council on Foreign Relations while at the White House. But he was not just a policy wonk: he had deployed multiple times to Latin America, the Balkans, and Iraq, where he was deputy commander of the special ops task force in Anbar Province. Hayes was motivated by a desire to succeed, but he was also a devout Catholic, and his religion—though he did not wear it on his sleeve—shaped his service ethic and his view of leadership. He wanted to make a difference in the world.

Hayes spent a great deal of time and thought preparing to take command in Uruzgan. Having just departed the White House, and still in close touch with his former colleagues there, he was all too aware that it was late in the war and that the administration was determined to draw down. Before he arrived in Afghanistan, Hayes laid out his guidance in twenty-five succinctly worded edicts that he thought conveyed the essential approach and mindset necessary for his team to succeed in a difficult task. His central message was to support Afghans and not act unilaterally. One edict, for example, was, "Every action should contribute to the creation of a self-reliant Afghanistan." He exhorted his team members to eschew meaningless metrics, writing, "Don't confuse outputs with outcomes." He insisted that they avoid civilian casualties at all costs: "Don't ask yourself, Can I shoot?" he wrote, but rather, "*Should I shoot?*" Hayes also reminded his troops to pay equal attention to governance and development and to engage with the population. He urged them to reach out to the youth, in particular, drawing a parallel that he hoped would resonate and make his men realize how profound their impact could be: "Every one of us remembers ... a teacher who positively influenced our lives....You will never know what small gesture of interaction will last a lifetime." He concluded with injunctions to behave collegially, reminding them of the sense of commitment that had led them to volunteer.[3]

Hayes's "Do unto others" ethic was tested right away when he discovered that his conventional counterpart, the US Army colonel in charge of partnering with the Afghan army brigade based at Tarin Kowt, loathed special operations forces. The army colonel made the depth of his animosity clear on their first meeting. Hayes bit his lip and bided his time. As the Afghans instantly took to Hayes's polite manner, the colonel found himself the least favorite player on the team.

Hayes established three clear objectives. One was to stop the "jet stream" of insurgents using Uruzgan and Zabul as their safe haven and transit route from Pakistan to Kandahar. He would concentrate his effort on securing the central corridor of Uruzgan. His second and related goal was to win over at least some of the Ghilzai Pashtuns from the Taliban side. The third goal was to transition a number of sites to Afghan control by the end of his tour and reduce the number of teams in Uruzgan. He knew that the US forces would be expected to draw down in the coming years, and he wanted to ensure that they were positioned to sustain their gains with fewer teams.

Though Hayes was driven, he was good humored, and his staff made sure there was time for hijinks to leaven the work. On his forty-first birthday, they surprised him in his room—parading through in Ninja costumes and foam-rubber headdresses while someone video-taped his reaction. That day's staff briefing featured outtakes spliced into the slide deck. As soon as the SEALs saw the decrepit base at Tarin Kowt, they petitioned for a new gym to replace the cramped, dark, one-room hovel that was jammed with equipment. A new gym as large as a warehouse, filled with CrossFit equipment and climbing and running machines, became a welcome retreat in which to escape for a few hours, day or night.

Stopping the insurgent jet stream was easy to say but hard to do. Special ops had been working at it for ten years already, but no one had taken a strategic approach to the problem. The critical central corridor was still not secure. The SEAL platoon assigned to the Chora District in Uruzgan was eager to find a solution that would stick, as the corridor was considered the Taliban's main highway straight into Kandahar. Any SEALs who thought that the work of foreign internal defense in Afghanistan would not stimulate one's adrenaline were in for a surprise. In their first weeks, the platoon in Chora was engaged in intense firefights on a regular basis. The Taliban did not shy away from close combat. These insurgents had been fighting over this ground for years, and they had every viable spot prepared for ambushes. One SEAL lost an eye due to shrapnel from a grenade. The deadly buried bombs also took their toll, blowing the legs off another SEAL. The platoon cast about for a change in tactics. Both Hayes and the special forces company commander were dubious when the platoon proposed building a wall to physically stem the flow of bad guys. Forging ahead despite the skepticism, the platoon built the wall, dubbing it "the wall of Chora." It was a 500-meter-long barrier made of dirt-filled Hesco structures, with three checkpoints.

To their commander's great surprise, the wall had a surprising calming effect once it went up. Feeling secure for the first time in years, the villagers came out to offer the SEALs fruit and give them tips as to where they might find buried bombs. The team began hearing less Taliban chatter on the shortwave radio. In perhaps the most telling sign that the tide was shifting, a Barakzai tribal elder who was known to be the elder in the village most sympathetic to the insurgents quietly moved away. The platoon believed it had reached a tipping point when another elder came forward one day to ask if he could be in charge of the wall. An offer of Afghan ownership, elusive for so long, had walked right up to their gate. The platoon leader readily agreed, and the team presented him with a plastic badge with a sheriff's star. He was keeper of the wall.[4]

Over the course of 2012, a year in which violence in Chora continued to subside, incidents still occurred that showed the Taliban had not given up—for example, a motorcycle rigged with explosives was found in the bazaar. But there was a notable change. Townspeople reported what they saw, and they supported the steps taken to disarm or blow up the bombs in place. Hayes believed this long troublesome district had finally been pacified, and that the partnership with the population seemed solid enough to endure. Progress in Chora was a good first step toward securing the central corridor of Uruzgan Province.

Zabul was another matter. Everything about that province was hard, beginning with the mountainous terrain. The logistics team at Bagram considered it hands down the hardest province to resupply, and the SEALs' site in Daychopan the hardest base to resupply in the entire country. It had a tiny drop zone ringed by houses, a cemetery, and steep mountains. When winter set in and supplies ran short, the SEALs rolled out in their all-terrain dune buggies and their heavier armored trucks in thigh-deep snow to wait for their food and water to fall from the sky. As they retrieved the scattered bundles, they would quite often find themselves under fire and would have to fight their way back home. Eighty percent of the supplies in Hayes's provinces—twenty-one sites in all—had to be dropped by air because of the rugged terrain and lack of landing strips. Helos, when available, would make milk runs. When it was not snowing, dirt became the pilots' biggest concern. They risked brownouts as they attempted to land in the swirling dust, a significant hazard, as the pilots could easily become disoriented. The solution devised for landing zones was "Rhino Snot": an acrylic copolymer mixed with water to produce a thick substance that was pumped through hoses to coat the landing zone. It took only a few hours for the Rhino Snot to harden into a kind of plastic lava field.

Zabul's human terrain was no easier than its physical terrain. The people were Ghilzai Pashtuns, which supplied most of the Taliban fighters. Its economy was so linked with Pakistan that the rupee was the common currency. Zabul was such a forgotten backwater that there was not one bank for the estimated 300,000 Afghans who lived there. Most of the Afghan soldiers posted there were Tajiks from the north, since few southern Pashtuns would join the army. The same was true of the police: only 20 percent of them spoke Pashto. The army stayed close to Highway One, and the police were largely holed up in the provincial capital of Qalat. The Taliban had virtually free rein in the rest of the province. Hayes was not so naïve as to think he could transform the entire province, but he wanted the teams to create and connect a few bubbles that Afghans could sustain. What he hoped to leave behind were districts with police chiefs who saw the value in the "pockets of excellence" that had been created in the villages where the teams had invested their efforts, and who had both the incentive and the knowledge to sustain them. "Once we've shown them how to grow it and connect it," he said, "Afghans can bring to scale the success we engender."[5]

The Afghan army brigade commander and the police chief in Zabul were considered professional officers, but the ethnic divide was a significant issue in an area where the population so deeply mistrusted the government and had relied on the insurgents for so long. Hayes hoped that the local police could be the wedge for a breakthough— but this was possible only if they could get some Zabul residents to come forward.

The SEALs had tried their best in the remote district of Daychopan in 2010–2011, but had been forced to admit defeat after braving a brutal winter. Instead of leaving it vacant, the Afghan army's corps commander sent a large number of troops from Kandahar to occupy that rugged district with the intent of conducting operations there the following spring.

Hayes adjusted course and sent a SEAL platoon to a less remote district, to the village of Bagh. It lay astride a dirt road paralleling the Arghandab River, which constituted one of Zabul's few easily navigable ratlines for insurgents traveling to and from Kandahar. When the SEALs first dug into their new site, it looked like it would be as hot as Daychopan had been. Every time they went on patrol they were attacked. The SEALs stood and fought, and the fierce gunfights eventually convinced both the people and the insurgents that they were there to stay. They slowly won over a few elders, who brought them a trickle of ALP recruits. The dirt road gradually became more secure, which produced their biggest dividend. The residents could travel unmolested to and from the bazaar, so business picked up and new stalls opened. The bazaar activity tripled over time, and the villagers attributed this visible, welcome change in their daily lives at least in part to the Afghan Local Police program—so more recruits began to volunteer.

As the local police program started to gain traction in Zabul, Hayes was pleased to see the provincial police chief take a great interest in it. He became very hands-on in his approach to overseeing the program, insisting on visiting the sites and approving them and any structures the special operators wanted to build, even roadside checkpoints. It was, Hayes thought, a promising sign.

While the teams in Zabul pushed out into bandit country, the teams in Uruzgan began to pull out of the villages and move to the district center. This was the necessary next step to connect the ALP with the district chiefs of police, and thus ensure that the latter would take ownership of the program in preparation for the day when the teams would no longer be there. Hayes envisioned that four teams would ultimately provide oversight from the province's four district centers, but as an intermediate step he would keep three additional teams in

Shahid-e Hasas, the biggest district in the west. A civil affairs team sergeant who worked in that district believed it had come a long way since the previous year. "This whole area was Taliban two to three years ago," he said.[6]

Over the course of 2012, Hayes closed four sites in Uruzgan as the teams repositioned to the district centers. The teams visited the vacated sites every three weeks to make sure the police were getting paid and supplied. Mentoring the entire police force would become increasingly the focus here and elsewhere, as it had been egregiously neglected throughout the war in Afghanistan, just as it had been in Iraq. The US government could not seem to get the police mentoring model right, even though policing is the single most vital task in counterinsurgency.

While the teams worked on security and village stability in the districts, Hayes dug deep into the tribal dynamics of Uruzgan and Zabul to understand the intra-Pashtun and Pashtun-Hazara conflicts. To help him, Dan Green, a naval reservist who had served on a provincial reconstruction team in Uruzgan, returned as his adviser. And he could rely on another storehouse of firsthand knowledge in Major Brian Strickland, an Air Force engineer who was an AFPAK Hand with over a year in Tarin Kowt in the Provincial Augmentation Team.[7]

Both men were well versed in the history of Popalzai domination in Uruzgan—a history that fueled much of the present conflict. The period when Karzai's friend, Jan Mohammad Khan, had served as governor had exacerbated the long-standing tensions. Even after Jan Mohammad Khan's assassination in July 2011, it looked like this engine of conflict could churn on in the person of his nephew, Matiullah Khan. The special forces teams had relied on him and his highway security force to guard convoys to and from Kandahar and generally beef up their defenses. But Matiullah appeared headed down the same road of "all for the Popalzai," nothing for the rest. He became acting provincial police chief, and his security force was grandfathered into the police force. At one juncture, Karzai sent a message from Kabul warning him to behave or he would have him fired.

Green was extremely skeptical that Matiullah Khan could be

redeemed. The central Popalzai-Barakzai blood feud looked set to continue when a Barakzai who was suspected in old Jan Mohammad Khan's assassination was killed. Some believed that Matiullah may have been responsible. Such blood feuds were all too common in Afghanistan. Strickland developed a different view from Green's as he sat in endless meetings in Uruzgan over two years, listening and watching the governor, the police, and other Afghans. He believed that the death of Jan Mohammad Khan, Matiullah's uncle and the main political boss and patriarch (who had fathered thirty-eight children from four wives), may have been one of those generational changes that made a different storyline possible.

Strickland told Hayes that he believed young Matiullah Khan wanted to go legitimate, just as the scions of America's bootleggers had reinvented themselves after Prohibition ended, and just as America's industrial "robber barons" had become philanthropists. Matiullah Khan had already amassed substantial wealth through his lucrative highway security company. After being named the provincial police chief, he told the Americans: "I have the job I want." The Afghan intelligence service viewed him as a source of stability in the province, and Uruzgan's literate and professional Afghan army commander was willing to collaborate with him on an operation to open up a road into Zabul, Route Whale, which had long been plagued by Taliban. Matiullah Khan, Strickland said, "had developed other tools and no longer needs to use the hammer." Green suspected that the Afghan's predatory instincts were only temporarily suppressed. Hayes opted for using his influence and resources to reinforce every constructive action Matiullah Khan took. He could not rearrange the players on Uruzgan's chessboard, but he could encourage any moves they made in the right direction.

Hayes was especially keen to find a chance to make inroads into the Taliban's base of support. The easternmost district of Khas Uruzgan was the unlikely scene of a major breakthrough. It was an impoverished, chronically violent area, riven by a Hazaran-Pashtun faultline and astride a pathway to Pakistan. The special operations team in the district got wind that a Taliban commander was ready to give up the fight. He turned out to be an important commander named Abdul Samad. He would be the most senior Taliban figure to have come into the reintegration program since it began. Hayes leaped at the opportunity and encouraged the team to explore whether he was in fact ready to make the break and to do so publicly. It turned out he was, and he would bring a number of his fighters over as well. His one condition was that the Americans guarantee his safety—a tall order. A Taliban commander who announced he was giving up in that area could be dead by dawn.

Hayes's first move was to get all the provincial officials on board and to activate the provincial reconciliation body that had been set up to provide a path back into civil society. A formal and fairly elaborate ceremony was held in which Samad exchanged his old turban for a new one and was given a Koran. The fighters brought an assortment of weapons and turned them over. A banquet was held and speeches were made; the provincial officials asked Hayes to sit at the head table with them. Hayes had held long talks with the now ex-Taliban, curious to learn more about his views and his fateful decision. He encouraged him to persuade other insurgents to follow his path.

Hayes settled on an unorthodox solution to the problem of Samad's security. He lobbied for an exception to the guidelines to allow Samad to form a local police unit with about twenty of his former fighters. The special operations team would keep tabs on them to ensure there was no backsliding. There were simply too few official Afghan forces available to provide Samad security, and Hayes was not sure they would do it if asked. So he took a gamble, judging that the greater danger was that if Samad was killed, any chance of more fighters in the area coming in from the cold would die with him. Samad survived and more fighters came in—eighty-four in all. Samad told Hayes that others were ready to quit, saying: "More will come in, if they see that I am being treated well. They are waiting to see what happens." Some glitches in pay and equipment caused the former insurgent leader to grumble about the provincial government's lack of support. The governor approved roads, a dam, and a new canal for the area; such development projects were part of the official US-funded reintegration program. Hayes's gamble had paid off so far, but the Afghan government would have to deliver on its side of the bargain. He hoped the seeds that had been planted would take root.[8]

Meanwhile, Hayes decided that the ALP in Zabul was ripe for expansion. He would send a team from Uruzgan to establish a new beachhead far enough from Bagh to incur some risk, but close enough that if the team succeeded, the two areas could connect into a much larger security bubble. Following the normal practice, Hayes first sent Afghan commandos with their combat advisers to clear the area of Taliban before the team embedded.

COMMANDOS RAISE THE BAR

A SEAL platoon served as the combat advisers for the Afghan commando kandak based in Uruzgan. Marshall, the platoon leader, had served on SEAL Team Six, but he harbored no prejudices about foreign internal defense. He did not see FID as a lesser mission. In many respects, conducting unilateral operations with fellow SEALs was easier than taking less capable partners through mission planning and going into combat with them. The SEALs' unofficial motto, "The only easy day was yesterday," applied in spades to this mission.[9]

Marshall had taken stock of the 8th Commando Kandak and its leader, Lieutenant Colonel Ahmadullah Popal, when he arrived in Tarin Kowt at the beginning of his tour. Popal was experienced: he had first served in a reconnaissance platoon and then in the first commando unit when it was formed. He was also politically well connected —since he was from the Popalzai clan of the president, as his name suggested. Popal's operations officer was especially competent; he carried his radio and notebook with him at all times and kept close track of his men. The unit's soldiers, however, were not nearly as tactically proficient as the Iraqi special operations counterterrorism force that Marshall had trained, advised, and fought alongside on five tours in Iraq. The difference was partly due to basic educational levels, which were much lower in Afghanistan than in Iraq. The 8th Commandos, formed in February 2010, was also one of the newest commando units.

The Iraqi force had benefited as well from much more intensive and longer mentoring by US special operations teams. A lot of money had been poured into Iraqi training facilities and equipment.

Marshall's platoon devised a way to boost the commandos' skills based on their own SEAL training. They held a competition within the commando kandak to select the best shooters, the strongest tacticians, and the fittest soldiers. These Afghans would be an internal elite cadre who would continue to train their fellow commandos when special operations teams where not there. They modeled the tryouts on the famous "Hell Week" at Coronado, a grueling week of endless running, swimming, obstacle courses, and punishing physical tasks designed to weed out the weak-hearted and leave the most determined and able SEAL candidates. The competition also spurred enthusiasm and developed esprit de corps. The Afghan Hell Week yielded fifty motivated commandos. The SEALs then worked with these men to refine their skills in close-quarter battle, the use of night vision goggles, and small arms marksmanship.

As the mission to Zabul approached, the SEALs took the commandos through every step of the preparation. They analyzed the mission order to search and clear the area, which was called Sayagaz, and then built a terrain model in a sand table to plot their scheme of maneuver. The Zabul mission into a Taliban stronghold would be difficult, as there were no forces nearby to come to their aid, and Popal wanted to be ready. He joked with Marshall, saying, "We don't know where the SEALs have been for the last nine years but we are glad to have them now." The thirty-year-old SEAL responded with a friendly quip, but he treated Popal with respect as his host and a senior officer in rank and age; he was very aware of the importance of dignity, honor, and position in Afghan culture. As the incidence of insider attacks mounted over the course of 2012, the US military command had pushed for tougher counterintelligence measures to weed out infiltrators, a necessary step, but also had conducted cultural sensitivity training for Afghans to help them understand the apparently rude American behavior. The ever-changing cast of conventional American units sent to Afghanistan did not help the US learning curve. Most special operators, by contrast, were on their fifth or sixth tours. Only a few attacks had occurred on special operations forces, despite the fact that the special ops soldiers lived in much closer proximity with their Afghan partners than conventional forces did—on the same compounds, and, in the case of embedded teams, often in the next room.

When dealing directly with the Afghans, Marshall emphasized his platoon's desire to help improve their commando skills without personally denigrating the individual soldiers. In their internal discussions, Marshall, Hayes, and Haas all expressed the belief that the commandos had grown too dependent on quick missions—they were normally ferried in on US helicopters for a quick op and then back out the following day. It was time to raise the bar and begin taking them on missions of three or more days. They would not always have access to helicopters; ground movements would need to be part of the mix.

In early March, Marshall's team and the commandos launched into Zabul, inserting by helicopter at night in the vicinity of Sayagaz on a three-day op. At midnight, the platoon and 107 commandos loaded their gear and crammed into two Chinooks and a Black Hawk at the Tarin Kowt flight line. They flew blacked out across eastern Uruzgan and into Zabul without incident, navigating mountain ridges and then dropping down into the valley. They were twenty-four kilometers away from the SEAL platoon at Bagh, so they were effectively on their own. Marshall put the commandos in the lead to see how they would do from start to finish. If things started to go south, he would step in, but he believed the Afghans were ready.

The commandos and SEALs offloaded in the planned sequence, with the lead element providing security at the landing zone until everybody was off and rucks were shouldered. So far, no incoming fire. They headed off, NODs on, to their predetermined strongpoint, a compound they would clear and move into until "BMT," as first light was known in military jargon. Since Karzai had banned night operations, the special operators had adapted their procedures so that they would arrive at the target location under cover of darkness. But they would hold off until the earliest permissible moment before launching their operation.

The Afghans occupied the preselected qalat, set up their security perimeter, and hunkered down to wait for a few hours. Just before dawn, they stealthily moved into the edge of the village of Sayagaz, heading for the mullah's house. Popal and Marshall had devised a new tactic that they considered a brilliant refinement of the usual practice. Normally, the Afghan commando leader would call on a bullhorn for the military-aged males to voluntarily come out of their homes, which was intended to sort the neutrals from those who would have to be fought. How much better would it be, they realized, if this call-out were done by the mullah of the village?

They stole silently to the mullahs' house and requested that he call all the males to come out and meet at the mosque for a shura. The commandos would then clear the homes and suspected stash sites. "Mullah Sahib, we are here to do an operation. We want to meet the tribal leaders, and we will treat any sick people," Popal told him. During the trainup, Popal had emphasized to his troops how essential it was to display deference to mullahs; they were the key to winning a welcome wherever the commandos were sent. "They teach our children, and we must show them we are the good Muslims, not the Taliban," he said.

The commandos and the SEALs were of course poised to fight if they were attacked, but their first recourse was to avoid gunfights that would further alienate the population. The mullah in Sayagaz agreed to call out the villagers. So far, so good. Nerves were stretched taut as they moved through the streets to the mosque under the fading cover of dark. The commandos and the SEALs positioned themselves defensively around the mosque, waiting to see if they would need to shoot, as the fingers of the dawn came up over the horizon. The troops were especially on alert, as riots had rippled through the country just days before in reaction to the burning of Korans at the US base in Bagram.

The Afghan men of Sayagaz came out of their homes, slowly, at least some of them. The SEALs were certain that others were stealing away under the cover of dark, perhaps to ambush them later. No one's guard dropped for an instant. The Afghans and the psychological operations soldiers moved to the fore to explain what was about to happen. "We want to meet and talk with you, and we are also here to look for the Taliban," they announced. "We are here because we want peace for our country." Popal explained that they planned to bring Afghan government, national police, and local police to the area. He described the Afghan Local Police program. The commandos completed the village search without incident that day, but the following day they came under constant harassing fire from across the river. They repelled those attacks without taking any casualties.

The commandos returned to base the following day, and Marshall and Hayes both considered the op a successful start to their Sayagaz campaign. A team from Uruzgan would move in shortly, and the commandos would go back to help if the Taliban decided to mount serious resistance to the arriving team. The team received some additional help in the form of a special forces team working with Jordanian special operators, who cleared IEDs from the road between Bagh and Sayagaz. The Jordanians were longtime US partners and had been coming to Afghanistan for years—105 were helping Hayes's men. They were worth their weight in gold; as Muslims they were frequently asked to meet with the local mullahs.

The team in Sayagaz made headway, but slowly. The men started by distributing humanitarian assistance. The road to Bagh remained dangerous. The team was able to raise Afghan Local Police recruits, but the recruits were too afraid to secure the road by themselves. The first Afghan Local Police volunteers were reluctant to man the checkpoints the team had built or to go on patrol by themselves. So the SEALs kept the training wheels on and stood guard with them, driving the highway with the Afghans in tow. The commandos continued to run operations elsewhere in Zabul and, when required, in Uruzgan. By summer's end, three hundred Afghans in Zabul had come forward to become local police. That was no small change in what had previously been a totally Taliban-dominated province outside of the city and Highway One.

Taking stock of the broader situation, Hayes realized that the coming drawdown would test the ability of US forces to continue to advise and mentor the entire Afghan security force—the military,

a panoply of police forces, and the growing Afghan special operations forces. He was particularly concerned that the US conventional
advisers embedded with the Afghan army were becoming vulnerable as the US combat formations departed, a prediction that came
true when two newly arrived advisers were killed by a suicide bomber
in Uruzgan. Hayes foresaw that the drawdown would put pressure
on special operations to become more efficient at all levels. So why
not combine the various special operations units and create a unified
battalion-level and brigade-level special ops command, as they were
moving toward doing at the top of the special ops hierarchy? Such
ideas were heresy within the stovepiped special operations culture, but
Hayes was ready and willing to help break the mold by floating such
ideas. When commanders realized how few special operators were
likely to be left behind after 2014, they might swallow hard and try
something new.

THE FALLEN

Hayes was approaching the end of his tour satisfied that he had
increased security in Uruzgan, but things were still dicey just to the
south, in northern Kandahar. A sister SEAL platoon in Kandahar was
partnered with the Afghan commando kandak based there. While
Marshall's platoon and Popal's commandos were hammering on their
part of the "jet stream," the part that ran across northern Kandahar
had remained problematic. The Mullah Dadullah Front had laid siege
to Route Bear five years before. The highway had been reopened in
2007 and a few footholds of Afghan Local Police had been created,
but their lines were not yet thick enough and the Afghan army had
not wrested control of the countryside from the Taliban.

Night operations were controversial in Afghanistan, but there is a
reason why special operators love the nighttime. Infiltrating under the
cover of darkness is always their preferred method of insertion because
it gives them the edge and reduces their own risk of casualties. In
response to Karzai's demands and the desire to minimize civilian casualties, night operations had been progressively reined in. Daytime ops

stripped the operators of their cloak of protection from the Taliban's machine guns, mortars, and especially, the ubiquitous and deadly rocket-propelled grenade launchers. The only confirmed helo downing by a surface-to-air missile had been in Helmand in 2007, but many other near misses were reported on the battlefield. These missiles posed a much more lethal threat, but a skillfully aimed RPG could bring down a helicopter, as Somali militia fighters had proven in the deadly "Black Hawk Down" battle of 1993 against Rangers, Delta Force, and special ops aviators.

The commandos and SEALs were operating without the cover of darkness on the morning of August 16, 2012, as they inserted into the rugged moonlike landscape of northern Kandahar's Shah Wali Kot District. The plan was to clear suspected Taliban locations there and work their way north and west, with other teams following behind to set up camp and recruit local police. As they came in for a landing, one of the UH-60 Black Hawks was hit by an RPG. It spiraled down to the ground and crashed, becoming consumed in a fireball. The other UH-60 took evasive action and then maneuvered to land near the flaming crash site so the men could try to rescue their comrades. They put out a security perimeter and feverishly searched the wreckage for survivors. There were none. Reinforcements arrived in helicopters, and the sad business of retrieving comrades' remains and investigating the crash began.[10]

Eleven men died in all, including seven Americans—the four crew of the Black Hawk helicopter, two SEALs, and a US Navy Explosive Ordnance Disposal (EOD) technician. Three Afghan commandos and an Afghan interpreter were also killed in the crash. After recovering the remains, the even grimmer business of identifying and separating them began. At Camp Simmons the following day, a soldier came into the operations center to ask a SEAL if he could help find a toothbrush or other item that would provide a DNA sample of his deceased teammate. All of the men had been through years of war and loss, but it did not dull them to the pain of loss. Hayes had been monitoring the crash and subsequent rescue, and he prepared to fly to Kandahar that night for the memorial service. General Allen and special operations commanders would fly in from all over Afghanistan to pay their last respects.

At Kandahar Airfield, those who would be carrying caskets gathered on the patio of Camp Brown to practice for the ramp ceremony that would be held that night as the caskets were loaded onto the plane. Major Angel Martinez, one of the special operations company commanders for Kandahar, arrived for a meeting at the command and stopped to watch the rehearsal for a moment. He noticed the commandos standing at attention, listening to instructions regarding the order of the night's ceremony. Then he saw that they were surrounded by American plainclothes security guards holding rifles. He shook his head. The special operators fought beside these commandos every day, and they had just lost three of their own. The security measures had been imposed because the US military command in Kabul was in a great turmoil about mounting insider attacks. So far in 2012, thirty-four Americans had been killed by Afghans dressed in uniforms. Two Marines special operations teams had just been hit by such attacks, and earlier in the spring an Afghan special operator had shot and killed a US team member before he was taken out. The special operations command was debating standing down all SOF operations and reverting every one of their partners, the Afghan special operators as well as their Afghan Local Police. Martinez thought that was an overreaction, but he was, above all, offended that these particular Afghans, grieving the loss of their comrades, had to be surrounded and guarded like suspects. He spoke briefly to one of the guards. "I just think that it is a shame that they have to do that so visibly," Martinez said. "I don't think it's necessary."[11]

This day of heavy loss reminded Martinez of the death of his best friend, Sergeant First Class Pedro Munoz, in 2005, in the western province of Herat. Recalling how he had failed to bring his teammate home safely to his wife and daughter, on that first of his four tours, he sat on a bench to reminisce about his friend, shedding a tear for him and the newly fallen. Reminders of special operators who had died were everywhere: their names were affixed to buildings, camps, and outposts all over Afghanistan. Pedro's was at the entrance of their camp in Bagram, and Camp Maholic was named for one of their teammates, Thom Maholic, an avid cyclist and Grateful Dead fan who had been with them in Colombia. Brown, Vance, Eggers, Montrond, and Simmons were all special operators who had given their lives in Afghanistan and had camps named after them. The deadly SEAL crash in Wardak exactly one year earlier, in August 2011, was also on everyone's mind that day. A Chinook full of SEALs and Afghans had been shot down as they came to the assistance of Rangers caught in a nighttime firefight. That was the worst mass casualty event in the history of naval special warfare; it took the lives of thirty-eight Afghans and Americans, including twenty-five special operators. It was also the deadliest single day of the Afghan war.

At 2 a.m. on August 18, 2012, hundreds of servicemen and women, and civilians, filed quietly out to the ramp, passing through the chain-link fence under the glaring white lights that lit the airfield and runway. Most of the people were staff and contractors who worked at the sprawling Kandahar base: their desk jobs meant that these ramp ceremonies were their most direct, visceral contact with the war going on outside the gates. The roar of transport aircraft and the occasional deafening scream of the fighter jets, the background noise of their lives, continued as people lined up in formation, two large blocks of troops at one end. The commanders formed a corridor through which the caskets would be carried into the open hatch of the massive C-17 transport plane that would bear the Afghan dead to Kabul and the Americans on to Dover, Delaware. Hayes and the other special operations commanders took their positions on the ramp. Then the field fell silent, as the takeoffs and landings were halted for the ceremony.

The hot summer wind blew over the crowd as ten RG armored personnel carriers crawled slowly along the concrete apron, their lights blinking in the night. One by one the giant vehicles turned in an arc around the plane to stop behind the assembled ranks, and the caskets were unloaded one by one. The troops were called to attention. Taps was played, then "Auld Lang Syne." A chaplain stepped forward to a portable podium beside the plane's belly, the ramp down and lights shining brightly within. He said a simple prayer and then read the name of each fallen warrior and his unit and hometown. One by one, the troops carried each flag-draped casket into the plane. A female soldier stood at attention off to one side. To no one but the desert night she whispered, "There are so many."

CHAPTER NINE

GOOD ENOUGH?

PAKTIKA 2012–2013

WEST PAKTIKA

In 2012 two new teams took over from Hutch's team in Paktika. His success in creating local police and growing security in a large swath of the province was a hard act to follow. It had been engendered by a good strategy, well-executed, with considerable assistance from an unorthodox Afghan partner, Commander Aziz. Aziz was a longtime ally of special operations forces who had been embraced by a multiethnic array of officials and elders in Paktika, but rival tribes kept up a barrage of criticism that periodically prompted yet another investigation. Hutch's team time was now over; it was the fate of the team leader to move on to the life of a staff officer. He was promoted to the rank of major and awarded a fellowship year to study for a master's degree at the prestigious Naval Postgraduate School. Eventually Hutch would make it back to the field, he hoped, to command a special forces company.

One of the two new teams was charged with consolidating Hutch's gains. But the focus now shifted to the western side of the province, and the second new team was sent there to extend the Afghan Local Police program to three districts.

Special Forces Operational Detachment Alpha 1114 was the team sent to western Paktika. Its jumping-off point was a base with a name that sounded like it belonged in a Seth Rogen movie: Super FOB. The team was to start there but move as quickly as possible into a mud-walled qalat in a village. The team's battalion commander insisted that teams should embed in villages to live next to the Afghans they were trying to mentor; he felt that too many teams under previous commanders had diverged from the stated methodology of embedding in the villages. The tradeoff, however, was that the teams would be farther from the district centers and the district police chiefs. The experience of the past years had also shown that it was hard for teams to connect their security bubbles as they grew if they remained too tied to one village. The tensions and tradeoffs between village stability operations and district stability operations were unavoidable.

Another consideration was the time it would take to find a qalat that was suitable from a security standpoint and that the owner was willing to rent. Villagers in insurgent-dominated areas were invariably nervous about the attention that the special operators attracted from the Taliban—and the likelihood that they would get caught in the cross-fire. In addition, the Afghans feared the men would see their women. Even when villages eventually decided they wanted the benefits of the program, the early days were usually marked by an understandable wariness.

During the first year or so of the program, special operations commanders had generally tolerated the long, slow courting period as Afghan villagers debated the risks and rewards of what the operators were offering them. But by 2012 there was a distinct air of urgency emanating from the top levels of the special operations command. Teams were being asked to show results, and quickly, and to move to a second site to repeat the process during one six-month tour. It was an extremely ambitious strategy that put the teams under enormous pressure.

ODA 1114 was commanded by a newly minted and extremely serious special forces captain named Jason Russell. His team sergeant, Russ, was a classic special forces senior noncom: confident, personable, and dominant in running his team of sergeants. The team's chief warrant officer was a studious guy who had memorized a social science encyclopedia's worth of information about Afghanistan, Paktika, and the districts the team would be working in. Russ's gregarious, hands-on personality would nicely balance the more introverted and academic nature of the other two leaders.

ODA 1114 and the rest of its parent 1st Special Forces Group normally deployed to Asia, but the manpower demands of the Afghan Local Police initiative required them to come to Afghanistan. A battalion command and other 1st Group teams had been deployed to western Afghanistan. The use of 1st Group in the region was not without precedent: Russ had been sent to Iraq to train and advise special police units in Kurdish Iraq, for example, and several other 1st Group teams had been sent to Mosul and Kirkuk. Russ, age thirty-nine, had deployed to ten countries in three regions, including Nepal and Somalia; he joked that he received his initial cross-cultural training from his Irish-Jamaican wife.

Although Afghanistan was a new culture for the team, much of their experience in foreign internal defense and the nuances of working with sensitive, prickly nations was fungible. Russ had taken his previous team, ODA 1112, to Jolo Island in the Philippines, where US special operations forces had been invested continuously but in relatively small numbers since 9/11. The Abu Sayyaf terrorist group had taken US hostages and had in general been running rampant through the heavily Muslim southern part of the archipelago. In an odd juxtaposition that showed the global reach of Islamic extremism, Abu Sayyaf was named for the Afghan Islamist leader Rasul Sayyaf. While nominally espousing militant Islam, the group had devolved into a largely criminal gang that carried out kidnappings for ransom, among other crimes. But Abu Sayyaf worried the Philippine government and US counterterrorism officials for two reasons. For one thing, such groups could find fertile soil among the Muslim population—the Moro

Islamic National Liberation Front was the long-standing separatist guerrilla movement that operated in the same general area. Equally worrisome, the Indonesian-based Jamaat Islamiya (JI) group, a more potent node of the worldwide Al Qaeda federation, was making inroads in the Philippines. JI had been responsible for the largest act of post-9/11 terrorism in Asia: the Bali nightclub bombings of 2002.

Special operators considered their past decade's work in the Philippines to be one of their unheralded successes, along with Colombia. They had made it a point to thoroughly analyze the mix of religious, tribal, and political conditions underlying the conflict before jumping into action, and they had worked closely with the Philippine government every step of the way. Those two steps could be considered the golden rules of a successful foreign internal defense program. After undertaking a thorough assessment of conditions in Basilan, in tandem with the Philippine government and US civilian experts at the US embassy, special operations teams, alongside Philippine forces, had begun to make contact with the population through civil affairs projects, information operations, and humanitarian assistance. That enabled them to gain a firsthand knowledge of the islands. Russ, who spoke both Tagalog and Thai, trained Philippine Marines and helped them track and eventually rescue American hostages held by Abu Sayyaf. The advisory mission, which involved US special operations units from the army, navy, air force, and marines, was commanded by a joint special ops headquarters (Joint Special Operations Task Force–Philippines, or JSOTF-P) that maintained a very close relationship with the US embassy. The Philippine armed forces retained all combat roles, but US forces provided a variety of direct support during operations, including intelligence, surveillance, and tactical advice. The only thing the US forces were not allowed to do, according to rules of engagement fashioned to respect Philippine sovereignty, was to pull the trigger of any weapon.[1]

In many of these respects, the Philippine mission very closely resembled what the US mission in Afghanistan was becoming. The Afghan government was asserting its sovereignty as the Filipinos had from the outset. Although Afghans appreciated American and coalition help, they wanted to run their own war. And they did not want foreign commandos storming into Afghan homes in the middle of the night; the Americans had never grasped how deep a cultural affront this was to the Afghans. The mission was becoming one of US support to Afghans taking the lead, an arrangement that would be formalized with the end to coalition combat operations by 2014, if not before. If the United States stayed on past 2014, its military headquarters would transition from being a war-fighting headquarters to being an advisory assistance group, and the US ambassador would become the primary interlocutor with the host government.

Russ and other 1st Group operators had ample experience working under similar restrictive conditions, not only in the Philippines but also in Thailand and Indonesia. Thailand had been a partner in regional security endeavors since the Vietnam War; it also faced its own brewing insurgency in its south that was rooted in historical, ethnic, and religious tensions. Special operators had been training and working alongside Thai military forces for decades; many of them had signed up for a grueling jungle warfare course as part of the relationship-building and to burnish their own fighting and survival skills. In the past decade, after a long-standing ban on military-to-military engagement was lifted, special operators had also begun to conduct training in Indonesia. This training provided critical on-ground contacts for the United States in the world's most populous Muslim nation (over 200 million)—the fourth most populous country in the world. US special operators also participated in a massive training exercise called "Cobra Gold" that was held in Thailand each year with half a dozen Asian nations.

The operators from 1st Group knew that their experience was highly relevant, so they shrugged off the wisecracks from other special operations units that had been heavily involved in the combat operations of the past decade. It was true that Afghanistan was a more lethal environment than Asia, but the degree of restraint needed as the United States shifted from a combat to an advisory role favored their background. In any event, Russ and most of the team members had tasted the combat environment on one or more tours in Iraq.

Before deploying, ODA 1114 studied Paktika's human and physical terrain, drawing on topographical maps and intelligence reports to identify the wadis and valleys that the insurgents used and the key chokepoints for heading them off. As the team settled into Super FOB, they made quick headway in the receptive district of Zarghun Shah. It was a good warm-up exercise for the team: the district was near the provincial capital and not very insurgent-infested. In addition, the deputy director of the Afghan intelligence service hailed from the district, and he wanted to ensure the program's success there. Soon the team had a burgeoning force led by an energetic Afghan who had worked with the Afghan intelligence service and on road-building projects. In consultation with the team, he arrayed his force in check-points to block insurgent traffic from the east, monitoring his charges daily. His only lament, he said, was that he did not know how to read or write; he hoped that the program would include literacy classes one day. His deputy was literate, however, so he handled the payroll and recordkeeping duties.[2]

The team's next target was a more difficult one, the district of Yahya Khel. The team members piled into their heavy armored vehicles, the MATVs, for one of their regular meetings with the elders there, but they avoided the direct route. Route Dodge, the main east-west road, was a notorious road seeded with mines that had killed and maimed coalition troops and civilians. They veered off the hardball asphalt onto a dirt road, and then off that road into a field, for a teeth-jarring ride over mounded irrigation channels. They would chart a different path for each visit to foil would-be attackers.[3]

Arriving at the district center, the team entered the gate and backed up the vehicles to "combat park" them for quick exit should an attack occur. A conventional unit had once been housed here, and the look-out tower above the concrete walls was pockmarked with bullet holes. The fighting here had been so fierce that the unit had been pulled out the previous year. As the meeting time approached, a steady stream of people filed in, including elders on foot or in cars, policemen in green trucks, and the district subgovernor, who lived elsewhere and came to work when he thought it safe enough.

As soon as the shura began, one elder complained about how the team had ridden roughshod over their fields. It was entirely understandable: repairing the damage would require backbreaking labor. The dirt mounds that channeled the water when they irrigated their fields would have to be reformed. "We would like to ask that you please not drive on the fields," said a wizened man in a pouf of a turban, with a tuft of cloth jauntily sticking out of the top like tail feathers on a bird. Each tribe wore turbans made of a different fabric, and each man expressed his personal style in the way he tied it. The fabrics were lustrous cottons with stripes and sheen, and a rainbow of subtle colors. The most numerous clan in the room all wore turbans of pale yellow cloth.

The elders who came to the meetings or spoke up were not always the most powerful figures. The latter often hung back to exercise their influence more discreetly. Several elders expressed concern that the ALP would be overrun. One especially vocal elder said, "Two hundred is not enough. There are four routes the Taliban can use." He recounted the attacks they had suffered in the past year. At the end of the discussion the official shura leader, Haji Yar Mohammed, sought to rally the others. Three of his sons had joined the ALP. "We will fight all of Pakistan if we have to, with your help," he said, and Russ started clapping to support him. After the shura, the sixty-year-old elder added, "I have a rifle in my house and am ready to fight, too."

The first of two objectives in the meeting was to nominate local representatives to link into the provincial offices that were responsible for bringing education, health, and other services to the district. The civil affairs officer who was the one-man District Augmentation Team explained the process and the requirements several times. Jason Russell, the team leader, tried to steer them to a choice based on merit: "You want to pick your best-qualified, most educated person because he will be able to bring the government projects to the village." During the meeting, the chief warrant officer unobtrusively snapped photos of villagers who had crammed into the room. The operators knew many Taliban were very likely in their midst.

The second objective was to select Afghan Local Police commanders.

The shura had already voted previously to form a local police force, but the Afghans were at odds over who would lead it, with their choices reflecting the rivalries among the three subtribes in the area. The elders were unable to reach a consensus. After a hearty lunch was served, the Afghans and the team set off to survey a vacant clinic nearby—no medical personnel were available to staff it. One of the sergeants who had been strolling in the bazaar while the shura was taking place returned, chewing on a warm piece of fresh nan bread. He marveled at how much had changed since the team had first visited Yahya Khel a month before. The bazaar had been closed, but now that local police had been nominated and trained, the shops lining the main street were open and bustling. Old men sat on chairs outside their little kiosks, selling vegetables, aluminum and plastic kitchenware, and clothing.

The team was feeling good. Russ and his weapons sergeants had overseen the training of the local police for the two districts. They had 174 recruits in their first class, which made the group the largest yet trained by any team in Afghanistan. The week before, the team's company, battalion, and CJSOTF commanders had all flown in to attend the graduation and validation ceremony along with a phalanx of Afghan officials. It was an auspicious start to the team's tour, but something bothered the company commander. His "spidey sense" went off as he surveyed the graduating class. He did not feel that all the looks in the crowd were friendly. That premonition proved to be correct. There was a bad apple in the barrel.[4]

Less than two weeks later, a contingent of the new local police settled in for the night shift at their newly constructed checkpoint. They sat in the crude plywood lookout tower drinking chai tea. One of the policemen had slipped a drug into the tea, and they were soon fast asleep. He picked up a gun and shot them all dead—nine in all—and then took their AK-47 rifles and fled in the new pickup truck they had been issued.

The team quickly discovered who the perpetrator was—a former Taliban fighter who had been accepted into the class on the insistence of the elders. The team had not wanted to include the man once they learned of his past. The youth had gone through the official Afghan reintegration program after being approved by the provincial peace council. Afghan intelligence vetted him and approved his admission. The elders believed he had been a wayward youth but was genuinely finished with the Taliban. He had been complicit in the killing of his own father, a friend of Yar Mohammed, but the elders believed the son's conversion was genuine. Russell's team was unaware of this familial treachery at the time of his recruitment. The operators were ultimately persuaded by the other recruits' willingness to accept him as one of them. But as they delved into his past after the killing, they learned that the son had approved the Taliban decision to kill his father, who was an outspoken critic of the Taliban. He was upset with his father for trying to get him to leave the insurgency. The Afghan police followed the fugitive's trail, but he was gone, very likely to Pakistan.

The crisis brought the provincial governor and the police chief to Yahya Khel. They summoned Commander Aziz from Orgun to accompany them. It looked as though the Yahya Khel local police might fall apart. Suspicion and recriminations rippled through the ranks. Who had supported the killer? How was he able to escape without help? The policemen, although they had known each other for years, began pointing fingers, suspecting each other of active or passive support for the insurgents. One of the nine killed was a commander, and as clan politics again surged to the fore, no one could agree on who should replace him. At the provincial police chief's request, Aziz stayed on for several days to provide additional security and participate in meetings with the elders. Aziz left behind a squad of his men to work with the team as they sought to find a new commander and shore up the shaky morale. Doubts sown here could affect their prospects throughout western Paktika.

Team ODA 1114 moved into a mud-walled compound they rented about two kilometers away from the Yahya Khel district center and worked to hold the line. Their priority was persuading the police not to quit, but they were diverted by attacks on their compound. The Taliban were not going to let them move in uncontested. The team members knew they were being watched, and they tracked the insurgents' chatter on the scanner. The special operators' movements over the wide flat valley were easy to spot. Fighting season had kicked off in earnest, and the team's qalat made a perfect target. Insurgents pummeled the compound with mortars, rocket-propelled grenades, and small arms fire. At night they would creep in to plant IEDs on the approach to the compound. The team repelled the attacks and, using the Afghan Local Police lookouts in their nearest checkpoint, spotted the holes that were dug the night before. The IEDs were the biggest problem; the victims were the very villagers whom the team was trying to protect. The team treated the wounded and petitioned for an ordnance disposal technician, who was sent to live with them. The villagers began to report IEDs to them as well.

The local police of Yahya Khel were put to the test not long thereafter, when the Taliban attacked the bazaar on May 10, 2012. The local police quickly shepherded the children in a nearby school to safety and helped repel the attack, along with Aziz's men and national police. It appeared to be a galvanizing moment, as the village rallied around its local defenders and expressed fury at the Taliban's assault. The US State Department lead at the provincial reconstruction team and a rare American fluent in Pashto, Jess Patterson, said that she read reports that the residents of Yahya Khel spat on the corpses of the dead Taliban that remained behind in the market. They left them there to fester, refusing to bury them. She followed events in Yahya Khel closely because two of her team members had been killed by a bomb there.[5]

Jason Russell, the team leader, feeling the pressure from his superior officers, decided to split the team and send half to a third district. He stayed with half the team to help Yahya Khel move ahead, while Russ took the other half to the third district to begin the process all over again. They did not have time to fully equip and field a force there, but Jason felt satisfied with what the team had accomplished. The local police had survived their worst insider killing yet and rebounded. Western Paktika had an Afghan Local Police force of 511 by year's end, which provided an indigenous line of defense separating the badlands of the border with Pakistan from Highway One.[6]

Later, looking back at the team's experience in western Paktika, Jason said, "I think there is a tipping point in each district where the realization sinks in, when enough recruits come forward, enough Taliban are killed, or enough attacks are repulsed, that they think they are going to win." He reflected, "Somewhere in there was a point when momentum shifted to the government side. The Taliban had had the power until then." The force he was leaving behind could count on some good commanders. "As long as they stick together I think they will make it," he concluded.

The sister team in eastern Paktika fared less well; in fact, it was a downright disaster. The team leadership of ODA 1112 was fired by the command early in their tour, but the team sergeant sent as a replacement was no better, and the captain was wounded. According to fellow special operators, the team sergeant was egregiously derelict in his job. That "retired in place" attitude is extraordinarily rare in the special operations community, but the toll of high operational tempo may have been partly to blame. In any event, leadership failure in small teams operating in austere environments is also risky in the extreme; special operators have to be alert to threats, and doing their jobs every day, or someone may well die. The team had been split in two halves and divided between Orgun and Sar Howza. A US soldier from a conventional unit was killed at Sar Howza one night in a friendly-fire incident. He approached one of the local police checkpoints and was mistakenly shot by an ALP policeman. The incident compounded concerns over poor leadership and lack of oversight, and the team leadership was relieved soon afterward. There were hard feelings, because the fate of this 1st Special Forces Group team was decided by the 3rd Special Forces Group leadership, but the potential consequences of *not* intervening were too important to ignore. Poor team performance could unravel several districts or an entire province, and incidents that caused a national or international outcry could jeopardize the entire program.[7]

AZIZ LEADS

Somewhat surprisingly, the progress that had been made over the previous two years by Hutch's team and Commander Aziz and his men
in eastern Paktika did not unravel despite the team turmoil. In the
fall, another team from 1st Special Forces Group, ODA 1411, led by
Captain Jae Kim, arrived to take up the reins. Part of the newly created
4th Battalion of 1st Group, the team had competed hard to be chosen
for the Afghan assignment. One of their members, an artist and aspir-
ing writer, had designed the team logo, a Japanese death mask with
the special forces dagger, and emblazoned it on caps and T-shirts.
Kim, at thirty-one, was a senior captain with two hard tours in Iraq
under his belt. It was a mature team, with a forty-one-year-old team
sergeant and a thirty-year-old chief warrant officer, and it was ready to
take on the hairiest parts of Paktika.[8]

They felt the clock ticking and the pressure for results from the
leadership above them, but Kim knew that "you make your own plan
or one will be given to you." It was a cardinal rule that strong teams
leaned forward and mapped out a game plan; the tradition in the special ops was to let the teams' ground knowledge guide the effort. If
schemes imposed from above bore no resemblance to the realities at
the grassroots, they were bound to fail. Kim made a 180-day plan: first
the team would fill one remaining gap in the security corridor that
Hutch's team had created, and then it would attempt to expand the
security bubble to the north. Finally, it would take on the Pirkowti
pacification that had eluded Hutch in the east. If the team succeeded,
he believed Paktika's defenses would be solid enough to endure.

Kim learned within days of his arrival in Paktika just how vital an ally
Aziz and his "Special Squad" of three hundred or so were. He already
knew from reading situation reports of previous teams that they had
been instrumental in persuading elders to form local police, in training the fledgling bands, and in coming to their aid when attacked.
Kim had arrived early, so on September 28 when the rest of his team
arrived, he headed back to the airfield to pick them up. On the road
trip from the team base at Orgun in eastern Paktika to the provincial

capital, he was accompanied by one of Aziz's main lieutenants, Lalu, and a contingent of his fighters.

The narrow mountain pass in the mountain range that divided Orgun from the capital was still somewhat dicey; some soldiers referred to it as the Gates of Mordor. As the small convoy wound through the pass, they were ambushed by Taliban lying in wait. Aziz's men, led by the long-haired twenty-something Lalu, opened fire with everything they had from the gunner's turrets of their Humvees. The Americans also returned fire; they were enclosed in their MATVs with their automatic remotely operated systems, which allowed them to shoot their guns unexposed.[9] But Lalu and his other two gunners were only shielded by a straight armored plate as they stood in their turrets manning the .50-caliber machine guns, and they were exposed on the sides and in back. Kim was awed by their fighting spirit. The Afghans fired a continuous hail of bullets as they pushed through the five-hundred-meter-long ambush. An RPG landed directly in front of one of the Afghan gunners, who did not flinch or stop firing for a second.

"They saved our lives that very first week," Kim said. On many occasions thereafter, he witnessed the esprit de corps that Aziz had fostered, in both battles and in their noncombat performance. They went about their business in a quiet, efficient way, and in battle they were deadly. That was viewed by critics as a bad thing. But in a land of relentless foes, the men who will stand up and shoot back are a necessity. Kim had heard of the criticisms and the earlier investigations, which ISAF had closed, but he did not see any evidence of indiscipline or abuses. His impression was that Aziz exercised more command and control over his forces than any other Afghan forces he saw. Aziz rotated his squads every two months to give the men a two-week break to visit their families, and he kept a close watch on the scheduled leave and attendance.

Kim and his team felt better knowing that this tightknit, battle-hardened group of Afghans would be with them in the field, augmenting their small band of twelve. But he also saw that the district police chiefs chafed at Aziz's position, which created an intermediate layer between them and the provincial chief of police, Dawlat Khan, who relied heavily on Aziz. Dawlat Khan had made him his "trusted agent," which meant that he was the official paymaster for the local police. His anomalous position was also recognized up the US chain of command, which was still nervous about the bad press Aziz had received.

With the clock ticking, Kim launched his plan. He was adamant that he would not split his team, so they moved together into a mud-walled qalat outside a village called Nawi Kalay. They had no running water, and lived cheek by jowl with a squad of Aziz's men. They made do with portable toilets and baby wipes, and on weekly visits to Orgun base they took hot showers and ate like wolves in the dining hall. This was the last hole in the security corridor that Hutch had created that still needed to be plugged; Kim intended to do it and move on. Nawi Kalay lay astride an insurgent ratline and still enjoyed a great deal of passive and active Taliban support. It was the spot where it all began, in 2010, when Hutch's team and Aziz's men had killed the local Taliban leader known as Chamtu. Kim's first step was to recruit more Afghan police from the surrounding villages and build a new check-point to fill in the gap between the checkpoints that already stretched from Shkin on the border to the capital.

To shore up this weak link in the chain, Kim sought to reward the surrounding villages that had been providing Afghan Local Police recruits for the past two years. His civil affairs officer surveyed the area and found that it had received far fewer benefits in terms of schools, clinics, and other development projects than other areas of Paktika. USAID's Office of Transition Initiatives had conducted 146 small-scale projects in the province, many in tandem with Hutch's push into hostile areas, but Kim felt the friendliest areas needed a little more love. He wanted to make sure these villagers would continue to support the program as the US drawdown proceeded—but he was not about to be duped into a massive handout program. After a slippery Afghan contractor submitted an exorbitant bid to put a roof on a school, Kim made clear that he was talking about improvements that cost about $5,000.[10]

Kim's men achieved something of a breakthrough in Nawi Kalay, but it took a small tragedy for the breakthrough to occur. A little girl who had been riding on a tractor with her father as he plowed his fields fell off, and the tractor wheels rolled over her before he could stop. The grief-stricken man gathered her up and drove pell-mell down the dirt track to the team's mud-walled compound, pounding on the gate and asking for help. The medic ran out with his bag and immediately began performing first aid and CPR. The child was already dead, but her little body heaved with trapped air, momentarily giving the father hope. "Ratina, Ratina," he called over and over, stroking her hair. The team could not save the little girl, but they took up a collection from their own personal funds to buy the family a sheep for the Muslim Eid holiday. The family and the entire village were touched by the gesture, and the relations became much friendlier thereafter. They were still not inclined to contribute volunteers for the checkpoint, however, so Kim would make do with other nearby villages.[11]

Kim also sought to encourage the district police chief to come outside the town more often to visit the villages in the populated valley. He especially wanted the police chief to embrace the local police as part of his larger force, as intended. He was a competent man, and not altogether without courage. He listened to Kim's relentless pitches to recalcitrant tribes from the western side of the valley. At a meeting in the district chief's office, Kim brought up the topic of local police to an elder from a village of known Taliban sympathies. "Oh, that again," the old man said, physically recoiling into the sofa. He laughed nervously. "We just want our school." Kim persisted, and the man became agitated. He felt that the Americans had reneged on the promise of a school, and he was angered by the implicit quid pro quo that Kim was offering. "I'm like one hand, waiting to clap," Kim said with a broad smile, raising his hand with his palm open. The meeting broke up and the old man stormed out.[12]

The district police chief frankly expressed his doubts about the Afghan Local Police. He believed they should all go through the academy and become regular policemen. Like many district chiefs, he saw his writ as largely confined to the district center, but he eagerly accepted Kim's suggestion that he should take over the job of scheduling the patrols and checkpoint duty shifts of the local police. Even if Aziz remained paymaster, at least for the moment, the district chief could assume control of their assignment and leave schedule.

The US conventional battalion commander in Paktika agreed with Kim that a move into Pirkowti was desirable to shore up the province's eastern districts, since the conventional forces were falling back from the border. He had his own ideas of how to do it. He wanted to use the Afghan army, not Aziz, even though the two Afghan battalions in Paktika had remained largely hunkered down in their bases for the past two years. The conventional battalion commander believed that Aziz had led US troops into an ambush, and tried to initiate yet another investigation of him. His primary assignment, however, was to withdraw conventional US forces and shut down their bases along the border. Combat Outpost Margah had already been shut, and he had begun to dismantle Forward Operating Base Tillman. As he did, the rate of shelling from the Pakistani side of the border escalated dramatically. The Taliban had posted videos of themselves moving into other vacated bases and celebrating, and the American command was determined to prevent a repeat of this scene.

The soldiers at Tillman were ordered to blow up everything that they did not carry away, to prevent it from being used by the insurgents or turned into a propaganda prop. The overtones of Vietnam echoed here, too, as the forces dwindled in Paktika. Tillman and Margah were bombarded over a hundred times each in November 2012, and Margah was already vacant. As the troops bulldozed Tillman and carted away every last container and piece of equipment, artillery and mortars rained down on the camp. A gory fascination gripped the highest levels of command as the daily reports came in. One commander in Kabul noted, "It was like, hey gringos, don't let the door hit you on your way out." Many Americans had been wounded and killed here, not just the famous pro-football player and Ranger Pat Tillman for whom the base was named. The Americans had never truly controlled Paktika's border with Pakistan.

The border would be left henceforth to the CIA's Counterterrorist Pursuit Teams, at least until the Afghan army was up to the task. The future of the not-so-secret CTPT force was up in the air as well. It would be up to the Afghan government to decide whether it should continue, come under effective control of the Afghan intelligence service, or be shut down. It was a sore topic with many in the US military. The existence of a separate armed force outside the military chain of command was a departure from US military doctrine. It created practical problems of coordination, since the CIA did not fall under military authority. Its chain of command ran from the Agency to the White House, with oversight from Congress. Congress, however, had been largely inert on this issue. Since 9/11, the Central Intelligence Agency had grown a shadow army—embraced by some Department of Defense civilians—that unbalanced the Agency, thrusting it into a tactical paramilitary role and diverting it from its core mission of collecting human intelligence and analyzing strategic-level threats to national security. Many in the US military, including special operations forces, saw that the CIA-led Afghan force created confusion among Afghans. That was the central problem, although spats flared up over personalities and prerogatives. The team at Shkin cooperated with the Agency on many operations, but the two also came to blows over an accidental fire and Agency evacuation plans that did not include them. Issues continued to fester and bubble up in the provinces where the Agency-created forces existed, in part because the forces were so large and operated not just on the border but well inside of it.[13]

At a security shura in Orgun in late 2012, the topic came into full view. The Orgun district chief of police raised the issue, saying he was concerned about the Afghan CIA force that operated in eastern Paktika. Some of its members regularly came to the bazaar high on hashish, and no one would control them. When complaints were brought to Commander Wazir, the Afghan head of the unit, he shrugged them off. Other Afghan officials then chimed in with their complaints. Aziz acknowledged the issue, adding that the Afghan Local Police commanders complained that they were losing men whom they had already trained to the CIA force, which paid triple the wages. Others chimed in on that point; national police and army soldiers were apparently also being lured away to join this force. The Afghans all seemed to agree that there were significant problems, but no one knew what to do. Absent from the discussion was the National Defense Service, Afghan intelligence, which nominally controlled the force. It did not appear that any of the Afghans around the table expected the NDS to address their concerns.[14]

A special operations officer in the room listened silently as the discussion proceeded. As the only American official in the room, he felt that it was important to clarify one key issue. He did not have authority to speak about the counterterrorism force, but he could see the consternation it was causing among the Afghan security forces. He leaned forward from his seat against the wall to make his only statement of the meeting. "You all are the government of Afghanistan. This is your country. If Afghans are violating your laws, you are completely within your right and responsibility to enforce the law. That is your job."

The special operations officer was well aware of the brewing complaints. This was not the first time he had heard them. He had tried to raise the issues with the CIA base chief, who blew him off. The existence of yet another armed entity operating under a separate chain of command was bound to trouble any military professional. A senior special operations commander in the United States had previously suggested a possible solution: the force should be folded into the Afghan military chain of command, perhaps under the tutelage and advisory oversight of special operations forces. If the US military left, and the CIA army remained, its loose command and control could result in the very militia running amok that the special operators were constantly accused of creating. The special operators tended to keep a tighter rein on their partner forces than the CIA did. Quite a few in the US military said the Agency's paramilitary operatives often behaved as if they were answerable to no one, and by and large they were not. The formal purpose of the force was supposedly to run cross-border intelligence operations, but in fact it was operating well inside the border. A small border force might be justifiable, given the likelihood that the threat from Pakistan would continue. But it had become something else entirely.

The CIA's future orientation became a point of discussion during the confirmation hearings for John O. Brennan's nomination as the next director of the Central Intelligence Agency in the spring of 2013. Brennan suggested that it might be time to recalibrate the Agency's focus away from its paramilitary endeavors of the past decade and back to its national strategic intelligence mission. This could entail changes in both the armed drone program run by the Agency and its on-ground paramilitary activities. Although he endorsed the need for some covert paramilitary capacity at the Agency, the question of scale, scope, and mission appeared to be open for reexamination. These same issues were raised, according to a *Washington Post* report, by the president's intelligence advisory board.[15]

For all the problems caused by the lack of coordination and command and control, the Agency force fulfilled its intended purpose of targeting insurgent leaders. Paktika's top insurgent leader, Mullah Nazir, had been living across the border in South Waziristan. In January 2013, he was killed by a drone strike. Given his prominence, his passing would likely change the dynamic of the insurgency in a large area. But would it be a change for the better? If the leadership vacuum was filled by the Haqqani network based in North Waziristan, it might not have the beneficial effect hoped for. In addition, Nazir had expelled foreign fighters from South Waziristan, and a new leader might allow them to move back in.

Kim pushed doggedly ahead with his six-month plan. After plugging the gap with a new checkpoint in Nawi Kalay, he built another checkpoint to further solidify the line in Surobi. Then he moved north to set up a checkpoint manned with new local policemen at a location that would support his move into the long-troublesome Pirkowti Valley. In early January 2013, he teamed up with the US conventional battalion and the Afghan army to make an assault into the valley. The ensuing fight seesawed back and forth for over a week. The battalion commander pushed the Afghan army to commit to stay there, and they built a fort using materials from the dismantled Tillman base. Kim thought the location, atop one of the highest hills in the valley, was perfect; it would give them visibility up and down the main route of the valley and would be hard to take by surprise. The team brought elders of Pirkowti together for a meeting and reminded them of the commitments they had made two years before to Hutch's team. The elders were doubtful that the Afghan security forces would stay to provide a security blanket for their sons, but finally they agreed to put forward twenty volunteers. Kim's team began training the first class of recruits in the last week of January.[16]

The elders were justifiably concerned about the possibility of being left to fend for themselves. In the winter months, the fledgling local police in the new sites were not attacked, but that was certain to change once spring arrived. Insurgent chatter about the new outposts spiked as soon as they were built, so Kim knew it was just a matter a time before they would be tested. The insurgents were likely to hit them hard in an attempt to take back their valley sanctuary. The border area was likely to be plagued indefinitely by attacks from the sanctuary in Pakistan. But Kim believed the Afghan solution might be coming together in Paktika. If the Afghan army, the local policemen, and Aziz began to cooperate routinely, he believed they could hold the bulk of the province. But in the spring, the ISAF command began to bulldoze the base in Sharana, the provincial capital, as the US forces drew down. The Kabul government intervened to stop them. Although the Afghan Air Force was still years from maturity, the government wanted to preserve the runway, which would help resupply and connect the province to the rest of Afghanistan.

As ODA 1411's tour was nearing its end in March 2013, the team was attacked upon returning from a patrol to the base at Orgun. In the crossfire, Kim was wounded in the head. He was evacuated to Bagram. His senior engineer, Sergeant First Class James Grissom, thirty-one, was more severely wounded. He was flown on to Landstuhl, Germany, where he died on March 23. Kim underwent surgery for shrapnel removal, but pressed the doctors to allow him to get back to Paktika. After keeping him under observation for his head injuries for a week, the doctors cleared him to return to his team. Kim knew the team was rocked by the loss of their teammate. Grissom, a quirky and witty Californian, had volunteered and come straight into the special forces after graduating from the San Francisco Art Institute. His creativity had blossomed early in life, and he had expressed it in art classes and construction projects. As a youth of eleven, he had built a tree house for neighborhood kids, and as a teenager he had singlehandedly constructed a set for a high-school musical. His teacher said, "It looked like the facade of Grauman's Chinese Theatre; it was three-dimensional. It was astounding. He did it by himself in about six hours. He was a wonderful artist."[17] Whenever the team deployed, Kim recalled, Grissom would immediately set about building something with whatever materials he could scavenge to make their locations more comfortable and fun.

Kim left Afghanistan with the conviction that Aziz had been—and would continue to be—an essential part of the Afghan security formula for Paktika. He credited Aziz with vital assistance in building Afghan Local Police in Pirkowti and other sites. His leadership was on display at a weekly security shura held at Aziz's compound adjoining the US base in Orgun. Aziz presided at the head of the table; the various commanders of the national and local police as well as the border police and army units were arrayed on either side. The district governor sat next to Aziz. Aziz was courteous to the officer representing the Afghan army, but the officer said very little. He sat with his head bowed, scribbling in his notebook, as Aziz succinctly framed the issues and asked relevant follow-up questions. Each security official took turns giving an update on his area of responsibility; the meeting was run as efficiently as any US military update briefing. When they reached the open discussion portion of the shura, Aziz tabled the most urgent issue for the group: whether Afghans were going to continue to man the border posts and attempt to keep them open, and what the consequences would be if they did not. He clearly wanted to rally support among the officials and persuade them to take up their responsibility to defend their borders. He did not blame the United States for leaving, but simply stated, "It is time for us to take over." He proposed that a vote be taken at the next meeting to force matters to a head.

Kim's boss hoped to shepherd the conversion of Aziz's force into an official Provincial Response Company (PRC) before his tour ended.

Other provinces had such paramilitary special police units, which were mentored by multinational special operations forces. Such a move would finally resolve the question of Aziz's status and make his men a formal part of the Afghan police. The role that Aziz had been playing in the province coincided with the PRC's functions. The provincial police chief was certainly in favor of the idea, but the question had languished for months. Aziz did not know it yet, but the plan was to move all of the special operations teams to Ghazni, along with the company command. He would be on his own in a very short while.

CHAPTER TEN

HIGHWAY ONE

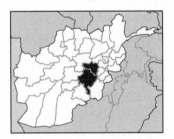

GHAZNI AND WARDAK 2012

UPRISING

In the second half of 2012, the special operations command became seized by the desire to focus on Ghazni Province. There were two reasons behind this change of focus. The first was a spontaneous uprising that offered a potential springboard for creating Afghan Local Police in the province, which had not been targeted in the initial program's design. The second was that the looming US drawdown and transition to a noncombat role in 2014 had galvanized the US and Afghan militaries to work on securing the critical arteries—Highway One between Kandahar and Kabul, and Highway Seven from Kabul to Nangahar. The latter was fairly secure already; the two gaping holes in security along Highway One were in Ghazni and Wardak provinces. The coalition had assigned security in Ghazni to the Polish Army, but its Task Force White Eagle, viewed by many Afghans as Soviets, had largely hunkered down, which did little to pacify the province. Wardak, the object of intermittent waves of intervention and neglect, remained a

203

bleeding sore, a virulent and mountainous insurgent safe haven less than an hour's drive from Kabul. So in the waning year of combat operations, the rush was on to turn both provinces around.

A special ops team sent to Ghazni quickly developed a sober outlook for their prospects. The history of the province had not been encouraging. The only prior attempt to build local police and conduct stability operations in Ghazni had been made by a SEAL team the previous year in a southerly district called Gelan. The population in Gelan had proved to be entirely unreceptive. Moreover, a conventional battalion attached to the special operations command in Ghazni provided little help and was plagued by internal problems of morale, discipline, and drug use. The only other special operations activity in the province had been raids conducted by Polish special operations forces that were partnered with the Ghazni Provincial Response Company, the paramilitary special police unit. The Poles were new and active members of a growing international special operations consortium, and the mission in Afghanistan, as in Iraq, provided them a valuable training ground to enhance their already considerable skills and to solidify their relations and familiarity with US special operations tactics and equipment. The same was true of the Romanian special operations forces, a newer but equally eager ally, which partnered with the Provincial Response Company in Zabul.

The spontaneous uprising against the Taliban, which occurred in April 2012, was triggered by a Taliban edict to close a school, which the villagers protested. The school was then burned down, prompting men in seven or eight villages south of the district center to take up arms against the Taliban. But by the time the special operations team arrived, several things had occurred to complicate the situation. The original leader of the uprising had been killed in the fighting, and a political figure associated with the Hezb-e Islami Gulbuddin (HIG) faction had subsequently insinuated himself to assert leadership over the movement. The Afghan intelligence service was also involved in backing the defenders, spurred on by the service's chief, Asadullah Khalid, who was a native of Ghazni and a former governor of the province.

In late September, three teams arrived in Ghazni: one in Andar District, where the uprising had occurred, and two in districts farther south on Highway One.[1] ODA 1326, led by Captain Terrence Jackson, moved into plywood huts in a small base adjoining the Andar district center, where the governor and police chief worked. The team launched into action to recruit, vet, and train local police according to the standard methods, and by mid-November it had trained and fielded thirty-nine policemen.

The team referred to these as "legitimate" ALP, to distinguish them from the original defenders. Jackson's police were selected, vetted, trained, and equipped in the manner approved by the Afghan Ministry of the Interior. The team was essentially trying to set up a competing local defense force that was not under HIG influence. In the face of the Taliban's concerted counterattack, that original group of defenders had dwindled from about 250 to 150. "They are not very proficient tactically," Jackson's intelligence officer said. "Basically they are a bunch of farmers on motorcycles." The Taliban had long held sway in northern Ghazni and would not leave without a fight. They killed and kidnapped several of the resistance fighters and burned two houses, and in October, three more men in the resistance were killed by a grenade. Jackson's intelligence officer offered up a grim overall assessment: the entire anti-Taliban resistance was quailing and might collapse under the steady barrage of counterattacks.[2]

The anti-Taliban factions needed help if they were going to hold the line. No Afghan commandos were available to go to Ghazni, but three Afghan special forces teams were sent there to reinforce the three American special forces teams. They were not there long before they came under attack. In November, the Taliban ambushed the new police and the US and Afghan special ops forces while on patrol. Amid the firefight, an IED exploded, and the Afghan special forces captain and his driver suffered concussions. As the captain recuperated in his plywood quarters at the spare base, he said that the outlook was not good. "The population here does not support the government, so they are not giving us information," he said. After his Humvee had been blown up, his team resorted to foot patrols to avoid IEDs. The captain had fought in seven different provinces over the past five years, and he said that the fighting in Ghazni was heavier than anywhere else he had been except for Helmand.

Greater optimism prevailed higher up the chain of command. The special ops company commander, Major Jason Clarke, had an ambitious plan for building Afghan Local Police in the four districts of Ghazni that straddled Highway One. His teams would have to carry out the plan without much help from US conventional forces, who were in the process of pulling out their small element of less than three companies, which were scattered at various outposts in the province. Clarke launched an intelligence effort to help his teams. Little collection or analysis had been done in Ghazni, as few US troops had been sent there over the past decade. What information existed was focused on the enemy. Clarke made an aggressive effort to collect and fuse data on the population, the community's economic needs, and the social and political leaders in the community using Palantir software, an expensive commercial system that created and organized open-source and classified data into searchable formats that could be manipulated, displayed graphically, and harnessed to the purposes of Village Stability Operations.[3]

The short timeline and the pressure to create Afghan Local Police limited just how much social science research could be conducted. Moreover, the questions that Clarke was trying to research were not easily answered, since they involved gaining a comprehensive understanding of province and district dynamics, not just who the bad guys were and where they were. Over the past decade, special mission units had perfected systems for rapidly fusing large and disparate sources of intelligence for the purpose of finding and capturing (or killing) enemy targets, but this was an altogether different type of intelligence problem. The task was not to find out "who and where," but rather "who and why." Dossiers of provincial-level figures did not exist, let alone dossiers of district-level leaders. The rural districts were where half of the population lived and where the Taliban had planted its roots.

The two competing local defense programs—one spontaneous but now controlled by HIG and/or Afghan intelligence, the other nurtured by the special ops team—made for a complicated vetting and recruitment process. Ultimately, the fate of the program would rest on whether the local government officials actively supported and sustained it. The provincial chief of police enthusiastically backed the program, attending the validation ceremonies and quickly supplying the arms and pay. In Andar, the governor was also effusively supportive, though his chief of police was less excited. The Andar district governor, Mohammed Kasim Diciwal, had embraced the anti-Taliban movement when it erupted in April. He had grabbed a gun and joined the anti-Taliban fighters at their first checkpoint south of town. Young men gathered around him, telling him they wanted to volunteer. "We are the first district to stand up against the Taliban. One hundred enemy have been killed," the governor said in November. "We are going to finish the Taliban next year."[4]

Diciwal's motivation was partly personal: his brother, also a district governor, had been killed by the Taliban in 2008. Diciwal had served as governor in western Ghazni until he was moved to Andar in September 2012, as Kabul decided it needed an experienced hand on the rudder there. Over a meeting in his office with the special forces team, the civil affairs officer, and his police chief in November 2012, Diciwal was abuzz with plans, suggestions, and queries. He applauded when the captain told him that the police slots for Andar had been increased from two hundred to three hundred. Polishing off a persimmon after dinner, he prodded the police chief to ask whether they could get heavy weaponry for the local police. "I hear the local police in Qarabah have been given a PKM and an RPG launcher to defend their checkpoint," he said.

The police chief, Ramazon, was a very cautious Hazara. He was an excellent police officer, but was mostly concerned with controlling corruption and preventing his men from getting killed. He came to the team to complain that ALP officers were eating at his dining hall. He did not have money in his budget to feed the extra mouths. The team leader, Jackson, assured Ramazon that the local police received a food stipend and did not need to eat his food. When brand new Hilux trucks arrived for the local police, Ramazon suggested that they be given driving lessons. His abiding concern was corruption; he was such a stickler that he re-counted the bullets and rifles after his staff took inventory. Since arriving in Andar seven months before, he proudly noted, he had fired seventy policemen. "Inshallah, it will soon be zero corruption," he said.

While Ramazon was a rather timid soul, at least for a police chief, the fact that he was a stickler for procedure and probity would help guard against the force going off the rails. With Diciwal as the cheerleader, the duo might just make a local defense program work. But the nascent effort would need mentoring. When word of Taliban massing arrived one night, the police chief asked the team to shoot some mortar rounds in their direction. The team occasionally fired illumination rounds so the defenders would feel like they had some backup, but they were not allowed to fire lethal rounds in populated areas. The only attack that materialized that night was a small ambush in the bazaar, with no casualties, but the team knew it would not take much to dent the new force's morale.

Nonetheless, the force continued to grow. The special operations command in Kabul characterized the program in Ghazni as "going viral"—growing rapidly—which was a somewhat exaggerated view of the situation. The defenders hung on, however, and did not collapse. By the end of January 2013, 139 US-supported ALP officers were on the payroll in Andar, and a total of 436 in the four Ghazni districts. Skeptics worried, however, that something built so quickly could just as rapidly unravel.

EXPULSION

If Ghazni might turn out to be a quick win, there was no such prospect in Wardak. The new US special operations commander in Kabul, Major General Tony Thomas, launched Triple Action, a series of major combat operations by combined special operations units in the fall of 2012. But in 2013 matters there went from bad to worse, just as the new four-star general, Joseph Dunford, replaced John Allen as ISAF commander, and special operators were at the center of the storm.

Given Wardak's strategic location as the southern gateway to Kabul, it was extraordinary that the province had not received the highest priority of the coalition's attention and resources. It was a nest of insurgency right at Kabul's doorstep. In 2010 the ISAF command had declared its intention to "expand the Kabul security bubble" outward. Despite those words, no surge of troops or resources was forthcoming in Wardak. Paradoxically, the province was treated like a backwater while troops and attention were lavished on remote provinces of secondary importance, such as Nuristan and Helmand.

Wardak featured the most rugged terrain in the country outside the Hindu Kush. Snowcapped peaks crept right up to Highway One, which was bisected by valleys so treacherous that conventional forces had shut down their few outposts after a tentative attempt to secure them. They built two bases along Highway One and a sprawling Afghan police training center, but insurgents moved freely through the Chak Valley, which paralleled the highway to the west.[5]

Wardak's governor until late 2012, Mohammad Halim Fidai, frequently lamented to US generals and other visitors: "You have treated Wardak like a petri dish for your experiments." One of those experiments was a pilot local defense program, the Afghan Public Protection Program (AP3), which General David McKiernan authorized in 2009. Initially the Afghans were trained and mentored by the special forces. According to Lieutenant Colonel Brad Moses, who had helped set up the original AP3, the force began going seriously off the rails after the conventional battalion sent to Wardak in 2010 took over the program in July. The battalion's oversight was lax, he said. The battalion allowed recruits to join from other provinces, turned them into static highway guards, and, worst of all, permitted a former Taliban commander, Ghulam Mohammad Hotak, to lead the group.[6]

The AP3 grew to some 1,200 police before it was disbanded. Some of the former members were later vetted and admitted into the Afghan Local Police over the course of 2011. But some five hundred former AP3—and their guns—remained unaccounted for. Over the course of 2011, special operations forces struggled without success to build the Afghan Local Police program on the ashes of the earlier AP3. The population was reluctant to volunteer for the local police no matter how hard the Americans tried. The special ops team finally made some headway in 2012, but it also suffered a number of casualties in the violent province. Team members managed to enlist several hundred volunteers, but it would later be confirmed that at least some of them were infiltrators.

The essential problem was that the province was divided between Taliban and HIG supporters. Most of those who supported neither of these insurgent factions had fled to Kabul. Some thought there might be a political solution to the province's conflict, by which they meant essentially peeling the HIG faction, led by the grey-bearded Gulbuddin Hekmatyar, off from the other factions. This divide-and-conquer strategy would eventually weaken the insurgency, or at least isolate its most hardcore elements. "That is all HIG territory," a senior Afghan security official commented, sweeping his hand across the map. Another faction of Hezb-e Islami had formed a party and elected representatives to parliament, and HIG had periodically put out feelers, accompanied by unrealistic demands. But despite several attempts at negotiation and reintegration, the United States and the Afghan government could not seem to find the formula to pacify Wardak.[7]

Thomas, the US special operations commander who arrived in July 2012 to replace Brigadier General Chris Haas, decided to launch a series of combined operations that fall. The history of combat in Wardak had not been encouraging, however. The worst loss of the war occurred in Wardak in August 2011, when thirty-eight SEALs and other Afghan and US servicemen were in a Chinook crash. This was followed a month later by a devastating suicide truck bombing at one of the two US bases there, Combat Outpost Syadabad. In the summer of 2012, in the Chak District, insurgents killed the governor and ten of the fledgling local police of fifty that special operators had recruited. They discovered that it was an inside job; elders allied with the Taliban had nominated Taliban fighters for the police. The toll suffered by special operations forces in Wardak continued: in September, Sergeant First Class Riley Gene Stephens was killed, and then Warrant Officer

Joseph L. Schiro. Staff Sergeant Justin Marquez died of gunshot wounds after a battle on October 6.

Thomas decided to focus the first set of operations in Chak. But he soon found that he would be doing it largely on his own: Regional Command–East was pulling out of its southernmost base in Wardak, and it would leave only a few advisory teams with the Afghan security forces based in the northern part of the province. Thomas sought to pull together all the special operations units to throw everything he controlled at the problem. "That one little [team site in Wardak] is the customer and we are arraying everything around them," Thomas said of his attempt to achieve a breakthrough for Afghan local policing and governance in the Chak Valley.[8]

He mounted the largest operation ever undertaken by the Afghan commandos, supported by a variety of US and coalition special ops units. The 6th Commando Kandak took to the shooting ranges for training and rappelled down walls at their base to brush up on their fast-rope techniques. On October 22, five hundred Afghan and coalition special operators flooded the Chak Valley for a three-day operation covering 150 square miles. It was the hardest the commandos had ever been pushed. They set up a perimeter and overwatch and moved through half a dozen villages and qalats in the valley, stirring up a hornet's nest. The combined force fought multiple battles, killing a total of forty-seven enemy fighters, including Taliban leader Mullah Gulam Ali. Special forces Chief Warrant Officer 2 Michael Duskin was killed in battle on October 23. The joint operation uncovered two large arms caches and several buried bombs, which the commandos helped defuse. The Afghan police chief of Wardak presided over a meeting at the district center at which the elders were again invited to contribute to their own defense. A few days later the provincial officials also visited Chak. It was the first time in three years that they had been there.

Thomas did not stop there. Over the coming months he launched additional operations in the districts to the north. He was still sore about the failure to persuade his RC-East counterpart to participate. Thomas said he was "literally flummoxed" at the general's resistance to join in. "Why didn't you tell us in September?" Thomas said. "We just lost a couple of guys. If [the conventional forces] don't come there, we are on a fool's errand." But he plowed ahead, launching special operators into Wardak's northern districts, where they detained numerous Taliban insurgents and Afghans suspected of facilitating attacks. At the same time, Afghan Local Police ranks expanded to 756 in Wardak.[9]

Two weeks after General Joseph Dunford took over the four-star ISAF command, Wardak blew up in his face. President Karzai's office issued a statement containing explosive allegations. "It became clear that armed individuals named as U.S. special force stationed in Wardak province engage in harassing, annoying, torturing and even murdering innocent people," the statement read. It didn't indicate who had identified the attackers as "U.S. special force." A Kabul delegation visiting Wardak had been besieged by complaints from elders and villagers, who accused the special operations forces and their Afghan partners of abuse, torture, and killing. A local provincial council member and family members of the missing Afghans also made denunciations to the press. Some of the family members traveled to Kabul, and the protests escalated. Nine Afghans were alleged to have disappeared; the ISAF command confirmed that it had detained four of the nine, but said that it found no evidence of misconduct by US special operations forces.[10]

According to one news report, a villager in Nerkh named Asadullah Aslamuddin said his son was detained on January 19, 2013, in a night raid by US special forces and Afghans, and found dead a short while later, shot three times in the head and chest.[11] Other villagers said they had received rough treatment by Afghans associated with the special operators based in Nerkh. A cell-phone video surfaced showing an Afghan, later identified as Zakeria Kandahari, kicking an Afghan repeatedly.[12] Kandahari, who was wearing a US military uniform in the video, had been an interpreter for the special operations team on its previous rotations in Kandahar, and the team had called him to come join the effort in Wardak. He was not yet on contract, however, when the incident occurred. According to the special ops battalion, he had been called to the Afghan intelligence service's office in Nerkh to identify someone when the videotaped incident occurred. Since the incident had allegedly occurred there in the presence of Afghan intelligence officers, one special operations officer wondered, "Why didn't they stop him if he was abusing a detainee?"[13] In any event, Kandahari left the NDS office, went to the special operations team's outpost, and then disappeared. The government in Kabul then asked for the Afghan to be detained. When Karzai found out that Kandahari was gone, he snapped. He ordered all special operations forces to be out of Wardak in two weeks, by March 10.

After prolonged meetings with Afghan officials, ISAF announced that it would open a joint investigation with the Afghan government. It stood by its previous statement that no coalition forces had been involved in abuses. An Article 15 investigation was conducted and no evidence of coalition complicity was found, but the report itself was not released. Allegations had been filtering up to Kabul since the intensive operations began, including through the NDS intelligence service. US special operations officers alluded to an extensive propaganda campaign being mounted through insurgent sympathizers to accomplish by slander what they could not achieve militarily: the removal of US forces from the battlefield. They did not name individuals, but a Wardak provincial council member, Haji Hazrat Janan, had denounced coalition combat actions on this occasion and previously.[14]

The reports of abuses fell on believing ears in the presidential palace. It was symptomatic of the state of US-Afghan relations. The deterioration in relations was underscored by another assertion by Karzai in a March 10 speech that left incredulous US officials sputtering with anger. "Those bombs that went off in Kabul and Khost were not a show of force to America. They were in service of America. It was in the service of the 2014 slogan to warn us if they [Americans] are not here then Taliban will come," Karzai said, referring to two suicide bombs that had gone off in Kabul the day before.[15]

General Dunford and various other high-ranking US officials immediately rejected Karzai's outrageous claim. A joint news conference with Chuck Hagel, in Kabul on his first visit as secretary of defense, was canceled. Karzai, who had been engaged in a prolonged standoff with the US government over detainees and control of the Parwan Detention Facility, was more determined than ever to assert Afghan sovereignty, playing to an increasingly nationalistic audience.

The team in Nerkh, the Wardak district where the alleged abuses occurred, believed it had been falsely accused by Afghan officials allied with the Taliban and Hezb-e Islami factions. The Taliban had successfully used elders' complaints before to take down army checkpoints that were interfering with insurgent movement. The team adopted a new policy: it would only go on patrol with a local official in tow, such as the district police chief, the Afghan intelligence representative, or the district governor. But these measures were too late to resolve the situation. The battalion operations officer, Major John Bishop, said, "We found ourselves in a power struggle between the government, HIG, and the Taliban." It was difficult to untaint the waters once allegations of abuse were made, he said.[16]

The March 10 deadline came and went. Dunford and the special operations command continued intensive closed-door talks with the Afghan officials and military command. US military commanders as well as many Afghan army officers, including the brigade commander for Wardak, warned that the Afghan security forces were not even close to being able to handle the province on their own. All the efforts of the previous months would likely be reversed if the coalition forces abruptly left Wardak, which was precisely what the Taliban wanted. The coalition had made a last big push to win back Wardak for the government, but the government did not appear to appreciate the effort. The special operations command spokesman acknowledged that it had failed to cultivate sufficient support from local officials to counter the wave of denunciations from Wardak. They had lost the battle of perception, at a minimum.[17]

On March 11, an Afghan national policeman in Jalrez, the district next to Nerkh, jumped into the back of a green Afghan police pickup truck and grabbed the machine gun mounted on the truck bed. He swiveled it into position, aimed at a crowd that included US special operators, and mowed them down. The Afghan 6th Commandos came to their aid, but Captain Andrew Pederson-Keel, twenty-eight, and Staff Sergeant Rex Schad, twenty-six, were killed. Nearly eight hundred people turned out for the officer's memorial service in his native Connecticut.

On March 20, ISAF announced that it had reached an agreement with the Afghan government regarding Wardak. The special forces team in Nerkh, ODA 3124, would depart from the district on March 30 and turn over its contingent of forty local police to an Afghan special forces team. That expelled team would move to Sayadabad, the district straddling a sixty-kilometer stretch of Highway One south of Nerkh. The command decided to bring the team in Chak in to work along the same corridor. The team in Chak had continued to fight an uphill battle there despite the huge operation in the fall, and the district still had no governor. The special operations battalion commander, Lieutenant Colonel Chris Fox, summed up the new approach to Wardak: "We are only going to work where we have a direct tie-in to the district police chief, the district governor and the Afghan army. If those entities do not deem it important, it will not work." Afghan Local Police only flourished in certain conditions, which did not exist in this province. Special operators had paid a high price in Wardak, yet the tide there still ran in the insurgents' favor.[18]

CHAPTER ELEVEN

WILL THE VALLEY HOLD?

KUNAR 2012–2013

A BAND OF BROTHERS

The successes in both Paktika and Kunar contrasted with the failures in Wardak. Indeed, like Paktika, Kunar emerged in 2012 as one of the clear successes of the Afghan Local Police program. The southern Kunar population was receptive to the local defense initiative, in part because it was anchored in the reliable and sober local police commander Nur Mohammed, whose good reputation extended beyond his district. He encouraged Afghans in the surrounding districts to join the program, and once their leaders were selected, he formed a close working relationship with them.

But the promising trajectory in Kunar was threatened by three factors: the safe haven available to the Taliban in Pakistan, haste, and ego. The Pakistan safe haven posed a particular threat because Kunar's populated areas were a few hours' march from the border. From Kunar's capital, Asadabad, it was less than a two-hour drive south through a broad valley to Jalalabad, the principal city of eastern Afghanistan—

and if those two cities fell it would be difficult to hold Kabul. Yet the safe haven in Pakistan was a fact, like the weather; for all the teeth-gnashing, intelligence operations, and pinprick drone strikes, there was little that could be done to alter it. Pakistan's internal dysfunctions had bred the insurgent stronghold, and only fundamental change would alter the country's self-defeating approach to security. Unlike Paktika, whose populated areas were farther from the border, Kunar's populated areas were right on Pakistan's doorstep, and the province would have to be more proactive in its defense if it was to keep the badness at bay.

That meant the local police force had to be solid, and it had to be backed up by the other Afghan security forces. Unfortunately, the coalition was in a hurry to leave Kunar. The culmination of two years of effort in Kunar was jeopardized by ISAF's plan to pull back to Highway One and Highway Seven and effectively abandon critical areas such as Kunar. No official would admit it, but the US military had adopted the same strategy the Soviets had twenty-five years earlier. US commanders rationalized their decision as necessary, however: they would focus on what the Afghans could hold, even though the Afghan military protested some of the moves. Afghans knew their history. The Soviet Army had withdrawn from Kunar in mid-1988, and by the end of the year its capital, Asadabad, had been in the hands of the mujahideen.[1]

The Taliban was certainly aware of the significance of this territory. Qari Zia Rahman, the Taliban commander for Kunar and Nuristan, told a Pakistani journalist in 2008 that "from the Soviet days in Afghanistan, Kunar's importance has been clear." He added: "This is a border province [with Pakistan] and trouble here can break the central government [in Kabul]. Whoever has been defeated in Afghanistan, his defeat began from Kunar. Hence, everybody is terrified of this region. The Soviets were defeated in this province and NATO knows that if it is defeated here it will be defeated all over Afghanistan."[2]

The second factor, haste, could lead US forces to depart too rapidly from Kunar, short-circuiting the emerging victory in the southern part of the province. The commanders had to carefully consider how much and what type of support the Afghans would need to hold it.

A third factor, ego, also threatened to derail Kunar's progress in the spring of 2012. After Matt's team left, Major Jim Gant was to move down from his mountain lair to Combat Outpost Penich in the valley to oversee the continued expansion of the Afghan Local Police. Gant had been one of the first special operators in Kunar. A paper written under his name, "One Tribe at a Time," recounting his experience of tribal engagement, had gained him a wide following and a degree of fame within the military community. He had been permitted to return to Kunar for a two-year tour in a somewhat unorthodox arrangement. Normally, a special forces major would be a company commander overseeing teams that were doing tactical missions. But Gant had grown deep roots in Kunar. His relationship with the "Sitting Bull," as he dubbed the tribal chief in Mangwal, was, by his own account, like that of father and son.

Gant styled himself as Afghanistan's Lawrence of Arabia, but turned out to be closer to Colonel Kurtz of *Apocalypse Now*. While he did lay some of the groundwork for the expansion of ALP in Kunar, he spent most of his time in Mangwal with his favorite tribe. There were rumors of unauthorized cross-border operations, questionable tactics, and unaccounted expenditures. His superiors grew uneasy, telling one visitor he had become "uncontrollable." Gant was seen zooming around in a Kawasaki dune buggy with antlers tied to the front. Finally, a young conventional infantry lieutenant attached to Gant's ad hoc team decided to blow the whistle after being asked to falsify a situation report. "This is just not right," he told Gant's superiors, adding that things were out of control in the camp. The command ordered an official "health and welfare" inspection of Gant's camp in early March 2012. It appeared that Gant had been living out some kind of a sex-, drug-, and alcohol-fueled fantasy, becoming, as one officer put it, "a legend in his own mind." Alcohol and steroids were found in his hooch, along with large quantities of Schedule II, III, and IV controlled substances and other drugs. Classified material was also found unsecured in his quarters, a violation compounded by the fact that Gant had been keeping a reporter-turned-lover at the camp, moving her around to prevent his superiors from learning of her presence.

Gant had suffered multiple head injuries, including from IEDs and other explosions, but it was unclear whether he was technically unfit for duty. He had suffered a concussion after a fall in January 2012. In any case, it was clear that Gant had gone off the reservation. He was so lost in his own misplaced sense of entitlement, his superior officers said, that he refused to acknowledge any misdeeds and had to be forcibly removed. The woman, a former *Washington Post* reporter named Ann Scott Tyson, also reportedly refused to leave. The US embassy in Kabul had to send personnel to remove her.[3]

Brigadier General Chris Haas wanted to throw the book at Gant, but Gant had many supporters in the higher ranks, which may have helped him stave off a court-martial. He spent months at Fort Bragg awaiting the outcome of the Article 15-6 investigation. No charges were brought in the end, but he was relieved for cause and ejected from the US Army Special Forces. One general said, "Breaking the arrows [the crossed-arrow symbol of the Special Forces] is a very serious step." He was taken off the promotion list for lieutenant colonel but allowed to retire with his pension—and to face whatever personal fallout would come with his wife and family.[4]

In his final months of command in Afghanistan, Haas had grown extremely concerned about discipline in general. The shootings allegedly perpetrated by Staff Sergeant Robert Bales on March 11 were an egregious example, but the Gant case hit home, too, given Gant's relative prominence within the military. He was an experienced officer who had been awarded a Silver Star for valor in Iraq, a seasoned combat adviser accustomed to working in all kinds of conditions, and had thus been given wide latitude. His behavior gave ammunition to critics of special operations forces and reinforced a stereotype of them as defiant of authority and scornful of procedure. The cowboy attitude of immature operators was not just unprofessional but, more importantly, could cost lives—and had cost lives on Haas's watch. He related one account of a team sergeant who, shortly after arriving in Afghanistan, had led his team into an ambush without doing the necessary pre-mission analysis. It cost him his life and the team its leader.

So Gant's fall was a blot on the reputation of special operators. But it had a concrete impact as well. It deprived Kunar's fledgling local defense forces of experienced guidance at a critical juncture. The special operators were seeking to triple the police ranks and their reach in the coming year. Because Gant was out of the picture instead of being moved to Penich, Nur Mohammed lacked the backup that he needed for the coming fighting season. This became especially evident one day in March, just as Gant was being ejected from Kunar, when Nur Mohammed's forces were attacked at one of their checkpoints. The boom of an RPG hitting the checkpoint could be heard across the river at COP Fortress, and a puff of smoke went up, followed by gunshots. The soldiers watched from the ramparts of Fortress to see if anyone would come to their aid, but no one did. Later that night, on the phone, Nur Mohammed said his men had had to fight off the attack alone. They had called Penich, where a rump staff told them to call another base. "We asked for air support" from Penich, Nur said, adding that his men had hit an IED in the course of going for help. As usual, Nur was calm and analytical as he pointed out the larger significance of the day's events. "If there is no backup, that only will encourage more attacks from the Taliban. We need a team at Penich if one is available," he said. Nur himself was also in the crosshairs: the NDS intelligence officer in Khas Kunar had twice warned Nur that suicide bombers had been sent to find him. The insurgents knew he was the lynchpin of the local police, and they were set on taking him out.[5]

It was a lot to expect of Nur Mohammed's lightly armed Afghan Local Police to hang out in their checkpoints, exposed to frontal attacks, IEDs, and ambushes, if they could not count on anyone to come to their aid. They were supposed to be one layer of a multilayered defense. So where were the other layers? The Afghans did need to start backing each other up, but Afghan army units were notoriously reluctant to come out of their barracks. When they did, they chose the safer western side of the Kunar River rather than the IED-laden route on the eastern side, much like the US conventional forces. The work of mentoring and stitching together the various Afghan police and army forces had been secondary for years as US forces focused instead on their own combat operations. Furthermore, the restrictions on border-zone operations had made it easier than ever for the insurgents to creep down the lateral valleys to the populated Kunar River Valley and then scoot back to their safe haven on the border.

To relieve the pressure on Nur and the populated valley, the special operations command won permission for their first near-border mission with Afghan commandos since the previous November, when Operation Sayaqa had precipitated the international crisis with Pakistan. The location was the Ganjgal Valley just north of Nur Mohammed's district, where the Battle of Ganjgal had taken place on September 8, 2009. For his heroism in that battle, Marine Corporal Dakota Meyer had become the first living Marine since the Vietnam War to receive a Medal of Honor. The 4-kilometer buffer zone established after the cross-border attack in November 2011 was still in effect; Ganjgal village, population 500, lay 4.7 kilometers from the border.

The 1st Commando Kandak and its partner special ops team, led by Captain Alex Newsom, lifted off in helicopters from Camp Dyer in Jalalabad at 1 a.m. on March 6. Their approved landing zone was 6.5 kilometers from the border, so the 140 men put on their NODs and stole toward Ganjgal in the darkness to preselected houses where they would await first light. Setting a watch, they hunkered down at these strongpoints at about 4 a.m. for a two-hour wait. The new rules for night operations would soon force them to infiltrate just before dawn, at "nautical twilight," which meant they and their aircraft would be visible to insurgents. At 6 a.m., the troops moved out toward the village, knowing that it was just a matter of time before they took fire. They took fire from the northern ridge at 9 a.m., and seconds later the ridge to the south opened up as well. Within eight minutes, they were taking fire from four or five locations. The ground commander declared troops in contact over the radio, which gave them priority for air support. Conventional forces and Afghan army troops blocked the route behind them along the highway. At Camp Dyer's op center, intelligence officer Captain Rick Holahan tracked the battle and updated his Google Maps laydown of the operation as it progressed.

It provided an excellent 3D model for after-action reviews. He put a digital "push pin" at every location where gunfire was reported.[6]

Fog created a low ceiling, so the attack helicopters were forced to wait for it to burn off before they could take off, which occurred at 11:36 a.m. But a blimp was up, with a camera and thermal sights, and it had spotted the hot barrel of a PKM medium machine gun on the north ridge at 9:51 a.m. The team called in the fast movers, and they dropped a bomb on the site, killing one insurgent. Shortly thereafter, another location on the south ridge was pinpointed and a second bomb was dropped, killing two insurgents.

The team's company commander, Major Kent Solheim, had come along on the mission and was up in the mountains on the north ridge, where he and his men spotted Taliban ducking in and out of a network of caves. They called in an A-10 Warthog, a slow-moving beast of a plane beloved by ground troops for its accuracy. It strafed the positions repeatedly. Solheim watched in amazement through his rifle scope as Taliban fighters popped out of the caves to fire off their AK-47s at the plane, hoping to bring it down. Solheim's own mettle awed his subordinates. An amputee from a previous combat deployment in Iraq, he was a dedicated runner and fierce competitor. He clambered through the steep mountains with the best of them.

The insurgent fire was suppressed for the time being, though the air weapons team overhead spotted reinforcements moving from the north. While the commandos entered the village below to begin meeting with elders, the troops on the ridges climbed up to the machine-gun nests to take photos of those killed in action. Solheim had learned the value of photographs on his very first commando op of this tour, in northern Kunar. Villagers alleged that commandos had killed women and children, and the provincial governor had repeated them, leading General Allen to ask the team for evidence of the operation. Luckily they had photos. The special operators with multiple tours in Afghanistan had grown used to all kinds of accusations anytime they conducted an operation. The troops in Ganjgal that day could not reach the highest point, about 6,100 feet up, which they believed was the Taliban commander's location. It lay 1.56 kilometers inside the forbidden buffer zone. But they did get photos of the others, as well as samples for DNA testing, which later led one fighter to be identified definitively as a Taliban IED maker.

As it turned out, Gant's departure did not stop the forward momentum of the Afghan Local Police in Kunar. Nur Mohammed soldiered on, and across the river, two special operations teams worked to build the program in two districts, Narang and Chowkay, over the spring and summer of 2012. One of those teams, ODA 3436, had been deployed to Uruzgan the previous year. The team members had hoped to return there, as they had mastered Uruzgan Province's intra-Pashtun and Hazara politics and knew the physical terrain like the back of their hands. But they took up the job in Kunar, grumbling aside, and found a ready ally in the acting district governor, a pharmacist who had lobbied for the Afghan Local Police program to be started there. An educated man, he volunteered to teach the class on the Afghan Constitution and Afghan law that was part of the ALP curriculum. The governor was impressed by the team's energy. "In a few months, they brought in solar-powered streetlights, built sidewalks and taught basic hygiene," he said. The team medic—who held a master's degree and spoke Pashto—conducted a health assessment, prepared packages of tailored supplies to be given out in the villages, and oversaw a $25,000-upgrade of the clinic, which saw some four hundred patients a day. "I think we're making a difference," the medic said. "Just by getting them to boil water, we are saving babies' lives every day. But they can't figure out the piss tubes," he added with a laugh, referring to the pipes that the team inserted in the ground as urinals. This was a simple method the special operators used in the field for urination to avoid contaminating the ground water, but Afghans were used to squatting and not inclined to use the tubes.[7]

ODA 3436 expanded the ALP force, running forty recruits at a time through the three-week class. The team reserved half of its two hundred approved positions for a second recruitment up Badel and Waygal valleys on the western side of the Kunar River. These bisecting valleys led to the Pech and Korengal no-man's-land farther north, and Taliban regularly traveled down them to stage attacks, lay mines, or cross over to Pakistan. As the operators trolled for recruits, they looked for Afghans with family ties in the valleys to help them move into those areas, and the district governor volunteered to go with them to recruit. The team sergeant, who planned to retire after twenty-three years in the army and six tours in Afghanistan—and many more in Africa, Haiti, and elsewhere—felt they had found a plucky ALP commander, Wazir. "He's a pipe-hitter," he said approvingly of Wazir's willingness to foray out into risky places. The team operating in the adjacent district also found ready recruits. The plan mirrored that on the other side of the river: to build a force that was strong and thick enough to hold the main populated area and seal off insurgents farther north among the tribes who wanted to be left alone to ply their timber-smuggling business.

THE LAST TEAM

By October 2012, the ALP program in southern Kunar was on a solid course. A new team, ODA 3131, arrived to pick up the baton for most of the province. This team was given the task of overseeing local police in four districts while also, in a fifth district, revetting and converting a force that had been formed by US conventional forces into Afghan Local Police.

Fortunately, the four ALP commanders of the districts of Narang, Chowkay, Khas Kunar, and Sarkani were sufficiently competent already. They were a band of brothers who could rely on each other even if the regular police or army did not come to their aid. Their relationship was evident one cold but sunny morning at the Chowkay district commander's headquarters located between the highway and the meandering riverbank. The commander, Asim Gul, pulled webbed cots outside into the sunshine to provide seating for the special forces team. And no sooner had the team members taken their seats than the Narang commander, Wazir, pulled up in his truck to see what was going on. His local policemen, who were posted along the highway, had alerted him to the gathering. Wazir and Asim Gul sat next to each other animatedly sharing the latest news. They had been friends since childhood and were on their way later that day to a funeral for Nur Mohammed's aunt across the river.[8]

The commanders had a functioning network that reacted when any one of them came under attack. Nur had responded with his men several times when Wazir and Asim Gul had called for help. The commanders stayed in touch with each other by cell phone, and their policemen stood watch day and night at the bridges, in the culverts, and in other areas that had been targeted. They enjoyed varying degrees of support from the district chiefs of police, although the pay did arrive regularly. The police chief in his district, Wazir said, was corrupt. Wazir's men had detained an insurgent leader at the bridge a month earlier, and the police chief, Wazir said, had released him. "He had 250,000 Pakistani rupees and a Pakistani ID," Wazir fumed, referring to the insurgent leader. The man, Wazir added, was a Taliban judge who had ordered the beheading of two policemen; he had also routinely sent out night letters to intimidate people in the valley. Just that morning, Wazir's men had seen a truck driver carrying a load of illegal timber pay a bribe to pass through a police checkpoint. Wazir had called the provincial police chief to report this, he said, since he did not trust the district chief.

The men had more regard for the Afghan army, but they wanted the army to help clear insurgents from the troublesome bisecting valleys. "The commandos came last summer, for the first time in a year," Asim Gul said. "Now the fighting up north is pushing the Taliban back down into our valleys." He and Wazir then excused themselves, saying they were late for the funeral.

After they left, Brandon, the ODA 3131 team sergeant, remarked, "Wazir is a heroin addict, but he's a functional one. He has guys posted at all the culverts, and every time we show up he comes to meet us in five minutes." The vetting rules established by the Afghan Ministry of the Interior permitted the Afghan Local Police recruits to test positive for hashish but not opium. However, the team was not inclined to derail an alliance with Wazir that seemed to be working well. Brandon assigned a sergeant to be the liaison to each district; the liaisons were to visit weekly with the ALP commanders and check in with them more frequently by phone. On a tour of the area, the team members stopped to talk with several policemen at their checkpoints. One man named Said Mohammed with a bushy white beard stood guard at the bridge across the river. "We are okay here; the Taliban is up in that valley," he said. The next checkpoint was manned by two men who thanked the team for delivering them a used "man can" so they could sleep in shifts.[9]

On the other side of the river, Nur Mohammed was adjusting to life without a special operations team in his district after Gant's departure. He was concerned that his men would not have any air cover in the event of a major attack. COP Penich had been turned over to the Afghans, who immediately began carting away equipment and furniture. "Khas Kunar is 98 percent secure," Nur said. "The government has been able to reopen schools in Walay and Shalay valleys." But the insurgents were still using Maya on the border as a base to launch from, and he believed another commando operation was needed in that area. "We've been attacked three times," he said, "but we have been able to repel them and kill four enemy." He was constantly struggling to get supplies for his men: the provincial police headquarters was slow to provide trucks and fuel, but at least, he said, his district police chief was now passing their requests up the chain.

The new team, ODA 3131, multitasked in a frenzy of activity to assist the police in these four districts while also getting their conversion project started in the district of Marawara. For the previous two years, teams had usually been responsible for one district, but this team would end up covering the entire Kunar Province. It would be a test of just how much one team could do. They were to convert Marawara's 120-member local defense force, which had been created by US conventional forces, into an ALP force. Previously, this would have been considered a full-time job. Marawara was a troubled district on the border with Pakistan that was also the refuge of Qari Zia Rahman, or QZR, as they called him. Rahman was the top Taliban commander in Kunar Province. His refuge, like Maya village, was conveniently located in the four-kilometer buffer zone in a village called Barawolo. The US forces were still banned from conducting combat operations there, but some Afghan development workers had been in the village.

ODA 3131 had its hands full in the southern half of Kunar, but another conversion was under way in the far northeastern corner of Kunar, deep in the Hindu Kush and smack up against the Pakistani border. Here a CIA-trained force was being converted into an ALP force because the Agency was closing down its base. No one would be left to conduct overwatch of that force except for ODA 3131, yet the team members could not possibly travel there and still complete their duties in the other five locations. Were they supposed to conduct overwatch by telephone?

Marawara was the team's priority for two reasons: first, it was the home of the top Taliban commander in Kunar, and second, it was a straight shot, thirteen kilometers, from the Pakistani border—and his lair—into Asadabad, the provincial capital. Qari Zia Rahman commanded insurgents throughout Kunar and Nuristan and across the border in Pakistan. He was Afghan, but the US military considered him an Al Qaeda affiliate, rather than just a Taliban leader, because his forces included a mélange of Central Asian and Arab fighters. "He is the nastiest guy around," said Holahan, the intelligence officer.[10]

Students of the Soviet war in Afghanistan were familiar with the fierce battle of Marawara in 1985. In the fall of Asadabad, the mujahideen had come through Ghaki Pass. Yet no special operations team had been assigned to Marawara for four years. Some villages in Marawara had asked for help in early 2012, after nine insurgents were captured, but there was no plan at that time to build an Afghan Local Police force there. Nor was there a local *tashkil*, or allotment of positions, for doing so. Holahan had fretted: "I worry that if we do not take it up we will miss the opportunity. The villagers stick up their head and ask [for help] and will not likely wait that long."

For their part, US conventional forces had launched repeated operations without finding a formula to hold the district. The solution to the puzzle, in a broad sense, was simple: unless an Afghan force remained behind, all their efforts would be for naught. Yet Americans continued to focus on combat operations rather than constructing this hold solution. In April 2010, the 2nd Battalion of the 503rd Infantry Regiment had fought at Daridam, the first insurgent stronghold in Marawara's Ghaki Valley, killing 100 of the enemy. Two months later, in June, the conventional battalion that replaced the 2/503, the 2nd Battalion of the 327th Infantry Regiment, returned to Daridam and again killed over one hundred insurgents. The sixty Afghan soldiers who accompanied the 2/327 retreated in the face of the withering battle. Even the US troops were fainting from lack of fluid and running out of ammunition. On the second day of battle, Afghan commandos were dropped in to assist. But no one remained behind to secure the village, and the police failed to show up. The next month, the battalion launched a one-day operation with 425 troops in search of Qari Zia Rahman in the village of Chenar, the next insurgent stronghold down the valley, but QZR was gone, along with most of the villagers. The following spring, the 2/327 launched another foray into the valley, this time as far as Barawolo, in a ten-day operation aimed at capturing QZR in his new hideout. It resulted in eighty enemy killed, but no QZR. Since then the village had been ruled off–limits, as it lay within the four-kilometer buffer zone.[11]

This final mission, operation Strong Eagle III, represented an advance in that the coalition had taken more Afghan army units out into battle for longer missions than ever before—and they had gone to multiple villages—but the Afghan army was not yet an expeditionary force. The Afghan army had many decent officers, but it was challenged by shortfalls in logistics and equipment; even the Americans had difficulty hauling ammunition to high-altitude combat locations. The Afghan Border Police post at Ghaki Pass, once resupplied by coalition air support, made occasional overland trips for supplies.

The team hoped, in the little time it had left, to fashion an enduring solution for the valley's, and therefore Kunar's, security. The operators believed that Asadabad's security required securing Ghaki Valley. They intended to do it primarily with residents of the valley, so they lobbied to double the Marawara local police allotment to 250 slots. That way, they could station 50 local police in the district center and recruit the rest from the villages leading down the Ghaki Valley to the border.

They would work their way down the valley, building local police forces one village at a time. The plan was ambitious, but if successful, it would do more for Kunar Province and beyond than the endless game of Whac-A-Mole that had been the status quo. If they could at least build local police halfway down the Ghaki Valley, they could buy Asadabad four more kilometers of defensive perimeter.

ODA 3131 was an experienced, cohesive team. The men had deployed together to Kandahar the previous year, with the exception of the captain, who was on his first tour in the Special Forces. The team sergeant, Brandon, thirty-five, had eighteen years of military service, and the chief warrant officer was a fifteen-year army veteran. Brandon was a giant redheaded bear of man with a steady manner and six deployments under his belt. He was a stickler for sound tactics and scrutinized everything the sergeants did to ensure there were no lapses. Their battalion had taken heavy losses since they arrived—they had been among the teams sent to Wardak and Logar—and Brandon was determined not to add to that count.

The team's chief warrant officer had deployed six times to Afghanistan and twice to Iraq. On two of the tours in Afghanistan he had been detailed to the CIA, and he had adopted the Afghan name Jawad for his undercover work. "Jawad" had been to "the Farm" for Agency training and taken the special forces Level 3 source development training (as had the team medic, Dave). Jawad led the team's planning and intelligence. He had an easy way with people and a talent for improvisation. From the moment he and Dave hit the ground they began to build a network of Afghans and colleagues in the province who would exchange information about people and events. Jawad's Agency time earned him immediate credibility with the CIA personnel in Kunar, and he met with them daily.

The team also was fortunate to have a civil affairs team working alongside it, led by Captain Tim Ambrose. Late in the war, special operations commanders had begun to revive this once-standard practice of using special forces, civil affairs, and psyops soldiers as a combined team. Ambrose dug into the Marawara human map and discovered some interesting connections. It appeared that one of the dominant elders of Marawara, Haji Hazrat Rahman, might be the uncle of QZR, and in any event carried great weight with the tribes in the Ghaki Valley. Rahman had been extremely standoffish, declining to attend any meeting or shura convened by the team. The Kunar provincial reconstruction team had built a model farm on land he owned, however, and Ambrose was eager to find a way to benefit from the knowledge of the US development workers and their relationships with the locals. He made overtures to the head of USAID's Office of Transition Initiatives, who had spent two years in Kunar and was now running the program from Kabul for the entire country. Ambrose hoped to tap into her network, although civilian officials were often reluctant to work with the military. In some cases, the reluctance was grounded in a concern for Afghan personnel working in remote conflict zones. Any sharing of names might expose them, and the insurgent retaliation would be swift and deadly.[12]

Just revetting and training the Afghan Local Police force at Marawara's district center was a fairly dicey proposition, to say nothing of recruiting police all the way to the border. ODA 3131 began training the first forty recruits in the abandoned police station at the district center, which sat at the mouth of the Ghaki Valley. The district governor had come back to work since the team had arrived, but it was still considered enemy territory. About an hour after arriving, the operators would usually come under fire from either a DShK machine-gun nest implanted in the ridge over the next village down the valley or 82 mm mortars launched from the mountain ridge.

As if on schedule, an artillery round exploded on the hillside next to the class about an hour into the session one day in early November 2012. Brandon snapped his head around to look at the puff of smoke made by the impact. "Did anyone shoot?" he said. He and other sergeants took cover and looked through their rifle scopes at the surrounding ridges. The gunners in the trucks swiveled their cameras over the horizon and down the valley. The captain called the conventional unit at the main remaining conventional base, FOB Joyce, which had an artillery section and attack helicopters, and asked for an air weapons team to launch and locate the insurgents. He requested a 155 mm artillery round to be fired in response. "Have you done a CIVCAS assessment?" the ops watch officer replied. The rules of engagement required an analysis of the potential for civilian casualties. After further discussion, Joyce decided that it could not fire in the populated area down the valley where the mortar had likely been launched. However, it could shoot a deterrence round into a nearby unpopulated hill. In twenty minutes, a distant thud marked the return of fire. Shortly afterward, two Kiowa helicopters flew into sight from the south and circled around the mountains. Whoever had been there was surely long gone. It was not exactly the kind of quick response that would strike fear into the insurgents' hearts.[13]

The team was also trolling for information about an Afghan soldier who had reportedly been captured by QZR's men the day before, on November 6, 2012. An Afghan arrived to report that the soldier had been taken down the Ghaki Valley, and that QZR had threatened to behead him the following day. Brandon sprang into action. He thought it sounded like a perfect mission for the Kunar Provincial Response Company, which was advised by Hungarian special operations forces and was based at FOB Joyce. But when he called, the US adviser there told him that the unit had not yet been validated for combat operations. He then called US advisers to the Afghan army battalion, which also declined to act. Next he called the district chief of police, who said he could not take action without orders from the provincial chief.

Brandon and the captain discussed their very limited options. The local police whom they were training were untested and were not supposed to go on offensive operations. The special ops team's Air Force combat controller was back at base recovering from surgery to remove wisdom teeth. Brandon's men wanted to load up and charge down the valley with their Afghan special forces partners, but it would not be wise to go into this heavily controlled insurgent area without a combat controller. They would very likely wind up in a fight and probably a big enough one to require air support. Brandon was frustrated that he could not goad Afghan forces into acting. "I made eight calls to eight different units and not one responded," he said. "I pulled the trigger and nothing happened."

The discouraging day ended on a bit of an up note. When the team arrived back at their base for the evening, Jawad, who had stayed behind, told them that the Afghan countermine group trained by special operators had found a mine and called the police. The countermine group also alerted the team base. It was a massive bomb, made of old antitank mines from the Soviet era, and buried in a hole in the road. A bomb of that size could take out the heaviest of the American armored vehicles. The Afghans planned to blow it up at dusk.

A few team members hopped onto their Kawasaki ATVs and zoomed up the rocky mountain trail behind their base, Camp Wright, to a picturesque red-brick turreted outpost overlooking the camp and the river. The mountains of Pakistan were clearly visible from the outpost, which was called OP Shiloh. To the north the breathtaking expanse of the Hindu Kush rose above the curving Kunar River. The outpost had been built by the Russians, as was the camp below, which the Americans now called Wright after Sergeant Jeremy Wright, a special operator (and all-American cross-country runner) who was killed in Kunar in 2005. After a frustrating day in which he felt his hands were tied, Brandon was pleased to see the far-off flash of the detonation in the valley below as the sun's last rays fell on the glistening river. "This is what we call success at our level," he reflected.

The team was eager to forge ahead with its push down the Ghaki Valley. Over the fall the team conducted several patrols to the first three villages. "If you poke the hornet's nest, you can find out who's who," Jawad said. Working in tandem with the CIA, the operators identified six or seven QZR subcommanders. Their visits into the first two villages had encouraged the residents to reopen their school. When they reached the third town, Daridam, however, they got into a heavy firefight. It was the site of the Soviets' Battle of Marawara in 1985, in which a Spetsnaz special forces company had been ambushed and pinned down on a reconnaissance mission that turned into a two-day battle, with thirty-one Russians killed. From the same mountaintop firing positions the Taliban let loose with DShK machine-gun and mortar fire raining down on the American special ops team. The team was in a bad tactical position, and the Taliban obviously did not care if they caused casualties among the villagers. The combat controller called in air support, which eventually chased the Taliban away. At the same time, Afghan commandos and their special ops partner team flew in from Jalalabad to hit Chinar, the next village, in a simultaneous helicopter assault designed to show QZR that they intended to bring the fight to him in a sustained way. In subsequent weeks, the team made two additional patrols into the valley, bringing the district governor and police chief, who had not visited the villages for several years, with them. In shuras they described the Afghan Local Police program and made a pitch for volunteers.[14]

But it was not to be. The higher command nixed the team's plan to recruit ALP in the Ghaki Valley. The team was told to focus the Afghan Local Police initiative on the Marawara district center and thicken the defenses there. They were not to build something that the Afghans would be hard pressed to sustain by themselves.

The company commander, Major Ben Hauser, did not have the heart to tell the team all the bad news. He had led ODA 3131 as a captain, and Brandon and others were his former teammates and friends. Hauser was under enormous pressure to move all the teams out of Kunar right away to begin building Afghan Local Police along Highway Seven down in Nangahar, as part of the pullback to reinforce the country's two main highways. The move to Nangahar was also a response to a political demand from its governor, Gul Agha Shirzai, a major Pashtun figure who was planning to run for president in 2014. At the special operators' blue-and-white tropical-muraled base in Jalalabad, Hauser relayed the order in a deadpan fashion. "This is a strategic withdrawal plan," he commented drily, pointing out the troop movements on the wall map in his office at Camp Dyer. A red marker showed the repositioning that was already under way and the scheme to move all teams in Kunar to create new ALP sites in Nangahar.[15]

The officers who had occupied this office at Camp Dyer before Hauser had all been in the business of expansion—more ops, more troops, more territory. Hauser instead faced giving up the gains for which they had bled. He did not like it; no commander would. He believed in the special operators' mantra of working themselves out of a job, but he was close enough to the ground truth to know that a total withdrawal from Kunar at that time was premature. His superior, Lieutenant Colonel Chris Fox, was so annoyed he would not even discuss it during a visit to his small base in Bagram's sprawl. "Kunar is not in the IJC plan," Fox said tersely, referring to the three-star ISAF Joint Command.[16]

When Fox's superior, Colonel Tony Fletcher, who was in charge of CJSOTF-A at Bagram, was asked to identify the threat that warranted the increase in special operations teams in Nangahar, he said, "It's an insurance policy. The idea is to thicken the defenses." And what was the plan to support Afghans in Kunar? Fletcher was equally terse: special mission units would run periodic disruption operations.[17]

It looked as though the province's future defense plan rested on pinprick strikes. Many operators knew that this was a weak reed, and even such sporadic operations would depend on intelligence gathered on the ground. They received a reprieve when the next conventional division arrived to lead Regional Command–East in the spring of 2013. The new command put the brakes on the total pullout of special ops from Kunar, allowing ODA 3131 to stay for the remainder of its tour.

That also gave the team and the special operations command the opportunity to compose a well-thought-out plan for maintaining a small footprint in Kunar for the immediate future. Such a plan would need to help the Afghans to pull their security forces together, and it would need to encourage district and provincial police chiefs to fully embrace the local police, leveraging them as a critical asset for village and valley security. It would also require reliable human intelligence for any counterterrorism operations and, more generally, the kind of situational awareness that can only be gained by having eyes and ears on the ground.

Camp Wright, in theory, could be maintained as a model of the small footprint presence that US special ops leaders discussed and which the US national defense strategy envisioned. Maintaining a team with the right enablers made a lot more sense than consolidating special operators at Bagram, where they would have no idea if insurgents were massing in Asadabad, much less be in a position to help orchestrate an effective Afghan response. Camp Wright was becoming the final frontier as US bases farther north, including Bostick, Monti, Falcon, and Honaker-Miracle, closed down one by one.

Camp Wright had everything needed to sustain operations; it was a small but sturdy base with solid mortar-and-stone walls built by the Russians, and was well positioned on a mountainside close to Asadabad. The two turreted observation posts above Wright provided early warning lookouts, coupled with two more posts on the other side of the river. They were manned by a CIA-trained Afghan force that was nominally led by the Afghan intelligence service. The camp was outfitted with a forward surgical team capable of treating the most severe wounds and stabilizing trauma cases for evacuation; it was also a forward ammunition and refueling point, with ammo and fuel for soldiers, helos, and drones. Giant bladders of fuel ringed the landing zone. It had generators and water purification equipment, and, at least for the time being, a route clearance unit of vehicles equipped with mine-detecting equipment. It could serve as a remaining outpost from which air and ground operations could be conducted if both the US and the Afghan governments decided that some stay-behind American presence was needed to bolster the Afghan forces for a time.

Camp Wright was an ideal small-footprint stay-behind base, but it would take the right people to pull it off. Namely, it would require a mature special operations team like 3131, led by someone like Jawad, with the understanding and credibility to interface with a CIA team, which the Afghan government might also choose to keep in place for the cross-border operations needed to gather intelligence. The basic situation resembled the one in Paktika, where special ops teams and the Agency occupied the same space. But in Kunar, the frictions between special ops forces and CIA teams were less prevalent than elsewhere because of Jawad's tours with the Agency and the relationships that he had forged. He spent a lot of time with the Agency team trading information. "Can you see how much better we'd all be if we shared everything we had?" he pleaded with them. Security classification and an institutional reluctance prevented his vision from becoming reality, but Jawad's friendly ways won over most of the CIA team in Kunar, one member of which was a woman codenamed "Rosebud." Since they would soon be the two remaining teams left in the province, both knew they would be more effective if they were on the same page. A clear division of labor was needed, however, and a clear chain of command under Afghan authority. Cross-border intelligence operations might be warranted, with Afghan concurrence, in a few critical spots, but they had to be contained and kept from contaminating the primary mission of enabling Afghans to secure their own territory.

The lack of US-Afghan agreement on these issues burst into the headlines in April 2013, following a battle in western Kunar's Shigal District. In this battle, a CIA officer was reportedly killed, and three other Americans employed by the CIA were wounded. Seventeen Afghan civilians, including twelve children, died when an airstrike was called in; according to an Afghan delegation later sent to investigate, a house had collapsed on them. President Karzai's chief spokesman, Aimal Faizi, made extensive comments to Western news media in which he criticized the CIA-run force. "It was a joint op at most in name, but really in fact a CIA-run parallel security structure, and such structures have been a factor of insecurity themselves," Faizi told the *New York Times*. "We are informed five minutes before they are conducting an operation, and our security agencies do not have authority over them." The Afghan intelligence chief for Kunar was fired, and Karzai ordered a review of all the counterterrorist pursuit teams.[18]

The division of labor became muddled as well in the selection of the ALP commander for Marawara, and the mingling of defensive and offensive missions and security and intelligence functions created confusion and potentially counterproductive effects. When it began the Marawara ALP program, the ODA 3131 team had spotted a candidate with good standing among his peers and the majority tribe there. The elders engaged in a long debate, but failed in three meetings to agree on a leader. They ultimately opted for a different fellow named Gudjer, who had worked for the CIA. He had a checkered past, one that had been extremely valuable for the Agency's purposes. He had fought in the war against the Soviets as part of a force led by the prominent mujahedeen commander Haji Qadir, and he subsequently had lived on the Pakistan side of the border in Bajaur as part of another militant group. He eventually broke with the group and its Pakistani intelligence handlers because they had wanted him to attack a target, which he would not name, that he refused to attack. In 2008 he returned to Kunar, where he was hired into the CIA force. He had conducted many cross-border missions to track and tag targets for the CIA. Gudjer's background made him less than ideal to lead the local police, however, which was defensive in nature and required close interface with the Kunar provincial police hierarchy. He was chosen anyway, perhaps because the elders expected his established American ties to deliver benefits, or because he reflected their own divided loyalties, as had occurred in Wardak's Chak Valley. At any rate, Gudjer seemed to think his main job was to go get QZR, the Al Qaeda–linked Taliban leader holed up in Barawolo, rather than help the population defend itself. "They expect me to stop QZR, and stop him from kidnapping people and taking livestock," he said.[19]

While side-switching was a deeply rooted part of Afghan culture, the selection of Gudjer made ODA 3131 uneasy. "If we don't make sure these are good guys," Jawad, the chief warrant officer said, "we'll be back here in twenty years having to fix the mess." Since the team could not overturn the elders' decision, the operators planned to watch Gudjer closely and work with him to influence his development. Their favored candidate was elected deputy commander, so he would provide a second channel to guide and monitor the evolution of the force.

If special operations forces were designing a dream team for a small-footprint stay-behind mission in Kunar, another desirable component would be civilian development experts. In El Salvador and Vietnam, aid missions had formed a useful triad along with the special operations and intelligence teams. The provincial reconstruction team at Camp Wright, housed in a funky wood-front building with a verandah that looked like a movie set for the OK Corral, was slated to shut down along with the rest of the PRTs in the country as the 2014 transition approached. But if a few civilian experts were to stay to assist with development and governance, that would provide a natural and productive link to the civilians while the military advisers focused on security.[20]

The idea of a small footprint with a combined military and civilian advisory team had precedents in both the CORDS model of Vietnam and in Central America in the 1980s, but the civilian agencies had become much more risk-averse since then and were often less inclined to work alongside the military. As of 2013, most US embassy personnel were being pulled back to Kabul. The US embassy's regional security officer had mandated that no Kabul-based personnel could spend the night at outlying bases. The USAID Office of Transition Initiatives reached the most remote locations of any civilian entity, and it still had a robust program in Kunar, but its director could not get out to oversee it. The intrepid personnel of OTI had conducted 112 different activities in Kunar as part of its Afghan Stabilization Initiative, ranging from water-management projects to civics education and training of local officials.[21]

In the waning afternoon sunlight as he sat on an Adirondack chair on the verandah, Jawad reflected on the type of people drawn to this type of work. The advisory mission was often dismissed as less important than the direct-action special ops assignments. Little glamor or career-enhancing incentives were attached to it, though it demanded a very high degree of skill and probably some inborn talent. Because it was not valued, often the US troops who were assigned to advisory missions were not cut out for the work. Jawad also lamented that Americans tended to look down on their Afghan comrades, and in many cases treated them poorly. They may be poor or have less formal education, he noted, "but they have a PhD in Afghanistan." The desired attributes for advisers were not hard to identify. "What we really are is teachers," he said. It was not possible to be happy in this line of work unless one enjoyed teaching, learning about foreign cultures, and dealing with people in general. The other dynamic he saw at work was the struggle over sovereignty. Most US commanders were trained to be in charge and to dictate the terms of a relationship. "But this is the Afghans' country," he said.

Jawad, Brandon, and many of their teammates were suited for these challenges, but many younger members of the special operations forces were not. Jawad recognized that the "commando" image that had drawn many young American men into special operations had left some of the newer operators feeling disillusioned. At least two members of ODA 3131 had decided to leave the service after completing their tours, a pattern repeated in other teams. One senior sergeant on a team in Paktika put it bluntly: "All of the guys on this team are leaving. They do not like this mission. They feel the recruiting video sold them a bill of goods." The recruiting video created at Fort Bragg emphasized a *Call of Duty* vision of special operations—direct action gun-slinging, popping targets in raids, jumping out of planes and helicopters. The future of special operations forces would depend on attracting and keeping people who were drawn to working with indigenous cultures—and good at it.[22]

CHAPTER TWELVE

THE ENDGAME

KABUL 2012–2013

UNITY OF COMMAND AT LAST

No one could say how the Afghan war would end, but by 2013 the Afghans were finally being given control of their war and their country. Special operations forces were substantial contributors to that effort, and they could lay claim to a certain amount of progress in the missions assigned to them. They had taken nearly 10,000 insurgents off the battlefield in the previous year. They had expanded Afghan Local Police to over 22,000, and they were building an 8,500-man Afghan special operations force that would eventually have its own intelligence, surveillance, and reconnaissance capacities and be able to conduct both air and ground assault on their own.

One of special ops' most important achievements was an internal change that was seemingly arcane but profound in its implications for the special operations community in the future. In July 2012, a single special operations command was formed in Afghanistan to orchestrate and lead all the different US and coalition special ops units running around the country. This had never been done in eleven years of war. An attempt had been made to create unity of command among special operations units late in the Iraq War, but by most accounts it was a formal gesture because no one forced the "SOF tribes" to play well together.

The man picked to lead this new command in Afghanistan was Major General Tony Thomas, a hard-charging Ranger who talked so fast that his aides had a difficult time writing down everything he ordered done. A lean man with a brush cut, Thomas was brutally honest, funny, and impatient—and, because of his background, the right person to lead the new command, which replaced Haas's one-star command in Kabul in July 2012. On his first day on the job, Thomas banned the "SOF tribes" metaphor and insisted on adopting a new term, "SOF nation," to represent the new ethos he wanted to instill. The diversity of special operations capabilities was its strength, but in its relatively brief history the community had not figured out how to orchestrate its different parts to achieve the greatest possible impact. The jealousies, rivalries, and superiority complexes fed by the Tier One, Two, and Three terminology and class structure ran deep, so deep that many special operators were either wedded to their parochialism or resigned to its permanence.

Thomas was charged with uniting three tribes: the US special mission units charged with hunting high-value targets, where he had spent twenty-one years of his career; ISAF SOF, which had grown to comprise special operators from twenty-five countries; and the US special operators of Combined Forces Special Operations Component Command–Afghanistan, or CFSOCC-A, until July commanded by Chris Haas. CFSOCC-A included the Green Berets, SEALs, and Special Tactics Airmen who were raising local police and combat-advising the Afghan commandos and special forces as well as the great majority of civil affairs and psyops units.

Thomas had lived through the anarchic situation, having been in Afghanistan for some portion of ten of the past eleven years, so he knew the problems were real. "We had people who were not talking to each other from ISAF SOF and task force. They would actually bump into each other on targets, and they thought that was okay. Really?" Thomas remarked, his voice heavy with sarcasm. In his first month on the job, Thomas traveled throughout the country to meet all the commanders. In Regional Command–East alone there were two SOTFs, three task-force elements, and nine ISAF SOF elements, which were partnered with special police units in nine provinces. "They all said, 'We're doing fine, marching to our own drummer,'" Thomas said archly. "Okay, first things first," he told them. "Let's build a common intelligence picture of what we're all seeing here, and then decide who should be going after what."[1]

Thomas had to wrestle with two basic fissures, one between the coalition and US SOF, and the other internal to SOF. The coalition SOF answered only to the coalition chain of command, and many of its member countries restricted the types of missions they could perform. To bring together coalition and US special operations forces, Thomas was dual-hatted, as commander of NATO Special Operations Component Command–Afghanistan and as commander of the US Special Operations Joint Task Force–Afghanistan. But that formality, which was accomplished by September 2012, was only the first step in creating an actual community of special ops forces, which did not yet even reside at the same physical headquarters.

The coalition special operators were the elite units of their countries, and they did not readily cede to a US boss, so the politics of the marriage were tricky. The British, Norwegian, and other top-notch allied special ops units had worked intensively with national special police units and the Afghan intelligence service, the National Directorate of Security, for years, and their Afghan partners were performing admirably. The nineteen Provincial Response Companies were SWAT-style police units in varying stages of maturation. Some of the ISAF SOF members felt that the other "SOF tribes" did not sufficiently appreciate the value of their contributions, which were considerable. Their operations were "warrant-based," reliant on gathering and preserving evidence—and on arresting suspects to be tried in Afghan courts. Under Afghan law, the NDS performed internal security duties akin to the FBI in the United States. This was not a sideshow to combat, but rather an important stepping stone to Afghanistan's postwar future and the rule of law. Furthermore, it was an important model for US special operators to learn from for use in countries where there was no declared war and no authorization for the use of military force.[2]

The special police units varied in quality, but as time passed they became more proficient with this intensive mentoring. By 2013, 86 percent of the police operations were Afghan-led and had a majority of Afghans on each operation. There was another important benefit to this endeavor: more and more countries that were allies of the United States began to send their special operations forces to Afghanistan as they realized their men could gain valuable experience working in a hot war zone. British, French, Australian, and Canadian special operators had long partnered with US special operations forces, but the more recently formed Eastern European and Baltic special forces from places such as Poland, Romania, Czechoslovakia, Hungary, Estonia, and Lithuania, and from other countries such as New Zealand, the United Arab Emirates, and elsewhere, were eager to gain experience and to work alongside Americans and other coalition partners. These forces were primarily trained for unilateral counterterrorism raids or hostage rescue, and many were acting as advisers to a foreign force for the first time. In order to mentor them in this particular art, the 10th Special Forces Group assigned a battalion to work alongside them and provide on-the-job training. This long-term investment, it was hoped, would expand a global network of willing allies for future advisory missions in other trouble spots.[3]

The second fissure that Thomas had to contend with, the one inside the US special ops community, was even more fraught. The US special mission units had traditionally operated with a direct line to the secretary of defense or the White House for missions of the highest level of importance and urgency. That remained true for many of their missions. But the use of special mission units had evolved over the past eleven years. Lieutenant General Stanley McChrystal had moved his TF 714 command group to Iraq in 2004, and when McRaven moved it to Afghanistan in late 2009, the special mission units had become a permanent fixture on the battlefield rather than the quick-in, quick-out force they had been in the past.[4] McRaven had pushed them to work with the other units in the field, but the separate chains of command remained.

The rationale for that separate chain of command became hazier, however, as special mission units in Afghanistan began servicing target lists that had less to do with the worldwide fight against Al Qaeda (of whom there were, at most, one hundred fighters of any rank inside Afghanistan at any given time) than with the effort to stabilize the country before US troops departed. This was not necessarily a bad evolution—Why keep your best hunters on a leash, waiting for that one shot at Osama bin Laden?—but it created a new imperative for collaboration that was not fully realized, despite McRaven's efforts. Special mission units were playing a role in the Afghan campaign but not fully integrated into it. A decade of operations had shown that failure to coordinate all the military and civilian pieces on the chessboard usually created problems and impeded progress, whether in a war zone, such as Iraq or Afghanistan, or in gray zones such as Yemen or Somalia, where there were many players but no common game plan.

If Tony Thomas could not bring the special mission units into the fold, no one could. Thomas had spent the previous two years (2010–2012) as the deputy commanding general of Task Force 535, first under McRaven and then under Lieutenant General Joseph Votel. Previously, he had been the task force's operations director and chief of staff, positions he held under McChrystal from 2003 until 2007. McChrystal, a fellow Ranger, acknowledged that his and Thomas's driven personalities were so similar that initially they often clashed. Both men epitomized the ascendancy of Rangers within the organization, and indeed, they had left indelible marks on its culture.[5]

When Thomas moved from the terrorist-hunting machine based at Bagram to take charge of the newly created unified SOF command at Camp Integrity in Kabul, the first thing he had to change was his body's clock. Special mission units operate at night and sleep in the day, and the Afghanistan that Thomas knew was the Afghanistan of the night. In his new job he sat in meetings with senior Afghan officials, taking their measure. He quickly realized how eager the Afghans

were to assert control over their own affairs. He had already been subject to the new rules that put Afghans in charge of night raids—and
limited their frequency—but his new position brought him face to
face with how fed up Afghans were with unilateral US behavior.

In the meantime, Thomas conducted his daily briefings in a
Quonset-style building at Camp Integrity, a little-known base on the
far side of Kabul's airport in a neighborhood of furniture makers, veg-
etable stalls, and rutted dirt roads. Inside, a few steps away from the
building that housed his cramped office, the men slept in concrete barracks known as "villas." Thomas's two American deputy commanders
were Scott Howell, an aviator from the task force, and Don Bolduc,
who had helped design and oversee the Afghan Local Police initiative.
The ISAF SOF commander, which rotated between an Australian and
a Brit, was Thomas's third deputy. Thomas had a staff of only 300
people to lead 13,700 special operators, and it was ad hoc staff formed
of individuals, rather than assigned as a unit that had trained together
for months before deploying. Thomas did request and receive two
dozen hand-picked staff members so he would have a core of known,
trusted subordinates in the group. His predecessors—Reeder, Miller,
and Haas—had labored under these same constraints, because there
was no standing command for these types of long-term special operations missions. Task Force 535, in contrast, had a standing three-star
command that was in a continual cycle of training and deployment. It
was the difference between varsity and a neighborhood pickup game.

When Thomas was appointed, some special operators under Haas's
command had feared that their advisory missions to Afghans would
be subordinated to the priorities of the special mission units, but
they soon found out otherwise. The price for progress would be paid
by the latter, since they had the most assets to be shared. There was
grumbling, but the steely-eyed Thomas cut it short, telling them in
no uncertain terms that their personal performance would now be
judged on how well they supported their special ops brethren. "Get
on board," Thomas told the special mission units, "and you will be
rewarded for it."

Thomas forced the various special ops battalion-level commanders in the same region to begin meeting regularly—some of them had never even met each other. He also required them to present a regular "deep dive" briefing update that they produced as a team—another mechanism to force them to collaborate. The disparate units were expected to look at Afghanistan as a common mission to which each was expected to contribute. This common planning entailed a common targeting and asset-allocation process as well as combined operations.

The change was epitomized by the nightly "JAAM" sessions—the Joint Asset Allocation Meetings led by Thomas's headquarters. Priority targets and operations were selected in a newly centralized process; decisions about which helicopters, gunships, and drones to use where, and which troops to insert or extract where, were subject to this same new centralized decision-making process. A portion of the two hundred aircraft and intelligence, surveillance, and reconnaissance platforms were apportioned for the entire spec ops force's use in this manner. Thomas made his priorities clear. "We are here to support the ISAF campaign plan, and Afghan Local Police is the priority SOF effort in that campaign," Thomas said in an interview.

Colonel Tony Fletcher, the CJSOTF-A commander, saw the immediate payoff for his sixty-two special operations teams, who were spread out in villages raising local police and fighting alongside Afghan special operations units. "I benefit the most," Fletcher said of the new command. "I get more airlift, gunships, ISR than ever before, and I have the benefit of his two-star influence." Air support for Fletcher's operations increased by more than 40 percent, and by 300 percent for ISAF SOF. One of Fletcher's subordinates, Special Operations Task Force–South (SOTF-S) commander Richard Navarro, also found the change was dramatic. Previously, he said, "for our priorities to make it onto their target list was a big event. And if we needed airlift, it was always 'space available'—if they had nothing better to do. After Thomas took over, the message was, 'We're here to help. Let us know who the heavy hitters are and we'll go after them.'"[6]

Thomas turned his efforts to planning a series of combined operations that brought all the special operations resources to bear on given problem spots, including the Triple Action, a series of operations in the gnarly province of Wardak. Winter was closing in, but the command was also eager to finish the tough Guardian series in Kandahar and apply the same formula of combined operations in Ghazni. Thomas aimed to bolster the anti-Taliban uprising in Ghazni's Andar District and increase recruits for Afghan Local Police all over the province along Highway One.

The special mission units also continued to target high-value insurgent leaders, facilitators, and the occasional Al Qaeda member or affiliate. Operation Haymaker in upper Kunar launched thirty-eight strikes over four months—a slower pace than earlier in the war—but Thomas considered it sufficient to keep the threat at bay. With only two orbits of drones, it was a test of what this type of small-footprint approach might look like in the future, when the conventional forces were largely withdrawn. The bigger endgame question for special mission units was whether a "judicial finish" could be arranged for the many combatants they had taken off the battlefield. The US government lobbied heavily to ensure that Afghanistan would not release a few dozen detainees that the United States considered highly dangerous, at least so long as coalition forces remained in Afghanistan. The task force had killed some 3,000 combatants and scooped up roughly twice that many in Afghanistan. All but a handful were turned over to Afghan control in 2013, and without trials this effort would turn out to be an ultimately fruitless game of catch-and-release.

Thomas's stepped-up pace of operations came at a steep price: 132 special operators and attached forces under his command were killed in action and 130 wounded in his first five months. Thomas did not always get the cooperation he sought from the special mission units: in the first Wardak operation, they decided not to join in. They could still opt out because they were only under the tactical control, not the operational control, of Thomas's command. Admiral McRaven wrote in an email, "I strongly believe the internal elements need to be OPCON to [i.e., under the operational control of] Tony. He must have the ability to reorganize and employ as he sees fit. While technically this isn't the case, practically, Tony feels he has that latitude *and* if any of the components were to push back, I would step in and get the issues resolved—to include with my NATO brothers over which I have a strong influence."[7]

All in all, Thomas believed that the combined command had proven its value. "If the baseline is creating ALP, something lasting and sustainable, then the question was how to align our forces to do that instead of random affiliations. Now the task force and [the British task force] are focused on that as opposed to targeting the subcommander of a subcommander of a Haqqani," he said. "The proof is in the pudding," he added, noting that the Afghan Local Police forces had continued to grow steadily, even with the two-month pause that he had ordered for revetting the force, as a measure to guard against infiltration and insider attacks. Four hundred local police were let go, but the net growth continued.

WHITHER LOCAL POLICE?

No one earned more sweat equity in the Afghan Local Police and Village Stability Operations than Don Bolduc. He signed on for another tour in Thomas's command as one of his deputy commanders to see the program through the crucial growth phase as he awaited promotion to brigadier general. He cared intensely about the program, which he had helped Scott Miller launch in 2010 on the back of the Community Defense Initiative. It was Bolduc who had pored over the weekly tracker, negotiated the district-by-district allotment of police slots with the Afghan Ministry of the Interior, and laboriously mentored the MOI police general who headed the program, General Ali Shah Ahmadzai, or ASA, as the special operators called him. It was one thing to say that the Afghan Local Police were under the command and control of Afghan's Interior Ministry, though, and another thing to actually make it so. That would be the acid test of whether the Afghan Local Police would endure, for whatever time the Afghan government decided, because the Afghans had to be able to raise, train, supply, and oversee the local police as the force grew and as the US special operations presence shrank in both relative and absolute terms. Even if some special operators remained in Afghanistan for years to come, they would number far fewer than the sixty-two special operations teams that Bolduc had to work with in 2012 and 2013.

Bolduc was focused on "beans and bullets" logistics tasks, because the Ministry of the Interior was still an immature bureaucracy that had a hard enough time keeping its regular police force supplied with ammo, fuel, and functioning vehicles and recruiting, training, and retaining a force that still suffered from high desertion, attrition, and casualty rates. Compounding this were persistent concerns that the MOI, and the Afghan government as a whole, was less committed to the ALP program than it was to its regular police and military. But Bolduc pushed ahead, dogged as ever. In December 2012, the deputy minister of the interior, Abdul Rahman, presided over a conference that issued updated procedures and guidelines for the local police, raised the ceiling on its eventual size to 45,000, and extended the lifetime of the program until 2025. A few weeks later, ASA and his staff moved from their cramped quarters into two floors of a new building.[8]

Bolduc had no doubt that the Afghan Local Police and Village Stability Operations initiative had delivered results, and his conviction was backed up by the quarterly assessments produced by the RAND team. Over 70 percent of Afghans with local police based in their area consistently told pollsters that they supported the police. The RAND analysis of violent attacks indicated a "significant reduction in kinetic activity" in a five-kilometer radius of a local police force within five to twelve months. Economic activity also tended to improve, with an average of one new market or bazaar opening within fifteen months. The special operations teams assessed that 70 and 80 percent of the district police chiefs and governors supported the local police, respectively, but only about half of the chiefs were deemed to provide sufficient logistical support.[9]

Even more important, Bolduc said, the Afghan Local Police had taken the brunt of the Taliban attacks, and they had successfully defended their posts 88 percent of the time. Their attrition rate, due to death or desertion, was only 2 percent. The local police had their share of problems: the teams reported bribe-taking, drug use, and other infractions, for example. But only 10 percent of the incidents were serious crimes such as rape or drug trafficking. Afghans who were polled reported greater bribe-taking by Afghan local officials and the regular police. All of these findings were a testament to the careful and close mentorship that special operators had exercised over their charges during the past two years. What was not known, however, was how well the police would do as the teams moved into "tactical over-watch" mode and then transitioned the program entirely to Afghan control. Where good local police commanders and Afghan mentors existed—such as Nur Mohammed in Kunar and Aziz in Paktika—the police might well survive and continue to provide security, so long as the pay, ammo, and supplies kept coming.

The United Nations Assistance Mission in Afghanistan (UNAMA) provided an independent barometer in its annual report on the protection of civilians issued in February 2013. Without detailing the exact polling methods used, it said that in its survey conducted over the year, "the majority of communities reported improvement in the security environment in those areas with ALP presence." It also praised the Afghan Interior Ministry for setting up a monitoring and evaluation unit to investigate allegations of misconduct. In an interview, General Ahmadzai vowed to keep a personal watch on trouble spots, such as Baghlan and Kunduz, and to sack ALP commanders for infractions, if necessary. But he and his team were dependent on US airlift to get to the districts, and his small staff of fifty was already overtaxed, as their duties had expanded from overseeing the biometric registry and validation process to investigating alleged crimes or misdeeds. The UN report concluded that further local oversight was needed: "While UNAMA observed considerable progress and commitment in 2012 to promoting accountability for violations by the ALP, UNAMA reiterates its concerns with insufficient implementation of existing policies resulting in cases of weak vetting, impunity and lack of local level ALP oversight and accountability mechanisms." UNAMA recorded fifty-five reports of human rights violations committed by Afghan Local Police forces, singling out three districts of Kunduz Province in the north and Khas Uruzgan in Uruzgan Province.[10]

As of April 2013, the Afghan Local Police had grown to encompass 21,886 officers in 104 districts, with another 1,180 vetted volunteers awaiting training. Over 8,000 of the local police were under "tactical overwatch"—meaning that special operations teams were making regular visits but not embedded at the ALP locations—and 4,700 had already transitioned entirely to Afghan control. Bolduc projected that at the current pace of growth, the force could reach 25,000 by year's end and 30,000 by July 2015. In Vietnam, by comparison, the Civilian Irregular Defense Group had reached a peak of 42,000 defenders, with 84 special forces "A camps."[11] Bolduc's plan was to shift the training location to the Regional Training Centers, where the regular Afghan Uniformed Police were trained. Both Thomas and Bolduc foresaw teams moving to districts and provinces as they positioned to take on a broader advisory mission to foster coordination among the various Afghan police and military units.

This rapid-production model was 180 degrees out from the original Village Stability Operations model, in which teams worked with village elders for months before any Afghan police were even recruited. The success of such quick handoffs relied heavily on the competence of the district chief of police, which was in many cases lacking. It also presumed that the force itself would solidify quickly. Many special operators were concerned that once teams left the field they would lose the intelligence and understanding of what was going on and how the forces were actually performing. "We have to stay tied to those guys going to the field or we'll be blind," one senior officer said. If not, the operators would be "unable to positively affect or assess what is going on where the insurgency thrives."[12]

But Thomas made no bones about wanting the teams to produce Afghan Local Police as rapidly as possible. "What I want is—hey fellows, the clock is ticking—you can expand this great tool you have given them that's viral now. I need them to say 'good enough, and I'm on to the next one,'" he said, noting that teams were reluctant to raise a local police contingent in one location and then move to a new district and repeat the process all in one six-month rotation. "That is the mark I am looking for, guys. It's really good production," Thomas said, describing his dialogue with teams in the field. In his rapid-fire delivery, he mimicked how he wanted teams to proceed: "When you train [your police], you get your DCOP [district chief of police] and say, hey bud, here are your boys....You own them now. Let's go through some battle drills on how you are going to sustain them." He continued, explaining how he wanted the teams to mentor the district police chiefs: "Now I'm going to start stepping back. You've got my phone and if you need me I'm right here. And by the way, your real chain of command is your PCOP [provincial police chief] or your MOI because I'm artificially here anyway."

Thomas was not wrong that Afghans had to assume ownership. The teams and others who were deeply invested in the program saw the worst-case scenario as tossing the ball only to see it fumbled—with wayward, criminal, out-of-control militias the end result. The "purists" believed that slower growth was better because it simply took time for villages to step up to defend themselves, resolve their internal disputes, and adopt sound governance practices. Others believed that the number of local police produced was a perfectly legitimate measure of effectiveness when investing scarce special operations teams. This tension created a certain churn as battalion commanders came and went, each one yanking teams here or there. Sometimes the demand of a conventional battlespace owner prevailed. Yet invariably, if local police were recruited in areas with heavy insurgent intimidation, progress would be slow and other problems could result.

Was the program a success? The Afghan Local Police forces generally appeared to enjoy the support of the people where they operated. They were receiving material support from the Ministry of the Interior, albeit fitfully in some cases. Swaths of the country, including important parts of the insurgent belt, had been pacified or largely secured. However, it would take time to see whether these positive trends would continue once the US training wheels came off. As Bolduc acknowledged, the looming question was how the transition to self-sufficiency would go. "Transitions have never historically gone well," he said, citing RAND's comparative historical research into civilian defense programs. Special ops forces, who were steeped in the doctrine of unconventional warfare,

raising or supporting indigenous forces to overthrow regimes or occu-
piers, were taught that the most important phase of unconventional
warfare was its seventh and final phase.[13]

Thus, the program would ultimately be judged by whether or not
its endgame was successful. Whether 20,000 or 40,000, the force
would need to be incorporated into the formal police in some fashion or formally disbanded. Either of those endgames, executed well,
would constitute a success. The gravest threat to the program was
that Afghans would divert funds and manpower into building a politicized militia and toss the ground-up vetting criteria out the window.
This had already happened to some degree in the north, at the behest
of Tajik leaders with clout in the security ministries and the cabinet.
The danger was that this kind of deterioration would accelerate once
the United States stepped back. The second threat was that the force
would degrade wholesale into a highway shakedown operation at the
service of corrupt district police chiefs or their own wayward leaders.
If the force appeared to be going off the rails, the United States could
always withdraw its promised funding for the initiative or tie further
funding to adoption of a demobilization plan.

Would weak spots or trouble spots grow worse or be contained?
Zabul, Khas Uruzgan, and Wardak could fall into these categories.
The Afghan Local Police were like the proverbial canary in a coal
mine. They might not survive a more organized enemy with superior firepower, and those areas riven by internal conflict would not
improve overnight. Leaving men with guns to run amok there made
little sense. In places like Baghlan, in the north, Pashtun enclaves
defended by Afghan Local Police could be easily overwhelmed by the
Tajik police and army, let alone the Taliban.[14]

What seemed more likely than wholesale success or failure was continued success in those areas where several conditions pertained—
where Afghan Local Police supported each other, where they were
well led, and where provincial police chiefs ensured the flow of logistical support, such as in Kunar, Paktika, and possibly Ghazni. In these
places, the Afghan Local Police had achieved an impact beyond the vil-

lage or district level. Where the scaling up occurred, economic activity increased and in turn generated more support for the ALP program.

Even in Kandahar's tough western districts, a surprising breakthrough occurred in the spring of 2013. Taliban thugs roughed up a couple of elders in Panjwayi District, and the population, long actively or tacitly supportive of the insurgents, suddenly decided it had had enough. The people of the district threw out the Taliban and began volunteering their sons for the local police. All but a few villages participated, supported by the new district police chief, who had been appointed about six weeks earlier. But could they hold the line or would the Taliban stage a comeback? It was impossible to know, but the mounting evidence suggested that the bottom-up approach was indeed a valid way to confront a rural insurgency in Afghanistan.[15]

Four conditions appeared to correlate with successful civil defense:

- A charismatic, strong local leader
- A scheme that connects a village to a larger cluster or area, so that, if nothing else, the ALP commanders can provide quick-reaction forces to support each other
- A district or provincial police chief or other entity able to ensure ongoing material support
- Communities not riven by severe intratribal or ethnic strife

As of mid-2013, the special operators had another year to continue to mentor Afghan Local Police—albeit from an increasing distance as the US presence decreased and the operators were moved farther away from ALP forces they had mentored. General Allen's successor, fellow Marine General Joseph Dunford, who assumed command in February 2013, was ordered to pull out 34,000 troops and a staggering number of vehicles and other equipment in one year's time. The other 32,000 troops would ramp-down to somewhere between 8,000 and 15,000. At least that was the plan. But if the United States and coalition partners were to provide funds, training, and advice after 2014, the roles of the foreign troops would have to be codified in a status of forces agreement (SOFA). The Obama administration made clear that it would insist on retaining legal jurisdiction for US troops—it would not turn over any troops accused of violations to the Afghan judicial system. Such a condition, while a standard part of SOFAs, had been the proximate cause of the collapse of negotiations for a postwar training and advisory mission in Iraq.

The Obama administration's top priority was retaining the ability to suppress any emerging threat from Al Qaeda, a job it felt could be performed by a small number of elite forces. Yet operating in Afghanistan's rugged terrain would require well-defended fuel and ammunition resupply points, and very likely more bases than just the one at Bagram. Thomas could not imagine that the Afghan government would allow unilateral counterterrorism operations on its soil. Already, under the agreement negotiated to allow night operations, Afghan Colonel Omar Fareed at the Operational Coordination Group (OCG) in Bagram vetted each proposed mission, and Afghan forces were part of each combat action.

Operators' views on the type of US advisory role that was needed varied. Thomas did not think it was necessary or politically viable for special operators to serve as advisers in the field after 2014. "If we SOF can't work ourselves out of tactical advise and assist two years from now, I gotta wonder how good we are," he said. Others viewed advising as a long-term endeavor that had less to do with the tactical skills imparted and more to do with influence and relationships. Proponents of long-term advisory missions argued that mentoring units over a decade or even a generation could encourage professionalism and allow ties to be forged that deepened as soldiers progressed in their careers. But Thomas, in his brisk and colorful way, pushed back against this view. "I'm challenging our guys, 'If there is a need tell me if you've got to stay that close. But if you are that good at training the muj, in this case training the ANSF [Afghan National Security Forces], you can't get them good enough two years from now, training their little butts off? How good is good enough?'" By 2015, he believed the only advisers needed would be at brigade or higher levels.

AFGHAN SPECIAL OPS TO THE FORE

Grappling with the exact size and scope of the US special ops follow-on missions—if there were any—would fall to Scott Miller, who returned to Afghanistan in June 2013 to replace Thomas. Miller had spent the previous year at Fort Bragg with a core staff preparing for his tour in Afghanistan. Although he arrived four months after Dunford, Miller hoped to help shape the best possible endgame. He would endeavor to ensure that control of the Afghan Local Police was successfully assumed by the Interior Ministry and the Afghan police hierarchy. His second task would be to rebalance the special operations effort to ensure that Afghan special ops forces were ready. That mission had taken something of a backseat to the ALP program, while most available teams were devoted to the villages. The Afghan government and military enthusiastically embraced the development of Afghan special ops forces, which would play a vital role in defending the country after 2014. The commandos were in high demand for combat operations. Afghan special forces teams, modeled on the Green Berets, were filling a critical gap as the ALP expanded and as sites transitioned to Afghan control. They were mentoring and monitoring Afghan Local Police as the US special operators transitioned to overwatch mode. The Afghan Ministry of Defense had agreed to provide this support to the Interior Ministry ALP program, at least for a while.[16]

The Afghan special operations forces were still relatively immature, however. In mid-2012, when Colonel Sean Swindell arrived to help oversee their development as the deputy commander for special operations at the training command, he was shocked to see how much there was to do. With a staff of two, he threw himself into the job. It was his first deployment to Afghanistan, but he had done this for years in Iraq and Colombia. In Iraq, he had been deeply involved in training and combat-advising the Iraqi special ops forces during a period in which they grew from one battalion to a brigade-sized force. In Colombia before that, he had been involved in building and mentoring Colombian special ops forces for years.[17]

Swindell naturally compared the Afghan special ops forces to the special ops forces in Iraq and Colombia. "In Afghanistan, the focus was on unilateral operations," he said. In Iraq, by contrast, there had been an enormous effort to create fully functional indigenous special ops forces, with no lack of funds for that purpose. Colombia's special operations capability had developed much faster than Afghanistan's precisely because it was the top priority: the US special operations mission in Colombia had never been about combat. Even after three American contractors in Colombia had been taken hostage by guerrillas, the United States had supported Colombia's search-and-rescue operation rather than attempt to take unilateral action.

Afghan commandos were progressing in their tactical skills, but the formation of the Afghan special forces in 2009 had set them back because the special forces had been recruited from the commandos' ranks. The greatest deficits were an intelligence capacity that would allow units to plan their own missions and mobility to transport operators in order to execute those missions. Development of senior leaders and staff also lagged: brigade and division headquarters staff were on the drawing board as Swindell arrived.

An Afghan helicopter wing was being formed, but it was a daunting challenge, given the technical skills involved. Pilots and mechanics had to be trained for the Mi-17 choppers. Swindell put Afghan mechanics on the floor of the bays turning wrenches alongside American contractors. As of late 2012, the new Afghan National Army Special Operations Command (ANASOC) had seven Mi-17s—on its way to thirty. For intelligence, surveillance, and reconnaissance, eighteen PC-12 aircraft outfitted with full-motion video were on order. As of mid-2013, five of a planned forty-seven pilots were being trained to fly with night-vision goggles.

Afghan military leaders were still not in the driver's seat in planning their own campaigns and operations. Swindell spent a lot of time briefing the head of Afghan special operations, General Abdul Karim, in order to hasten this transition. He helped him craft a special operations plan that would become a component of the overall campaign plan, and he worked with Bolduc to ensure that the Interior Ministry and the ALP were incorporated into the plan. "It is the only tool for safe haven denial that they have," he said of the ALP. Swindell helped Bolduc on the logistics supply process. No detail escaped him: astonished that no one had created "Mission Essential Task Lists" to drive the commandos' training and equipment needs, he corrected this shortcoming and sent out contractors to train the units in these processes.

The growth plan for the Afghan National Army Special Operations Command was ambitious. The division headquarters had been activated on July 16, 2012. Under ANASOC's authority, two brigade headquarters would each oversee 928 operators in four commando and special forces kandaks, with fire support and military intelligence units at their disposal. Another component of the Afghan special operations force was "Kteh Khas" ("Special Force," in Dari), originally called the "Afghan Partner Unit." At first it was merely an "Afghan face" for US operations, but the Rangers took up the task of training the Kteh Khas operators in earnest, and they became more and more capable. Kteh Khas would have 373 operators organized in four squadrons, each with its own military intelligence company. Another unit was also being formed, a mobile strike force of two companies equipped with light armored vehicles. All of this was possibly too ambitious and complex an organization, given the limited human capital available.

The Afghans would make these decisions—provided the United States, as the primary donor, found enough political will and spare cash to continue underwriting the development of Afghanistan's security forces. There was certainly the possibility that the United States would pick up and leave—it had done so numerous times after interventions. All were braced in Washington for another steep cut in defense spending. Swindell was no expert in Afghanistan, but he had quickly picked up on the bruised sensibility of the proud Afghans. He had witnessed several slights suffered by the affable and courtly chief of the Afghan army, General Sher Mohammed Karimi, and did his best to repair that damage in his weekly briefings with the top general. Sitting in his office at the modern Defense Ministry building, nestled in the park surrounding the presidential palace, Karimi reviewed the course of the bilateral relationship. "It took Americans a long time to listen to Afghans," he said, noting that the earliest US ties had been formed with the Tajiks, and this had tinged the Americans' perceptions. "There is an unfortunate tendency to think the Pashtuns are the enemy," he said. A Pashtun himself, he had been passed over for defense minister because, he believed, the Tajiks controlled the security ministries. But despite this, he rejected the idea that his country would devolve into civil war.

The sixty-seven-year-old general was ready to pass the torch, after forty-five years of military service and two very narrowly survived attempts on his life—one of them outside his office door on the third floor of the ministry. Unlike Afghanistan's nouveau riche, he noted, he had no passport, so he would not be hightailing it to Dubai or America. His son Zia, a tall and thoughtful young man, was about to depart for school at Fort Benning, just after his first child, a daughter, was born. He had been his father's aide-de-camp for the past three years and had absorbed every chapter of the saga. He was ready, he said, to carry on in his father's stead.

CHAPTER THIRTEEN

THE FUTURE OF SPECIAL OPERATIONS AND AMERICAN WARFARE

Special operations forces have played an increasingly prominent role over the past decade in many ways, and that trend is likely to continue in the future for two basic reasons: technology and political preference. A highly skilled, small military force is more cost effective than a large one and less likely to cause attendant political and diplomatic complications—if it is used with care and sophistication. Part of that caveat points to the need for special operations forces to mature, to view themselves differently, to be—and to be seen as—a more integral part of the nation's arsenal, rather than a secret tactical tool that is brought out on occasion and then again tucked away. Their future evolution will be multifaceted, but some signs of the changes are in evidence.

Beginning in 2010, special operations forces started making an important pivot away from the heavy immersion in combat that had subsumed them for the decade following 9/11. This was true of all operators, not just those sent to the villages of Afghanistan. They were all forced to retreat from the unilateral application of their skills, to learn how to function alongside partners from a very different culture, and to cope with the myriad restrictions and tensions besetting the United States' troubled relationship with Afghanistan.

In some respects, this change mirrored what special operations forces were already doing elsewhere. In between tours to Afghanistan, they came and went to Libya, the Levant, the Horn and the Sahel of Africa, Colombia, Southeast Asia, Korea—in all, seventy-five countries over the course of a year. Some were special mission units sent to hunt the increasingly dispersed Al Qaeda affiliates, but most often they consisted of small teams of SEALs, special forces, or civil affairs or military information soldiers who were sent to work with another country's forces. In some cases, individual special operations officers were assigned to long tours in US embassies in Lebanon, Yemen, Turkey, and Mexico. This diverse range of small-footprint deployments would probably be the shape of the future, barring an unexpected crisis that would drag a very reluctant America into another all-out war. Even large-scale operations might resemble Libya and Somalia more than Afghanistan or Iraq, with a minority US contribution to a multinational endeavor—a formula that was also contemplated in Mali.

What was profoundly different about the latter years in Afghanistan was that special operators were tasked to engage deeply with civilian populations in remote areas and then to lead those willing to bear arms. They were forced to learn new skills and to stretch themselves in entirely new ways. Prominent among these skills was the art of sitting with elders to figure out the complicated web of rivalries and alliances that were at work in individual villages, and listening carefully to find out how the people of these villages could be motivated to come together for a common purpose. This assignment made the use of firepower the last resort—though the operators kept their spears sharp and by their side—because their partners would only learn to trust themselves if they took the lead. The center of gravity shifted decisively to this task of empowering partners and becoming teachers. Deploying in small teams in remote locations also instilled in the operators a new confidence that they could survive in hostile or guerrilla-controlled territory, lonely and sometimes very lethal environments. They learned to trust not only their technology and firepower, but the bravery of the likes of Abdullah Hakim, a bereaved father willing to risk it all.

How might this experience be relevant to the future? Though special ops are not likely to be deployed anytime soon at the scale of their footprint in Afghanistan—13,700 troops, with 17,000 support personnel, including 9,000 for aviation alone—the skills are fungible on any scale and in many places. The tactical teams, led by men such as Dan, Hutch, Matt, Marshall, and Brad, proved to be extremely adept at the skills of bonding, understanding, and maneuvering. They recaptured skills used by old-timers in Vietnam and learned how to become chess players in a complex culture. They exercised initiative in unusual ways every day, far from any superior officer. Contrary to those who thought special operators had irrevocably lost their way, the evidence suggests that the raw talent and instinctive ability to conduct political-military warfare are not in short supply.

What is needed is for their commanders—and US policymakers—to set the future course and mold the force. It is up to them to ensure that raids are not synonymous with special operations. As all special operators know, raids are the most conventional aspect of the toolkit, and should not become the tail that wags the dog. The same applies to drone warfare, which is merely a tactic. The challenge, then, is for these senior leaders to absorb and apply the experience of these last years to get the future direction right. The following observations may help in setting the azimuth.

Too little time is spent on learning, and applying what is learned, with correspondingly slow progress up the learning curve. As many of those interviewed for this book acknowledged in hindsight, many years were lost in Afghanistan through the failure to apply what operators already had learned elsewhere.

The unilateralism too often seen violated another cardinal rule that special operators should have long since internalized: it is not their country. Recognition of sovereignty entails appropriate rules of engagement and a basic sense of humility. Many US officials bore responsibility for the acts and omissions that created an increasingly fractious relationship between the US and Afghan governments at the national level, and it is worth noting that interactions at the district and village levels were generally far less tendentious.

Special operations forces and conventional forces now get along much better than they did before 9/11, but frictions persist, and these frictions should not be dismissed as situation- or personality-dependent. In particular, command relationships are still problematic despite efforts to develop collaborative networks and "mutually supporting" arrangements. The military is fundamentally a hierarchical organization, and as such the single most important question will inevitably be, "Who's in charge?" Unity of command is also recognized as the best guarantee of coordination and synergy. Therefore, when overall command is exercised by a conventional forces officer, that officer must understand special operations and must not display prejudice or parochialism. Conventional forces may not be commanding large battles in the near future, but the US military's activities, of whatever type, will be conducted through geographic combatant commands that are largely led and staffed by conventional forces, and therefore the imperative for greater understanding and interoperability will not disappear.

One of the most important innovations in SOF-conventional operations in Afghanistan was the attachment of fifty-four conventional infantry squads to sixty-two special operations teams who were conducting village stability operations and raising local defenders. Without such collaboration, the special ops initiative could not have been conducted on such a wide scale or in as many highly contested and remote areas. This is a highly fungible experiment, since there is a great demand for advisory support around the world, and only a limited number of special operators. The conventional unit's performance was not uniformly good, however, and must be improved. Personnel must be carefully selected and trained, and those chosen will perform best if they have habitual—even career-long—relationships with the regions in which they are stationed and with the operators with whom they work.

A deeper issue that surfaced in Afghanistan was a lack of appreciation for what political-military warfare is and how it should be prosecuted. One special operations officer confided his dismay at seeing a terrain model in a senior general's office in Afghanistan that was festooned with labels such as "block," "attrit," and "isolate"—a pretty clear indication that the general viewed the contest as a fight over physical terrain that could be addressed with a conventional scheme of maneuver. Special operators, for their part, were plagued by contradictory and shifting assessments of what people and places mattered most in their human-centric campaign, and the parlance of "jet streams" and "ratlines" indicated an ongoing focus on chasing the enemy.

Continuity of planning and execution nonetheless improved dramatically. After years of seesawing back and forth, successive special ops commanders embraced the same game plan and rulebook for Afghan Local Police and Village Stability Operations. These leaders learned from their ad hockery of the early years in Afghanistan and stopped using indigenous forces as blunt offensive weapons, militias by any other name. They codified the best practices and ensured that successive rotations of ground-level teams understood and applied them. There was some variation and some churn—and a heightened risk of failure as the endgame decisions in Washington accelerated the calendar. But the essential vision of a ground-up, elder-validated defense force providing security in major belts of the rural insurgent zone was embraced, implemented, and expanded by special operations commanders and their staffs.

Unity of command within special operations forces' competing tribes remains a work in progress. Internally, special operations forces face a choice between learning to operate together, to combine their various competencies in new and creative ways, or retreating to their separate stovepipes. The latter mode is wasteful and counterproductive. The internal tensions are sharp indeed, but the experience of the past decade has given a new generation of generals and admirals the ability to see the promise and benefit of creating a fully unified special operations community. It may become a community less dominated by a strict "tier" or caste system, where more officers or operators attain a wider range of qualifications than in the past. These new commanders not only need to be leaders of the entire community, but also to deliberately and systematically raise the bar on preparing for and exercising leadership.

To improve civil-military relations, these new leaders should strive to ensure that policymakers understand the ways in which their forces may be used, because most policymakers lack sufficient knowledge of what they can and cannot do. The latter—*not* doing something—is possibly the most important, and most difficult, type of counsel to offer, since by nature this breed wants to wade into the troublesome spots and try to make a difference. But it would be extremely dangerous if the newfound visibility of special ops caused them to be mistaken for a panacea. Application of special operations forces is one option between doing nothing and engaging in a major military operation. Policymakers will always be forced to weigh whether US interests or a larger moral imperative dictates sending troops into hostile zones.

Special operations forces will gain credibility if they develop criteria that help policymakers evaluate and weigh options for their use. There is nothing easy or guaranteed about building viable, legitimate security forces to support governments in places such as Yemen, Somalia, or the Maghreb, or, in some cases—where the harm of backing an illegitimate government may argue for a stopgap—backing tribes who have greater standing than the government among their own people. The option of conducting unconventional warfare, one of the special operators' core missions, to throw off despots in places such as Taliban Afghanistan will always be controversial, whether conducted covertly or not. In the end, civilians will make judgment calls that cannot be reduced to a science, but an effort to define the elements required for degrees of success would be useful.

Security force assistance is a fundamental tool of national security and foreign policy, but neither the US military nor policymakers prioritize it. Perhaps the most important lesson to be learned from Afghanistan is that the United States did not place enough importance on getting Afghan security forces ready to shoulder the responsibility of defending their land against internal and external enemies. The US military remains an institution that is geared toward major combat operations and that prepares and rewards combat leaders. To rectify this imbalance, special operations forces should systematically embrace and integrate their role in this vital mission of security force assistance.

Although many military leaders have learned to quote T. E. Lawrence—better known as Lawrence of Arabia—over the past decade, his maxims did not form the central spine of the American outlook or approach to Afghanistan, or anywhere else for that matter. Almost any country can be substituted for "Arabs" in one of Lawrence's most astute and applicable injunctions in his "Twenty-Seven Articles": "Do not try to do too much with your own hands. Better the Arabs do it tolerably than that you do it perfectly. It is their war, and you are to help them, not to win it for them. Actually, also, under the very odd conditions of Arabia, your practical work will not be as good as, perhaps, you think it is."[1]

Strategic patience does pay off. The United States rarely musters the kind of patience required for these ventures to produce results, but that does not render invalid the argument for taking a long view. The United States may find its way to an enduring and affordable formula to support Afghanistan over the coming decade. In doing so it would be following US policy toward El Salvador and Colombia, a model that might be called "go small, go long." Such a model entails a realistic assessment of the government and an appraisal that it is in the long-term interest of the United States to support it, warts and all, as well as to exercise whatever leverage and influence the United States possesses to help the recipient improve. It should be noted that countries can change substantially in a decade's time due to demographic, educational, and social shifts.

A middle road must be charted between pure expedience and excessive aspiration if foreign policy and national security objectives are to be achieved. On the one hand, special operations forces have often leaned toward expedience as the more "realistic" posture for averting near-term danger—but taking this path involves risks and possible pitfalls that must be more explicitly acknowledged and weighed. On the other hand, the latter years in Afghanistan witnessed some ill-advised excursions into overly aspirational development and anticorruption crusades. That is not to say the United States should turn a blind eye to malfeasance by those whom it aims to help. It must simply decide whether it is, on balance, supporting or attacking a given government, and refrain from waging war on both the government and the enemy simultaneously.

A more routinized approach to conditionality and accountability would help. All US assistance should be attached to minimum requirements for transparency and accountability, with auditing mechanisms that can be performed by third-party professionals. Such mechanisms work very well, for example, in the National Solidarity Program, with checks administered by both the World Bank and grassroots community development councils. The auditing in the case of Kabul Bank, in contrast, was clearly deficient. If standards are universally applied, they will be less contentious—and more effective—than when individuals, such as the president's brother or close advisers, are singled out.

This appeal for principled pragmatism as a guide to foreign engagement encompasses a wide range of possible approaches, though it eschews the unilateral use of force except in the case of the direst threats to national security. After war, this nation often veers into isolationism, but it should be ready to fight when it identifies grave, existential threats from concrete plots of identified foes. In most if not all other cases, it can find other ways of winning without fighting—to paraphrase Sun Tzu—and be better off for it.

AUTHOR'S NOTE

A little over two years ago I set out to chronicle the special operations forces' largest-scale initiative since Vietnam as well as their evolving approach to war. The number of operators involved and the geographic extent of the operations made this a challenging project. It was not possible to capture the scope and complexity of Village Stability Operations and the associated civil defense program called Afghan Local Police at a single site, but it was not feasible to visit all the sites, which numbered 106 as of April 2013. So I developed an approach aimed at gaining the best possible appreciation of what special operations forces were doing in the villages and districts in which they "embedded" and what had resulted from this close interaction with the population.

I selected three locations for repeat visits, made random visits to other sites, and obtained countrywide data about the program from the commands, including a weekly tracker of the number and location of local defenders who were enrolled in the program, weekly reports summarizing the latest developments, and other documents, such as "fragmentary orders" (FRAGOs) and program procedures. The command also shared analytical papers with me as well as formal quarterly assessments that were produced by RAND. In addition, I consulted the official record of the program in the semiannual "1230 Reports," prepared by the US Department of Defense, and two independent reports, one by Human Rights Watch and the other by the United Nations Assistance Mission in Afghanistan. My original research, which is the primary material on which this book is based, consisted of more than three hundred interviews with US special operations personnel at all echelons, other US officials, and Afghan citizens and officials along with my field observations.

The interviews and my personal observations form the basis for the scenes described and the quotations used; in some cases, participants recounted conversations they had with others. To the greatest extent possible, I have consulted more than one source when reconstructing scenes that I did not witness; in other cases, I used secondary sources. Some of the interviews were conducted on a background or off-record basis, so the interviewees cannot be named. In the case of team-level special operators, except for those not returning to field-level duty, for security reasons I have used only first names or nicknames rather than full names.

The International Security Assistance Force (ISAF) granted my access to the units in the field and the various echelons of the commands above them. I used commercial transportation and lodging whenever possible, but my visits to the sites entailed reliance on US military transport as well as lodging and meals at US military sites, including *qalats* rented by the US military in Afghanistan. My access to sites and individuals was generally unfettered. In a few cases I was not permitted to visit certain sites at certain times: during the ouster of Jim Gant, which occurred while I was in Kunar; during the massacre at Belambay, which took place a few hours before I arrived in Maiwand; and when a team's leadership had been fired in eastern Paktika. Subsequent to those events, however, I was granted the interviews I requested.

The leadership of the US Special Operations Command (USSO-COM), first Admiral Eric Olson and then his successor Admiral Bill McRaven, permitted access to special operations units in the field and following their tours, as did their subordinate commands and commanders. I am grateful to Colonel Tim Nye, USSOCOM's director of public affairs, who cheerfully championed my endless requests, understanding how much access is required to produce a book. He and his able deputy, Ken McGraw, helped me at every turn over the past ten years as I sought to understand this closed—and now much less closed—world.

I was most fortunate to have two welcoming perches from which to research and write this book. One was the Woodrow Wilson

International Center for Scholars, where I was a public policy scholar. This center is a treasure of an institution, headed by Jane Harman and led by a thoughtful band of intellectuals and directors, including Rob Litwak, Bob Hathaway, and Mike Van Dusen. A special thanks to my research intern, Ben Arnett, who braved the deadline pressures along with me. I am immensely grateful to Richard Haass and Jim Lindsay, president and vice president of studies, respectively, for welcoming me as an adjunct senior fellow at the Council on Foreign Relations, where I spent fifteen months, ably assisted by Jane McMurrey, my research associate, in the company of many fine professionals. I thank the Smith Richardson Foundation for its grant to support this research and my study on the future of special operations forces at the Council on Foreign Relations, and in particular its program director, Nadia Schadlow, an astute colleague and scholar of the military.

I relied on the sage advice and moral support of the best agent and friend anyone could hope to have—Flip Brophy, president of Sterling Lord Literistic. Clive Priddle is also a friend as well as an utterly unflappable editor, now publisher of PublicAffairs, which is publishing my work for the third time; thank you for your deft pen, your cool head, and your terrific team, including Melissa Raymond; Robert Kimzey; Jaime Leifer; Kathy Streckfus, whose conscientious copyediting greatly improved the book; and Susan Weinberg, now Group Publisher of Basic Books, Nation Books, and PublicAffairs. Pete Garceau did a beautiful job with the cover.

In the writing of any book, especially one relying so heavily on interviews, literally hundreds of individuals have given of their time and shared their insights. My effort to thank all of the individuals who consented to interviews, in many cases multiple times, will inevitably leave out someone, but I have attempted to recognize all those who can be acknowledged. Any errors, misjudgments, or omissions are of course mine alone.

The principal interviews conducted in southern Afghanistan were with Chris Riga, Bill Carty, Richard Navarro, Brian Rarey, Justin Sapp, Brian Mack, and other members of their staffs; Scott White, Angel Martinez, J. R. Jones, Dan Hayes, and Operational Detachment

Alpha (ODA) 3314; Tyler Oliver, Brad Hansell, and ODA 7233; J. R. Anderson and his staff; Mike Hayes and his staff; Ben Jahn, SEAL platoon leader Marshall, Brian Strickland, Dan Green, Beau Bezouska, and team members in Kajran and Gizab; officials from the US Agency for International Development (USAID), the US State Department, and the US Department of Agriculture; Abdullah Niazi, Fazil Ahmad Barak, Obaidullah Barwari, Najibullah, and ODA 112; Azizullah Rahman Tutakhel and ODA 115; Jan Mohammed, Abdullah Hakim, Dawood Mohammed, Ahmadullah Popal, and Shah Janan.

The principal interviews conducted in the east were with Bob Wilson, Bob Davis, Bill Linn, Chris Fox, John Bishop, Eddie Jimenez, Pat Rotsaert, Kent Solheim, Mike Holahan, Ben Hauser, Jay Pope, ODA 3316, Jake Peterson, Craig Kunkel, Mike Perry, Tim Ambrose, ODA 3436, ODA 3131, Mike Bandy, Jason Clarke, John Meyer, Michael Hutchinson, and ODA 3325; Jason Russell and ODA 1114; Jae Kim and ODA 1411; ODA 1326; and Mary Kettman, Jess Patterson, Hanif Kheir, Waliullah Hamidzai, Wali Mohammed, Nur Mohammed, Gudjer, Asim Gul, Wazir, Commander Aziz, Major Osman, Kasim Diciwal, Ramazon, and Noor Mohammed.

At the headquarters commands in Kabul and Bagram, the principal interviews were conducted with Don Bolduc; Scott Miller and his command group, including Geno Paluso, J. R. Stigall, Fred Krawchuk, Scott Whitehead, and Scott Kesterson; Chris Haas and his command group, including John Evans, Wes Spence, Heinz Dinter, Beau Higgins, Alec MacKenzie, Pat Stevens, Ken Gleiman, Gail Yoshitani, Jack Stanford, and Chris Foltz; Billy Shaw, Doug Rose, Randy Zeegers, Duke Christy, Tony Thomas, Scott Howell, Art Kandarian, Andrew Pence, Jim Linder, Sean Swindell, Ed Reeder, Pat Mahaney, Chris Castelli, Mike Sullivan, Mark Schwartz and his staff, Brad Moses, and Tony Fletcher and his staff. Others interviewed included General Sher Mohammed Karimi, Ali Shah Ahmadzai, Dadon Lawang, Nooristani, Zia Karimi, David Petraeus, John Allen, James Terry, John Campbell, Curtis Scaparrotti, Jim Huggins, Ryan Crocker, Fred Johnson, Noorzai Ahmed Hamdard, Nader Nadery, Abdullah Abdullah, and Shahmahmood Miakhel. Scott Mann, Dave Phillips, Clare Lockhart,

Tom Barfield, Todd Greentree, Harj Sajjan, and Neamat Nojumi generously shared their knowledge and perspectives on Afghanistan.

The past decade has seen many Americans in uniform in war zones, and in many ways their experience creates a great gulf between them and their fellow Americans who have not gone to war. I hope this book may serve as a bridge between those two sets of Americans as well as a source of understanding for anyone interested in what special operations forces do—and what they may be asked to do in the future. I have grasped the trunk and maybe the tail of the elephant, and I recognize that there are many other vantage points from which to tell the story.

Finally, I must thank, above all, my beloved husband, Scott, who put up once again with my long absences. I made it safely home, but many others did not. Since 9/11, 434 special operators have been killed in action and another 2,021 wounded. Their sacrifices and their families, and all of those killed in these wars, should be remembered.

NOTES

CHAPTER 1: HITTING TARGETS

1 This number is cited in Stanley McChrystal, *My Share of the Task: A Memoir* (New York: Portfolio, 2013), 265.

2 Ahmed Rashid, "Afghanistan: Taliban's Second Coming," BBC News, June 2, 2006.

3 Mahaney's words and the account of Operations Nish and Adalat are drawn from an email exchange with the author on March 13, 2013; an author interview with him on March 8, 2013; and a written account of Special Operations Task Force 71's service achievement in Operation Enduring Freedom that was submitted for a unit citation.

4 McChrystal, *My Share of the Task*, 265.

5 The statistics are cited in the unit citation narrative cited above; the account of the enemy situation and the battle is drawn from an author's interview and email exchanges with Chris Castelli, March 13, 2013. According to Castelli, the three principal Taliban leaders operating in this area were Mullah Shakur, Haji Lala, and Mullah Tahir.

6 Author interviews with Castelli and Mahaney.

7 "Taliban Launch Rare Frontal Assault," Associated Press, August 8, 2007.

8 Author interviews; unit citation narrative.

9 Author interview with Mahaney; Patrick J. Mahaney Jr., "Observations for Practitioners of Complex Operations," in Christopher M. Schnaubelt, ed., *Complex Operations: NATO at War and on the Margins of War*, NDC Forum Paper 14, NATO Defense College, Research Division, July 2010.

10 The quotation is from an author interview with a special operations officer, June 10, 2011. Numerous special operations officers characterized the early approach taken in Afghanistan in this way in author interviews. Lieutenant General John Mulholland was interviewed on February 15, 2012. There is a large literature on Afghan militias and the demobilization, disarmament, and reintegration process in Afghanistan. See the work of Antonio Giustozzi, especially his *Koran, Kalashnikov, and Laptop: The*

Neo-Taliban Insurgency in Afghanistan, 2002–2007 (New York: Columbia University Press, 2009.

11   The two forces linked up in Tarin Kowt in Uruzgan to ready their drive to capture Kandahar from Taliban control. As Karzai's men and the special forces gathered to stage their attack on Taliban-held Kandahar, they came under attack from Taliban forces. Karzai and the team were bombed after the GPS device reset; the aircraft was incorrectly given their coordinates instead of those of the enemy in trucks bearing down on them. Karzai survived unscathed, though others died, and shortly thereafter he received the call from Bonn informing him that he had been chosen by the Afghans gathered there as the interim president of the new Afghanistan. See Eric Blehm, *The Only Thing Worth Dying For* (New York: Harper, 2010). Reeder's statements and his recollection of Eikenberry's statement are from an author interview conducted on November 16, 2011.

12   Another short-lived initiative was the Afghan National Auxiliary Police, formed in 2006. Afghans were recruited in six provinces to supplement the Afghan National Police. They were given ten days of training and assigned to static security duty. The program received minimal support, with few safeguards to properly vet recruits, weed out opportunists, and prevent tribal imbalances, according to Mahaney. See also Seth G. Jones, *In the Graveyard of Empires: America's War in Afghanistan* (New York: W. W. Norton, 2010), 175–176; Mathieu Lefèvre, *Local Defence in Afghanistan: A Review of Government-Backed Initiatives* (Kabul: Afghanistan Analysts Network, 2010).

13   One of the polls showing Taliban support at about 10 percent of Afghans was conducted by the Program on International Policy Attitudes and posted on WorldPublicOpionion.org on January 30, 2006; possibly 8 percent of Afghans surveyed expressed favorable views of the Taliban. Some poll results—for example, one by the Asia Foundation in 2011—show higher levels of support (29 percent) for the "aims of the Taliban." This result may reflect support for conservative Muslim values or for Pashtun representation, or opposition to a foreign presence in Afghanistan. In the 2012 Asia Foundation survey, only 10 percent of respondents expressed sympathy for armed opposition groups, and of those, 34 percent said they supported them because they were Afghans and 33 percent said they supported them because they were Muslim. Four out of five Afghans supported reintegrating the Taliban fighters, and 52 percent believed the country was headed in the right direction. See "Afghanistan in 2011: A Survey of the Afghan People," Asia Foundation, available at http://asiafoundation.org/publications/pdf/989.

14 See Seth G. Jones, *Counterinsurgency in Afghanistan*, RAND Counter-insurgency Study vol. 4 (Santa Monica, CA: RAND National Defense Research Institute, 2008); Seth G. Jones and Arturo Munoz, *Afghanistan's Local War: Building Local Defense Forces* (Santa Monica, CA: RAND Corporation, 2010); Thomas J. Barfield, *Afghanistan: A Cultural and Political History* (Princeton, NJ: Princeton University Press, 2012).

15 Author interviews with Eric Olson, January 27, 2012, and an IJC official, April 4, 2012.

16 Author interviews with Lieutenant Colonel Brad Moses, Bagram, October 7, 2011, and March 29, 2012.

17 Author interview with Reeder, November 16, 2011.

18 This account of the Community Defense Initiative is drawn largely from the author interviews with Reeder, November 16, 2011, and Scott Mann, November 21, 2011.

19 According to Reeder, at his request Karzai's half-brother Ahmed Wali used his Popalzai network to secure the proof that Bergdahl was still alive. Rateb Popal, a member of the tribe and a cousin of the Karzais, agreed to go to Pakistan to find out whether he was being held by the Taliban. Popal had been an interpreter for the Taliban ambassador to Pakistan during the Taliban's rule. In 2005, to cash in on the spigot of US funds entering Afghanistan, Popal and his brother formed Watan Risk, a private security company that received lucrative contracts from the military to provide convoy security for trucks resupplying US forces in the south; his brother pleaded guilty to heroin trafficking in a US court. Inquiries into contracting corruption began in 2009. An agreement was finally reached in 2011 that barred Watan from further contracts. However, the Popals remain active in many other businesses. See Associated Press, "Fraud Fighting Effort in Afghanistan Criticized," updated September 14, 2011.

CHAPTER 2: INTO THE VILLAGES

1 Scholars such as American anthropologist Tom Barfield have noted that the largest militias tended to be Tajik and Uzbek. A demobilization program after 2001 had seized most of the Uzbek and Tajik heavy weaponry, and most of the foot soldiers had been sent home or inducted into the army or intelligence service. Most of the senior leaders of the politico-military groups were given high posts in the government, although Abdul Rashid Dostum was eased out of the country for a time. Northern Alliance leader Mohammed Qasim Fahim Khan became chief of the army and later vice president. On the Pashtun side, Gulbuddin Hekmatyar had joined

forces with the Taliban. He continued to fight from his base in Pakistan, along with the Haqqani network that belonged to the Mohammad Yunus Khalis faction of the Hezb-e Islami Party. The Durrani of southern Afghanistan are the wealthier, landholding Pashtuns and have traditionally played political roles, while the Ghilzai Pashtuns that predominate in eastern Pakistan are more martial in nature and will fight to defend their valleys and small farms.

2 In an interview with the author in Kabul on October 30, 2011, Nader Nadery of the Afghan Independent Human Rights Commission expressed concerns that politicization, corruption, and lack of professionalism in the government would hamper the ability of the Ministry of the Interior to play its intended role. Furthermore, he noted, it would be difficult for the special operations personnel to understand all the political crosscurrents in a given area.

3 Eric Schmitt, "U.S. Envoy's Cables Show Worries on Afghan Plans," *New York Times*, January 25, 2010. This article quotes the cables, which were also published by the paper. For a fuller account of the policy review, see Bob Woodward, *Obama's Wars* (New York: Simon and Schuster, 2011), and for the ensuing bureaucratic sniping, Rajiv Chandrasekaran, *Little America: The War Within the War for Afghanistan* (New York: Random House, 2012).

4 The description of Miller's contributions and approach to command are drawn from interviews and email exchanges with the author, including on June 11, 2011, and November 21, 2011, and direct observation at the commander's conference and in Afghanistan. See also Stanley McChrystal, *My Share of the Task: A Memoir* (New York: Portfolio, 2013).

5 Author interview with special operations officer, September 14, 2011.

6 Michael Hastings, "The Runaway General," *Rolling Stone*, June 22, 2010, www.rollingstone.com/politics/news/the-runaway-general-20100622. See also Helene Cooper and David Sanger, "Obama Says Afghan Policy Won't Change After Dismissal," *New York Times*, June 23, 2010.

7 Author interview with General David Petraeus, August 22, 2011.

8 Details of the program are from a copy of Afghan Presidential Decree No. 3196, August 16, 2010; Afghan Interior Ministry guidelines; and author interviews with Afghan and US officials, including Afghan Ministry of the Interior Brigadier General Ali Shah Ahmadzai, October 29, 2011.

9 Author interview with J. R. Stigall, June 10, 2011, during weeklong visit to CFSOCC-A.

10 This short-lived experiment in village stability operations as part of Operation Restore / Uphold Democracy was chronicled in Bob Shacochis, *The Immaculate Invasion* (New York: Viking, 1999).

11 This account of the formulation of the Village Stability Operations and Afghan Local Police plan design is compiled from multiple author interviews with Brigadier General Austin Scott Miller and his staff; author interview with Lieutenant Colonel Scott Mann; attendance at SOF Academic Week in Eglin, Florida, September 13–14, 2011; and multiple videos and written products created by the command for training operators in the procedures to be used.

12 The civilian surge statistics come from the Special Inspector General for Afghanistan Reconstruction's September 8, 2011, report, SIGAR Audit-11-17 & State OIG AUD/SI-11-45 Civilian Uplift. The DST personnel were earnest and committed people—and in some cases extraordinarily experienced and effective—but by and large they were young or even temporary civilian government hires on their first deployment in a war zone. Moreover, they were severely restricted in their ability to move around the countryside. So the Village Stability Operations / Afghan Local Police (VSO/ALP) initiative was in many places the first sustained village-level outreach to rural Afghanistan—that is to say, most of the population of the country. One exception was USAID's Office of Transition Initiatives, which worked in some villages through local hires to conduct the Afghan Stabilization Initiative and its follow-on program, the Community Cohesion Initiative.

13 Don Bolduc cited this number in an article he wrote for *Special Warfare* magazine and in author interviews. See Donald C. Bolduc, "Forecasting the Future of Afghanistan," *Special Warfare*, October–December 2011.

14 Mann became Mr. VSO/ALP for the rest of his active-duty career, setting up the predeployment academics training described later in this chapter. He was a patient and indefatigable promoter of the concept and champion of the equal role that governance and development efforts should play. He founded a networking website, www.stabilityinstitute.org, to build and maintain a community of interest among current, future, and former participants as well as a widening circle of academics, NGOs, and other interested parties.

15 Author interview with Geno Paluso, Kabul, June 11, 2011.

16 Author interviews with Miller and Petraeus.

17 Personal observations and interviews during trip to Balkh and Kunduz, June 9–10, 2011.

CHAPTER 3: THE TALIBAN'S HOME

1   Author interview with Colonel Art Kandarian, commander, 101st
    Airborne, 2nd Brigade, November 5, 2012; DOD News Briefing with
    Colonel Art Kandarian, April 14, 2011; visit to Zhari district center and
    Forward Operating Base (FOB) Pasab, February 23, 2011.

2   This account is principally based on author interviews with Colonel Chris
    Riga, February 15, 2011, and May 8, 2013, and his operations officer for
    1st Battalion, 3rd Special Forces Group, Lieutenant Colonel Michael
    Sullivan, May 14, 2013. See also Joshua Partlow and Karin Bruillard, "U.S.
    Operations in Kandahar Push Out Taliban," *Washington Post*, October 25,
    2010, and, on Tarok Kolache, Joshua Foust, "How Short-Term Thinking
    Is Causing Long-Term Failure in Afghanistan," *The Atlantic*, January 24,
    2011.

3   The allegations against Raziq are detailed exhaustively in Matthieu
    Aikins, "Our Man in Kandahar," *The Atlantic*, November 2011. See also
    Yaroslav Trofimov and Matthew Rosenberg, "In Afghanistan, U.S. Turns
    'Malignant Actor' into Ally," *Wall Street Journal*, November 18, 2010;
    Matthieu Aikins, "The Master of Spin Boldak," *The Atlantic*, December
    2009.

4   Megan McCloskey, "Petraeus Promises Villagers U.S. Will Rebuild What
    It Has Knocked Down," *Stars and Stripes*, December 21, 2010.

5   All the quotations for this section on ODA 3314 and Maiwand are from
    author interviews with the team members and local Afghans or my direct
    observation, October 2011 and February 2012. Brant is quoted from an
    author interview conducted on October 23, 2011.

6   Major Tyler Oliver, "The Economics of Opium Poppy and Substitution
    of Wheat in Maiwand, Kandahar," District Augmentation Team Maiwand
    Information Paper, February 2012. Oliver's paper is based on interviews
    he conducted with Maiwand farmers. He found that "the low price for
    wheat [19 cents per pound] is the result of massive wheat distribution
    programs in Afghanistan artificially affecting the market. The inefficient
    planting techniques used locally cannot produce wheat cheaply enough
    to compete with wheat grown by modern production methods." He con-
    cluded, "The vastly higher profitability of opium poppy, combined with
    the high costs of wheat production, makes the large-scale adoption and
    substitution of wheat as a licit crop virtually impossible in Maiwand."

7   This assessment of moderate corruption on the part of Barwari comes from
    author interviews with US officials, including the team leader. Sources for
    this section also include author interview with Barwari, October 21, 2011,
    and multiple shura meetings in October 2011.

8 Author interview, March 13, 2012.

9 Author observations on visits to Kandahar Province. Fazluddin Agha's death was reported by Reuters on January 12, 2012. He was killed by a suicide car bomber along with two sons and two bodyguards.

10 This account is principally based on author interviews with Dee on August 18, 2012, and Bill Carty on February 1, 2013, and email exchanges. See also "Kandahar Police Chief Survives Suicide Attack," Aljazeera.com, January 11, 2012.

11 Author interviews with Bill Carty, October 28, 2011, and February 15, 2012.

CHAPTER 4: PAKTIKA

1 The team members' quotations and actions in this chapter are principally drawn from direct observation and author interviews with Hutch, Greg, Dustin, Cameron, and other team members, October 9–10, 2011; with Hutch and Greg on February 14, 2012; and with Hutch and Cameron on October 24, 2012.

2 Bob Woodward revealed the existence of the CIA's Counterterrorist Pursuit Teams in *Obama's Wars* (New York: Simon and Schuster, 2010).

3 Author interviews with ODA 3325 members in October 2011, and with Aziz in Paktika, October 11, 2011, and March 27, 2012. Aziz's history with the special forces, his role in Paktika, and his hospitalization were also discussed by Brigadier General Chris Haas in an author interview on October 4, 2011.

4 In addition to interviews with Hutch and other team members about their views and approach, this characterization draws on an unpublished paper written by Hutch entitled "Twenty Tribes at a Time."

5 These events in Rabat and Nawi Kalay, and the first battle in Pirkowti, were recounted by team members in the author interviews cited above. Details of Aziz's actions were also provided by him in the separate author interviews cited above.

6 Hutchinson, "Twenty Tribes at a Time," and Powerpoint presentation prepared by ODA 3325.

7 Author interview with Lieutenant Colonel John Meyer, October 10, 2011. The quadrupled rate of fire from the Pakistani side of the border is also cited in a DOD News Briefing given by ISAF Joint Command Lieutenant General Curtis Scaparrotti on October 27, 2011. He said, "With respect to the number, in the south along Paktika's Khost—Patika border area with Pakistan, the cross-border fires this year are about—are over four times higher than they had been in the past year, so considerably higher."

8 Author interview with Mary Kettman, October 27, 2012, and subsequent email exchanges regarding her experiences and OTI activities in Paktika. Additional information about the Afghan Stabilization Initiative was supplied by the USAID Office of Transition Initiatives in Washington, DC, on March 18, 2013.

9 Details about Abbasin and his role are cited in a US Treasury Department press release, "Treasury Continues Efforts Targeting Terrorist Organizations Operating in Afghanistan and Pakistan," dated September 29, 2011. This account of the operation is based on the author's observations.

10 Julius Cavendish, "Afghanistan's Dirty War: Why the Most Feared Man in Bermal District Is a U.S. Ally," *Time*, October 4, 2011. An earlier version was published by *The Independent* on March 18, 2011, which includes the ISAF statement that its investigation could not substantiate the UN report: "A NATO spokesman said that its own investigation of Azizullah turned up nothing. 'There was a derogatory report via UN channels last summer, but when we tried to research it, there was really little information to substantiate what were essentially claims,' said Lieutenant-Colonel John Dorrian, chief of operations at NATO's public affairs unit in Kabul. As a matter of due diligence, we subsequently tried to backtrack to the origin of the claim, but nothing credible could be found."

11 Author interviews with team members and Aziz. US State Department official Jess Patterson and an Afghan intelligence official in Kabul confirmed this description of the Paktika government and the elders' response to the allegations about Aziz. The latter interviews occurred on December 30, 2012, and April 4, 2012.

12 Author interviews with Aziz, October 11, 2011, and March 27, 2012.

13 Author interview with Aziz, March 27, 2012.

CHAPTER 5: ON THE BORDER

1 Author interview with Steve Townsend, Bagram, February 26, 2011.

2 Jim Gant, "One Tribe at a Time," Nine Sister Imports, Inc., 2009. Some readers, such as former Ambassador Ron Neumann, were concerned by Gant's account, saying that he had taken sides in a dispute that pitted one tribe against another. According to the official VSO methodology formulated by the special operations command, the teams were to rely on the consensus of elders and to seek a tribal balance in areas populated by a variety of groups. Moreover, Afghan Local Police were supposed to

perform purely defensive functions and promptly turn over any detainees to police custody.

3 Author interview with CFSOCC-A official, June 8, 2011.

4 The dialogue and action recounted in this section are based on the author's observations during visits to Kunar in August and October 2011 and interviews with team members and Afghans, including Nur Mohammed and local police, the Afghan Interior Ministry in-processing team, acting district governor Shah Mahmoun, NDS intelligence official Abdul Shah Wali, District Augmentation Teams, and US district support team civilian officials. Post-tour interviews were conducted with the team leader and team sergeant at Fort Bragg on February 15, 2012.

5 In addition to the interviews cited above, author interview with Lieutenant Jake Peterson, October 16, 2011.

6 Author interviews with Jay Schrader on August 5, 2011, and February 15, 2011.

7 Quotations are from author interview with Mark, senior communications sergeant, August 6, 2011, and Nur Mohammed, August 5, 2011.

8 The quotation is from an author interview with Lieutenant Colonel Bob Wilson on February 14, 2012; he also discussed the issue in an interview on August 4, 2012, as well as in interviews with 3310 commander Major Eddie Jimenez and Sergeant Major Rotsaert on August 7, 2011, and October 14 and 15, 2011. Wilson also said he experienced the same "red-centric" or enemy-focused approach when he tried to persuade the brigade commander based in Khost to conduct operations to close two passes on the Pakistan-Paktiya border to support efforts to establish Village Stability Operations there. A senior US officer recounted that Jack Keane, an influential but unofficial adviser to General Petraeus, had urged that brigade commander to focus on enemy kill-and-capture operations. Several US officers related accounts of such pressure during battlefield circulations conducted by Keane.

9 Author interviews with Wilson (cited above); Colonel Mark Schwartz, October 6, 2011; and Lieutenant General Curtis Scaparrotti, ISAF Joint Command, April 2, 2012.

10 Author interview with 3310 commander Major Eddie Jimenez and Sergeant Major Rotsaert on August 7, 2011, and October 14–15, 2011.

11 The account of the operation and dialogue in this section is principally drawn from author interviews with the ODA 3316 team leader, Matt; the chief warrant officer of ODA 3313; 3310 company commander Jimenez; and battalion commander Wilson.

12 This account draws principally on author interviews with the participants

and secondarily on the unclassified version of the official investigation, known as the Clark Report. The Pakistani government has never acknowledged that its personnel fired first on the American and Afghan troops. See Stephen A. Clark, "Investigation into the Incident in Vicinity of the Salala Checkpoint on the Night of 25–26 Nov 2011: A Report," United States Central Command, 2011, www.centcom.mil/images/stories/Crossborder/report%20exsum%20further%20redacted.pdf.

13 Clark Report, as well as author interviews with Mike, chief warrant officer 2, who was the ground force commander for the operation, February 15, 2012; his battalion commander, Lieutenant Colonel Bob Wilson, February 14, 2012; the CJSOTF-A operations officer, Lieutenant Colonel Brad Moses, March 29, 2012; and Colonel Heinz Dinter, CFSOCC-A, March 10, 2012.

14 Quotes are from author interview with Mike, February 15, 2012; additional information was supplied by interviews and email exchange with Wilson.

15 Initial press reports contain Pakistani government denials, as in Dion Nissenbaum, Tom Wright, Owais Tohid, and Adam Entous, "Airstrike Ravages U.S.-Pakistan Ties," *Wall Street Journal*, November 28, 2011. Press questions of Clark are in his DOD News Briefing on the report, December 22, 2011, www.defense.gov/transcripts/transcript.aspx?transcriptid=4952. For Pakistan's official reply to the Clark Report, see "Pakistan's Perspective on Investigation: Report Conducted by BG Stephen Clark into 26th November 2011 US led ISAF/NATO Forces Attack on Pakistani Volcano and Boulder Posts in Mohmand Agency," published by Pakistani military's Inter-Services Public Relations (ISPR), January 23, 2012, available at www.ispr.gov.pk/front/press/pakistan.pdf.

16 The report states that "RC-E did not forward the CONOP to NBCC [the Nawa Border Coordination Center] or ODRP [the US Office of Defense Representative in Pakistan]." Clark Report, p. 21, paragraphs (4) and (5).

CHAPTER 6: THE BURDENS OF COMMAND

1 Author interview with General John Allen, Kabul, April 3, 2012.

2 This account is based on author interviews with General John Allen, April 3, 2012; Brigadier General Chris Haas, April 3, 2012; Colonel Heinz Dinter, April 5, 2012; and three other US officials with direct knowledge of the events.

3 ISAF press release 2011-11-CA-013, dated November 26, 2011. The text of

the release read: "The International Security Assistance Force is investigating an incident that occurred early this morning along the Afghanistan-Pakistan border."

4 See Stephen A. Clark, "Investigation into the Incident in Vicinity of the Salala Checkpoint on the Night of 25–26 Nov 2011: A Report," United States Central Command, 2011; DOD News Briefing with Brigadier General Clark on December 22, 2011, posted at www.defense.gov.

5 The observations from Haas are from author interviews with him on August 9, 2011; October 4, 2011; October 31, 2011; and April 3, 2012.

6 Author interviews with Ryan Crocker, August 8, 2011; October 30, 2011; and April 1, 2012.

7 CJSOTF-A ALP Weekly Tracker, October 31, 2011.

8 Author interview with Dinter, Kabul, March 10, 2012.

9 Author interview with Colonel Mark Schwartz, Bagram, October 6, 2011.

10 RAND used a polling firm that hired and trained Afghans to do the polling. The firm conducted three "wave" polls between November 2010 and June 2011. The sample size was 10,000 in 26 districts that had Afghan Local Police, with an average of 430 Afghans interviewed per district. See "Assessment of Opinion Poll and Team Reporting for Village Stability Operations in Afghanistan: Wave 3," RAND unclassified briefing, October 30, 2011. Wave 2 was produced in April 2011.

11 Author interviews with team leader in Kunar, October 17, 2011, and with Chris Haas, October 31, 2011.

12 Author interview with member of Haas's staff, April 7, 2012. The issues and events in this section draw on interviews with Haas, Dinter, Colonel Beau Higgins, Captain Wes Spence, Colonel Pat Stevens, and other members of Haas's staff.

13 Author interviews with the Group Support Battalion commander and numerous CJSOTF-A staff, October 2011 and March 2012.

14 James R. Marrs, "Findings and Recommendations of AR 15-6 Investigation: Credibility Assessment of Allegations of Human Rights Violations Appearing in a Human Rights Watch Report," USFOR-A-DJ2, United States Forces–Afghanistan, 2011; author interviews with Schwartz, Bagram, October 6, 2011, and March 29, 2012.

15 Author interviews in Kabul, October 3 and 5, 2011, and March 9, 2012.

16 This account is drawn from author interviews with Haas, Dinter, Schwartz, Higgins, Spence, Stevens, and other members of Haas's staff as well as two Afghan officials.

17 Author interview with Haas, Kabul, April 3, 2012.

18 Author interview with Dinter, March 10, 2012, and Haas, April 3, 2012.

CHAPTER 7: ON THE SAME TEAM ... OR NOT

1 This incident was related in an author interview with Brad Hansell, March 12, 2012. The issue of corruption and the drug eradication campaign in Maiwand and Kandahar Province generally was also discussed with Major Brian DeMarzio and other members of the SOTF-S staff, VSCC-South's Lieutenant Colonel Brian Mack, and Major Sean Walrath in briefings on March 11, 2012. The information in this chapter is primarily based on author interviews with ODA 7233 and local Afghans, as well as personal observation during March and August 2012 visits. Other sources are noted below.

2 Author interviews with Najibullah and Hansell, March 2012. The quotation is from an author interview with Najibullah on March 13, 2012. Some Afghans, like Najibullah, only use one name.

3 Author interview, March 14, 2012.

4 Author interviews with Hansell and direct observation in a meeting with Kala Khan.

5 Author interviews with Abdullah Niazi and Hansell; direct observation.

6 Author observations of events in Maiwand in the immediate aftermath of the massacre.

7 Author interview with Chris Haas, April 3, 2012, and direct observations of command staff lawyer.

8 Author interview with Lieutenant Colonel Richard Navarro, August 13, 2012.

9 Author conversation on patrol, March 14, 2012.

10 This incident is cited in the preliminary and final reports of the United Nations Assistance Mission in Afghanistan (UNAMA) on the protection of civilians. The final report says, "According to reports, the ALP commander along with two other ALP members beat and kicked the detainees, tied the detainees to their car and dragged them behind the moving car, killing both detainees. ALP members informed international military forces that the detainees had escaped." See United Nations Assistance Mission in Afghanistan and UN Office of the High Commissioner for Human Rights, *Afghanistan: Annual Report 2012. Protection of Civilians in Armed Conflict* (Kabul: UNAMA, 2013), 44. See http://unama. unmissions.org/LinkClick.aspx?fileticket=K0B5RL2XYcU%3D&tabid=12254& for online text of the report.

11 This account is based on author interviews with Hansell, Navarro, Angel Martinez, Jim Huggins, and other US officers, as well as email communications.

12 Author interviews with team members and Afghans and direct observation, August 2012.
13 Author interviews with J. R. Jones, Martinez, Navarro, and Brian Rarey, August 2012.

CHAPTER 8: SEALS DO FOREIGN INTERNAL DEFENSE, TOO

1 Author interviews, August 1–3, 2011, with the command master chief senior enlisted adviser; the N3 operations officer; the senior chief petty officer in charge of ALP program support; the Support Center director of Special Operations Task Force–Southeast, Uruzgan; and command group and team members in Tarin Kowt. The official name of SEAL Team Six was changed in 1987 to United States Naval Special Warfare Development Group (NSWDG), or DEVGRU. It and the army's Delta Force are also referred to as "special mission units" or "tier-one" forces.
2 Author interviews with SEALs in Tarin Kowt; author interview with a retired senior special operations officer in charge of the Philippines operation, August 31, 2012. The author also viewed a videotape of the operation that killed Abu Sayyaf commander Abu Sabaya on June 21, 2002. See also Geoffrey Lamber, Larry Lewis, and Sarah Sewall, "Operation Enduring Freedom–Philippines: Civilian Harm and the Indirect Approach," *Prism* 3, no. 4 (2012): 117–135; Colonel David S. Maxwell (ret.), "Foreign Internal Defense: An Indirect Approach to Counter-Insurgency/Counter Terrorism, Lessons from Operation Enduring Freedom–Philippines for Dealing with Non-Existential Threats to the United States," paper delivered at Foreign Policy Research Institute conference, Washington, DC, December 6, 2011. For SEAL activities in Africa, see *Ethos*, published by Naval Special Warfare Command, Issue 8, n.d., 4–9, www.sealswcc.com/pdf/navy-seal-ethos-magazine/ethos-magazine-issue-8.pdf.
3 Author interview with Mike Hayes, Uruzgan, March 17, 2012, and copy of his commander's guidance.
4 The events of 2012 recounted in this chapter draw on author interviews with Hayes, members of his command group, teams under his command, the Village Stability Coordination Center director, and a company commander in March and August 2012, as well as the author's direct observation. Some interviews were conducted by video teleconference.
5 Author interview with Hayes, Uruzgan, March 19, 2012. See Ann Marlowe, "The Back of Beyond: A Report from Zabul Province," *World Affairs Journal*, March/April 2010. A battalion of 4/82 BCT posted in Zabul and Uruzgan in 2009 was ordered to pull back to focus on Highway One

in January 2010. One of the two Afghan battalion commanders, however, did make the effort to learn Pashto, as Carlotta Gall reported on May 23, 2011, in the *New York Times* in "A Slice of Afghanistan Well Secured by Afghans."

6 Author interview with civil affairs team sergeant, August 2012.

7 Author interview with Dan Green, March 20, 2012, and numerous author interviews with Brian Strickland in August 2011 and March 2012. The Strickland remark is quoted from a March 19, 2012, interview.

8 Maria Abi-Habib, "SEALs Battle for Hearts, Minds and Paychecks," *Wall Street Journal*, August 29, 2012.

9 The training of the commandos and the mission in Zabul were recounted in interviews with Marshall, the SEAL platoon commander; Lieutenant Colonel Ahmadullah Popal; and operations officer Shah Janan, March 18, 2012.

10 Information in this passage is from author interviews. See also Tom Vandenbrook, "Black Hawk Crash Kills Seven U.S. Troops," *USA Today*, August 16, 2011; Bill Roggio, "11 NATO, Afghan Troops Killed in Helicopter Crash in Kandahar," *Long War Journal*, August 16, 2011.

11 This account is based on author observations and conversations, August 17, 2012.

CHAPTER 9: GOOD ENOUGH?

1 Details on career from author interview with ODA 1114 team sergeant Russ, March 24, 2012.

2 Author interview with ALP commander Abdullah Khan, Zarghan Shah, March 25, 2012. Two of his brothers had joined the regular police and army and had been sent to Balkh and Farah provinces in the north and west, respectively. One of them had been killed. The ALP commander said he was determined to stay in Paktika to take care of the widow and his mother.

3 This account is drawn from author observations at the shura, the lunch, and a tour of Yahya Khel and author interviews with Haji Yar Mohammed and other Afghans on March 26, 2012.

4 The quotation is from an author interview with company commander Major Mike Bandy, Sharana, March 25, 2012. The account is based on interviews with team members and Jess Patterson. See also Kevin Sieff and Javed Hamdard, "Rogue Afghan Police Officer: A Taliban Infiltrator's Road to Fratricide," *Washington Post*, April 1, 2012.

5 Author interview with Jess Patterson, December 30, 2012.

6   Author interview with Russell, December 17, 2012.

7   Author interviews with 1st Special Forces Group team members. The Sar Howza shooting, which occurred on March 26, 2012, was reported in a US Department of Defense casualty report press release dated March 28, 2012. Sergeant William R. Wilson III of 2-28, 172nd Infantry Brigade died of his wounds suffered in the shooting.

8   This section is based on author interviews with Captain Jae Kim, other members of ODA 1411, and Afghans in Paktika in November 2012, in addition to follow-up emails with the team leader.

9   The MATVs were equipped with the Common Remotely Operated Weapon System, or CROWS.

10 The information on OTI projects was supplied by the USAID Office of Transition Initiatives.

11 Author interviews with ODA 1411 members.

12 I witnessed the meetings described in this section in Surobi and Orgun and conducted interviews with Afghans and team members who were present on November 11 and 12, 2012.

13 Kimberly Dozier and Adam Goldman, "Counterterrorist Pursuit Team: 3,000 Man CIA Paramilitary Force Hunts Militants in Afghanistan, Pakistan," Associated Press, September 22, 2010; Mark Mazzetti and Dexter Filkins, "U.S. Military Seeks to Expand Raids in Pakistan," *New York Times*, December 20, 2010; Greg Miller, "CIA Digs In as Americans Withdraw from Iraq, Afghanistan," *Washington Post*, February 7, 2012.

14 Author observations at the shura, Orgun, Paktika, November 11, 2012, and interviews with Afghan and US officials.

15 Greg Miller, "Secret Report Raises Alarms on Intelligence Blind Spots Because of AQ Focus," *Washington Post*, March 20, 2013. A webcast of Brennan's confirmation hearing on February 7, 2013, is posted at the website of the Senate Armed Services Committee.

16 The events in these paragraphs are largely based on the author's email communications with Captain Kim and phone interviews with battalion and other special operations officers.

17 Rebecca Parr, "Special Forces Soldier James Grissom, of Hayward, Remembered by Friends, Family," *Mercury News*, April 1, 2013, www.mercurynews.com/breaking-news/ci_22917925/special-forces-soldier-grissom-hayward-remembered-by-friends.

CHAPTER 10: HIGHWAY ONE

1   In August 2012, a special operations team was sent to Andar from northern Afghanistan for the final weeks of its tour.

2   Author interviews with team intelligence officer in Andar, November 10, 2012.

3   Author interview with Major Jason Clarke, AOB 1320, Sharana, November 9, 2012. The degree of Taliban control in the districts of Andar and De Yak was outlined in a *New York Times* article, and RC-East officials at the time verified the accuracy of this article for the author. See C. J. Chivers, "Afghanistan's Hidden Taliban Government," *New York Times*, February 6, 2011. See also Joshua Foust's post, "The Push into Andar," at Registan. net, February 2, 2011.

4   The quotations from Andar officials Diciwal and Ramazon are from author interviews with them and personal observations in Andar, November 10–11, 2012.

5   The conventional forces were pulling back their small footprint from Maidan Shah, Sayadabad, and Jagatu to FOB Shank in Logar. They would have small advisory Security Force Assistance Teams (SFATs) at FOB Airborne in northern Wardak and at Shank to mentor the Afghan army corps and kandaks.

6   This account is drawn from author interviews with Lieutenant Colonel Brad Moses, Bagram, October 7, 2011, and March 29, 2012. See also Jean McKenzie, "War by Other Means," Part 3, "Guardians of Wardak," *Global Post*, June 28, 2010, www.globalpost.com/dispatch/afghanistan/100625/ us-aid-afghanistan-taliban-3-qaeda?page=0,0.

7   Author interview with Afghan army chief General Sher Mohammed Karimi, April 3, 2012. The description of Wardak and of the events that took place in that province is drawn from numerous author interviews with Afghan officials and US officers responsible for operations there at different points in time, including Major General John Campbell and his RC-East staff on February 25–27, 2011; Lieutenant Colonel Bob Wilson on October 6, 2011, and February 14, 2012; Lieutenant Colonel Brad Moses on October 7, 2011, and March 29, 2012; and CJSOTF-A J-3 on November 14, 2012, as well as other interviews cited in this section and personal observations.

8   Author interview with Major General Tony Thomas, Kabul, November 6, 2012.

9   Ibid. Statistic from the CJSOTF-A ALP Weekly Tracker, January 28, 2013.

10   The statement issued by Karzai's presidential office is quoted in Thom Patterson, "NATO: No Evidence for Afghan Claim of Possible Torture, Murder by U.S. Forces," CNN, February 25, 2013.

11   Yaroslav Trofimov, "U.S. Set to Pull Forces from Afghan District," *Wall Street Journal*, March 20, 2013.

12 Dylan Welch and Hamid Shalizi, "Insight: Afghan Move Against U.S. Special Forces Tied to Abuse Allegations," Reuters, February 26, 2013.

13 Author phone interview with Major John Bishop, US Special Operations Task Force–East, March 30, 2013.

14 The chief public affairs officer of NATO Special Operations Component Command–Afghanistan, Lieutenant Colonel Tom Bryant, said in an email on April 28, 2013, in response to the author's query, that the ISAF investigation had found that "there were no US Special Forces involved in any way with misconduct or any other alleged misdeeds that may or may not have occurred in Nerkh district." Janan's role was also reported by Ben Brumfield and Thom Patterson in "ISAF Begins Pulling Out of an Afghan Province with a Legacy," CNN, March 20, 2013.

15 Mirwais Harooni and Phil Stewart, "Afghan's Karzai Blasts U.S., Marring Hagel Visit," Reuters, March 10, 2013.

16 Ibid.; author phone interview with Bishop, March 30, 2013.

17 Ibid.; Bryant email exchange.

18 Author phone interview with Bishop, March 30, 2013.

CHAPTER 11: WILL THE VALLEY HOLD?

1 See Lester W. Grau, "Breaking Contact Without Leaving Chaos: The Soviet Withdrawal from Afghanistan," *Journal of Slavic Military Studies* 20, no. 2 (2007): 10; Brian Glyn Williams, *Afghanistan Declassified: A Guide to America's Longest War* (Philadelphia: University of Pennsylvania Press, 2012), 64; Barnett Rubin, *Afghanistan in the Post–Cold War Era* (Oxford: Oxford University Press, 2013), 87–88.

2 Qari Ziaur Rahman, quoted in interview with Syed Saleem Shahzad, "At War with the Taliban: A Fighter and a Financier," *South Asia Times*, May 23, 2008. QZR also acknowledged how the terrain of upper Kunar and Nuristan put the Americans at a great disadvantage, fixing them in bases that the guerrillas then attacked. He said, "Thank God that this is a mountainous region. NATO has a presence in the bases only, other than that they do not control anything. The mujahideen patrol everywhere and they carry out attacks freely....Koranghal is our main operation theater in Kunar. It is a slaughterhouse for the Americans. Many Americans have been killed there. Kamdesh in Nooristan is our main operation front. We killed many Americans there as well. Similarly, we are very active in Sarkano, beside many other areas."

3 This account is based principally on author interviews with Gant's superior officers, including Lieutenant Colonel Bob Wilson, Colonel Mark Schwartz, and Brigadier General Chris Haas. In addition, the author was

provided with email communications between senior US Army officers regarding the detailed allegations about Gant and the events in Kunar.

4   Comment made to author by general officer at Fort Bragg.

5   Author phone interview with Nur Mohammed, March 21, 2012.

6   Captain Rick Holahan and other members of Major Kent Solheim's company staff provided a detailed briefing on, among other things, the plotting of the battle on Google Maps, in Jalalabad, March 22–23, 2012.

7   This section is based on author interviews with members of ODA 3436, Waliulah Hamidzai, and other Afghans, Kunar, March 21–22, 2012, and Major Kent Solheim, Nangahar, March 22, 2012.

8   This section is based primarily on the author's direct observations during a November 2012 visit to Kunar and author interviews with members of ODA 3131, Afghan Local Police commanders, and other Afghans.

9   Author interviews with Afghans and members of ODA 3131, November 2012, and personal observations.

10 Information on Qari Zia Rahman can be found in NATO ISAF press releases and *Long War Journal* articles by Bill Roggio. See "Afghan, ISAF Forces Secure Eastern Afghan Town," International Security Assistance Force, press release, July 20, 2010; Bill Roggio, "Afghan, US Forces Hunt Al Qaeda, Taliban in Northeast," *Long War Journal*, August 2, 2010; Bill Roggio, "US Hunts Wanted Taliban and Al Qaeda Commander in Kunar," *Long War Journal*, July 20, 2010; "Several Insurgents Killed, Two Detained by Afghan and Coalition Force in Kunar," August 2, 2010, www.dvidshub.net/news/53811/several-insurgents-killed-two-detained-afghan-and-coalition-force-kunar#.UZvKhqJJOAg.

11 Operation Strong Eagle I is recounted in the three-part series "Fight and Flight," by Dianna Cahn, in *Stars and Stripes*, September 20–21, 2010. Operation Strong Eagle II was reported in several press releases issued by US Army public affairs, including "Marawara District Shura After Operations Strong Eagle II," July 22, 2012. Operation Strong Eagle III details were reported in "Forces Conclude Operations Near Pakistan Border," American Forces Press Service, April 7, 2011.

12 Author interviews with Captain Tim Ambrose, November 7–8, 2012, and with OTI official in Kabul, November 15, 2012. USAID OTI subsequently provided additional information about its projects.

13 Author's personal observation of events in Marawara, November 7, 2012.

14 Vladimir Grigoriev, "Facts of the War History: Marawara Company," June 23, 2006, Art of War, http://artofwar.ru/g/grigorxew_w_a/text_0080.shtml.

15 Author interview with Major Ben Hauser, November 9, 2012.

16 Author interview with Lieutenant Colonel Chris Fox and his command staff at Camp Montrond, November 14, 2012.

17 Author interview with Colonel Tony Fletcher at Camp Vance, November 14, 2012. I also interviewed his operations and plans officers.

18 Rod Nordland, "After Airstrike, Afghan Points to C.I.A. and Secret Militias," *New York Times*, April 18, 2013. In another account, Faizi told a reporter that a decree Karzai had issued in late February 2013, following another civilian casualty incident caused by the CIA-led force in the same district, abolishing parallel structures, "was aimed primarily at dismantling CIA-controlled teams." See Emma Graham-Harrison, "Hamid Karzai Seeks to Curb CIA Operations in Afghanistan," *The Guardian*, April 19, 2013. A press release on Karzai's February order is posted on the Afghan presidential office website; see "President Karzai Assigns Delegation to Merge All Armed Units Outside Government Structure into Afghan Security Institutions," February 28, 2013, http://president. gov.af/en/news/17849. It reads, in part: "President Hamid Karzai has issued an executive order assigning a delegation tasked to bar operation by any armed grouping or units outside the formal government security structures and to completely merge them into government security institutions. The delegation chaired by National Security Advisor Dr. Spanta shall be responsible to identify and merge into government structures all those armed units and groups run and operated by international coalition forces as local security units. The delegation will be responsible to demand from the international coalition to hand over all such armed groupings to Afghan security institutions within three months." See also Kate Clark, "What Exactly Is the CIA Doing in Afghanistan? Proxy Militias and Two Airstrikes in Kunar," April 28, 2013, Afghanistan Analysts Network, http://aan-afghanistan.com/index.asp?id=3370.

19 Author interview with Gudjer, November 7, 2012.

20 An argument for such small combined civil-military teams is made in Carter Malkasian and J. Kael Weston, "War Downsized: How to Accomplish More with Less," *Foreign Affairs* 91, no. 2 (2012): 111–121. The inflated role assumed by regional security officers at US embassies often overrides the ambassador's intent, and in any event prevents civilians from operating freely throughout the countries to which they are assigned. Without a revised approach, the military-intelligence-civilian triad model outlined here cannot be realized. It was a key feature of the CORDS program in Vietnam and subsequent Cold War conflict zones. In the wake of the Benghazi fatalities and subsequent recriminations, however, the trend toward more restrictive policies for civilians may increase rather than decrease.

21 Information on OTI provided by USAID OTI officials, March 18, 2013.
22 Author interview, November 12, 2012.

CHAPTER 12: THE ENDGAME

1   Quotations by Tony Thomas are from author interviews, Kabul, November 6 and 15, 2012. "Task force" is special ops' shorthand for special mission units; although many military formations are task-organized, the term refers to those special mission units organized for rescuing hostages or hunting terrorist leaders. This task force has been given different numbers over the past decade, so to minimize confusion this account will simply refer to special mission units. When commanded by General Stanley McChrystal, it was Task Force 714; it was later renamed Task Force 535. A subordinate task force is Task Force 310. See Stanley A. McChrystal, *My Share of the Task: A Memoir* (New York: Portfolio, 2013), 92; Donald C. Bolduc, "Forecasting the Future of Afghanistan," *Special Warfare* 24, no. 4 (2011): 22–28.

2   Brigadier Mark Smethurst, National Defense Industrial Association conference, Washington, DC, January 28, 2013; author interview with Colonel Duke Christy, deputy commander of ISAF SOF, Kabul, April 7, 2012.

3   Major Michael E. Gates, "Creating SOF Networks: The Role of NATO Special Operations as a Testing Ground for SOF Integration" (Thesis, Naval Postgraduate School, 2011); Lieutenant Colonel Buck Dellinger, "Special Operations Command Europe: Strengthening Partnerships for Global Security," *Special Warfare*, April–June 2012, 12–15. One of McRaven's initiatives as commander of the US special operations command in Europe in the mid-2000s had been to found a NATO SOF headquarters to provide a permanent venue for common education and training of NATO special operators.

4   McChrystal, *My Share of the Task*, 367.

5   In *My Share of the Task*, McChrystal describes his relationship with Thomas but uses his initials instead of his name (p. 99). Thomas's profile on the networking site LinkedIn includes the titles and dates of his command and staff assignments. Some of his positions are also described in his "Department of Defense Press Briefing with Maj. Gen. Thomas from the Pentagon," May 15, 2013, the transcript of which is posted at www.defense.gov.

6   Author interviews with Colonel Tony Fletcher, November 14, 2012, and Lieutenant Colonel Richard Navarro, August 18, 2012.

7 Email exchange with the author, May 3, 2013.

8 Comments attributed to Bolduc are from author interviews in Kabul, November 6 and 15, 2012, and subsequent emails, and two unpublished, unclassified documents from the command, "ALP Information Paper & Talking Points" (undated), and the ALP Map weekly tracker, January 28, 2013.

9 Meeting with RAND, December 19, 2012, Arlington, Virginia, and briefing deck.

10 UN Office of the High Commissioner for Human Rights, *Afghanistan: Annual Report 2012. Protection of Civilians in Armed Conflict* (Kabul: United Nations Assistance Mission in Afghanistan [UNAMA], 2013), 9, 42–47; author interview with Ali Shah Ahmadzai, Kabul, April 7, 2012. The UNAMA report noted that the Afghan Interior Ministry had acted promptly to investigate and detain Afghan Local Police officers accused of murder in Zhari, but the suspects were subsequently released by local officials.

11 The statistics are from the Military Assistance Command Vietnam–Studies and Observations Group website, www.macvsog.cc.

12 Email communication with senior special operations commander, January 10, 2013.

13 The official US military definition of unconventional warfare is: "Activities conducted to enable a resistance movement or insurgency to coerce, disrupt, or overthrow a government or occupying power by operating through or with an underground, auxiliary, and guerrilla force in a denied area." See Joint Publication 3-05, "Special Operations," and Joint Dictionary 1-02. For comparative historical research on transition of civil defense, see Austin Long, Stephanie Pezard, Bryce Loidolt, and Todd C. Helmus, *Locals Rule: Historical Lessons for Creating Local Defense Forces for Afghanistan and Beyond* (Santa Monica, CA: RAND/National Defense Research Institute, 2012). In an April 3, 2012, interview with the author, Brigadier General Christopher Haas, then commander of Combined Forces Special Operations Component Command–Afghanistan, observed that the planned growth of the Afghan Local Police would test the special operations forces' span of control.

14 A good description of ALP in Baghlan is in Luke Mogelson, "Bad Guys vs Worse Guys," *New York Times Magazine*, October 19, 2011.

15 See DOD News Briefing with Major General Robert Abrams, Regional Command–South commander, March 13, 2013, transcript posted at www.defense.gov, and Carlotta Gall, "Afghan Villagers Take on Taliban in Their Heartland," *New York Times*, March 20, 2013.

16 Eighty-two percent of the Afghan army and police patrols in southern Afghanistan were conducted unilaterally—without coalition forces—in the period from July 2012 to March 2013, according to Major General Robert Abrams, Regional Command–South commander, in a March 13, 2013, press conference with the Pentagon press corps. The 205th Afghan Army Corps conducted six large-scale operations and in the last one was able to sustain continuous operations for sixteen days. One of its brigades sustained a battalion-sized operation one hundred kilometers away for three weeks. The air wing serving southern Afghanistan was still tiny, however, consisting of five Mi-17 and Mi-8 helicopters. It conducted its first independent air-assault operation in October 2012. It took thirty hours to mount two sorties of Mi-17s to respond to an attack by an estimated two hundred or three hundred Taliban in Day Kundi, but the Afghan army did successfully resupply its troops and evacuate the most serious casualties. The confusing terminology adopted by ISAF made it difficult to understand which units were capable of fully independent operations. Development of sufficient lift and logistics capacity had lagged as ISAF had focused on building infantry units, so an infantry unit might be well trained and led but still not capable of "independent operations" since it could not support itself. See the semiannual, congressionally mandated reports entitled *Report on Progress Toward Security and Stability in Afghanistan*, Report to Congress in Accordance with Section 1230 of the National Defense Authorization Act (Washington, DC: US Department of Defense, 2009–2012).

17 Author interview with Colonel Sean Swindell, November 4, 2012.

CHAPTER 13: THE FUTURE OF SPECIAL OPERATIONS AND AMERICAN WARFARE

1 T. E. Lawrence, "Twenty-Seven Articles," *Arab Bulletin*, 1917; republished as e-book (Seattle: Praetorian Press, 2011).

SELECTED BIBLIOGRAPHY

BOOKS

Barfield, Thomas J. *Afghanistan: A Cultural and Political History*. Princeton, NJ: Princeton University Press, 2012.

Bergen, Peter L. *The Longest War: The Enduring Conflict Between America and Al-Qaeda*. New York: Free Press, 2011.

———. *Manhunt: The Ten-Year Search for Bin Laden from 9/11 to Abbottabad*. New York: Crown, 2012.

Berntsen, Gary, and Ralph Pezzullo. *Jawbreaker: The Attack on Bin Laden and Al Qaeda: A Personal Account by the CIA's Key Field Commander*. New York: Three Rivers Press, 2005.

Blaber, Pete. *The Mission, the Men, and Me: Lessons from a Former Delta Force Commander*. New York: Berkley Caliber, 2008.

Blehm, Eric. *Fearless: The Undaunted Courage and Ultimate Sacrifice of Navy SEAL Team SIX Operator Adam Brown*. Colorado Springs: WaterBrook Press, 2012.

———. *The Only Thing Worth Dying For: How Eleven Green Berets Forged a New Afghanistan*. New York: Harper, 2010.

Boot, Max. *Invisible Armies: An Epic History of Guerrilla Warfare from Ancient Times to the Present*. New York: Liveright, 2012.

Bradley, Rusty. *Lions of Kandahar: The Story of a Fight Against All Odds*. New York: Bantam Books, 2011.

Briscoe, Charles H., and Richard L. Kiper. *U.S. Army Special Operations in Afghanistan*. Boulder: Paladin Press, 2006.

Chandrasekaran, Rajiv. *Little America: The War Within the War for Afghanistan*. New York: Random House, 2012.

Connable, Ben, and Martin C. Libicki. *How Insurgencies End*. RAND Corporation Monograph Series. Santa Monica, CA: RAND, 2010.

Felbab-Brown, Vanda. *Aspiration and Ambivalence: Strategies and Realities of Counterinsurgency and State-Building in Afghanistan*. Washington, DC: Brookings Institution Press, 2012.

Fishel, John, and Max Manwaring. *Uncomfortable Wars Revisited.* Norman: University of Oklahoma Press, 2007.

Frederick, Jim. *Special Ops: The Hidden World of America's Toughest Warriors.* New York: Time Books, 2011.

Fury, Dalton. *Kill Bin Laden: A Delta Force Commander's Account of the Hunt for the World's Most Wanted Man.* New York: St. Martin's Press, 2011.

Gerges, Fawaz A. *The Rise and Fall of Al-Qaeda.* New York: Oxford University Press, 2011.

Giustozzi, Antonio. *Koran, Kalashnikov, and Laptop: The Neo-Taliban Insurgency in Afghanistan, 2002–2007.* New York: Columbia University Press, 2009.

Jalali, Ali Ahmad, and Lester W. Grau. *The Other Side of the Mountain: Mujahideen Tactics in the Soviet-Afghan War.* Reprint, Kirkland, WA: Tales End Press, 2012.

Jones, Seth G. *Counterinsurgency in Afghanistan.* RAND Counterinsurgency Study, vol. 4. Santa Monica, CA: RAND National Defense Research Institute, 2008.

———. *Hunting in the Shadows: The Pursuit of Al Qa'ida Since 9/11.* New York: W. W. Norton, 2012.

———. *In the Graveyard of Empires: America's War in Afghanistan.* New York: W. W. Norton, 2010.

Jones, Seth G., and Arturo Munoz. *Afghanistan's Local War: Building Local Defense Forces.* Santa Monica, CA: RAND, 2010.

Kelly, Terrence K., Nora Bensahel, and Olga Oliker. *Security Force Assistance in Afghanistan: Identifying Lessons for Future Efforts.* RAND Corporation Monograph Series. Santa Monica, CA: RAND, 2011.

Kilcullen, David. *The Accidental Guerrilla: Fighting Small Wars in the Midst of a Big One.* New York: Oxford University Press, 2009.

Long, Austin, Stephanie Pezard, Bryce Loidolt, and Todd C. Helmus. *Locals Rule: Historical Lessons for Creating Local Defense Forces for Afghanistan and Beyond.* Santa Monica, CA: RAND National Defense Research Institute, 2012.

Luttrell, Marcus. *Lone Survivor: The Eyewitness Account of Operation Redwing and the Lost Heroes of SEAL Team 10.* New York: Little, Brown, 2007.

Maurer, Kevin. *Gentlemen Bastards: On the Ground in Afghanistan with America's Elite Special Forces.* New York: Berkley Books, 2012.

McChrystal, Stanley A. *My Share of the Task: A Memoir.* New York: Portfolio, 2013.

McRaven, William H. *Spec Ops: Case Studies in Special Operations Warfare. Theory and Practice.* New York: Presidio Press, 1996.

Naylor, Sean. *Not a Good Day to Die: The Untold Story of Operation Anaconda.* New York: Berkley, 2005.

Owen, Mark, and Kevin Maurer. *No Easy Day: The Autobiography of a Navy SEAL.* New York: Dutton, 2012.

Phillips, William R. *Night of the Silver Stars: The Battle of Lang Vei.* Annapolis, MD: Naval Institute Press, 1997.

Rabasa, Angel, John Gordon IV, Peter Chalk, Audra K. Grant, K. Scott McMahon, Stephanie Pezard, Caroline Reilly, David Ucko, S. Rebecca Zimmerman. *From Insurgency to Stability,* vol. 2, *Insights from Selected Case Studies.* RAND Corporation Monograph Series. Santa Monica, CA: RAND, 2011.

Rashid, Ahmed. *Descent into Chaos: The U.S. and the Disaster in Pakistan, Afghanistan, and Central Asia.* New York: Penguin, 2009.

———. *Taliban: Militant Islam, Oil and Fundamentalism in Central Asia,* 2nd ed. New Haven, CT: Yale University Press, 2010.

Robinson, Linda. *Masters of Chaos: The Secret History of the Special Forces.* New York: PublicAffairs Books, 2004.

Rothstein, Hy S. *Afghanistan and the Troubled Future of Unconventional Warfare.* Annapolis, MD: Naval Institute Press, 2006.

Sanger, David. *Confront and Conceal: Obama's Secret Wars and Surprising Use of American Power.* New York: Crown, 2012.

Scahill, Jeremy. *Dirty Wars: The World Is a Battlefield.* New York: Nation Books, 2013.

Schmitt, Eric, and Thom Shanker. *Counterstrike: The Untold Story of America's Secret Campaign Against Al Qaeda.* New York: Times Books, 2011.

Schroen, Gary C. *First In: An Insider's Account of How the CIA Spearheaded the War on Terror in Afghanistan.* New York: Presidio Press/Ballantine Books, 2007.

Stanton, Doug. *Horse Soldiers: A True Story of Modern War.* New York: Little, Brown, 2005.

Tucker, David, and Christopher J. Lamb. *United States Special Operations Forces.* New York: Columbia University Press, 2007.

Wasdin, Howard E., and Stephen Templin. *SEAL Team Six: Memoirs of an Elite Navy SEAL Sniper.* New York: St. Martin's Press, 2011.

West, Bing. *The Wrong War: Grit, Strategy and the Way Out of Afghanistan.* New York: Random House, 2012.

Woodward, Bob. *Obama's Wars.* New York: Simon and Schuster, 2011.

Wright, Donald P., with the Combat Operations Studies Team. *A Different Kind of War: The United States Army in Operation Enduring Freedom (OEF), October 2001–September 2005.* Washington, DC: Government Printing Office, 2010.

Zaeef, Abdul Salam. *My Life with the Taliban.* New York: Columbia University Press, 2010.

OTHER SOURCES

Bolduc, Donald C. "Forecasting the Future of Afghanistan." *Special Warfare* 24, no. 4 (2011): 22–28.

Chesser, Susan. "Afghanistan Casualties: Military Forces and Civilians." Congressional Research Service, February 3, 2011.

Clark, Stephen A. "Investigation into the Incident in Vicinity of the Salala Checkpoint on the Night of 25–26 Nov 2011," December 18, 2011. United States Central Command. Available at www.centcom.mil/images/stories/Crossborder/report%20exsum%20further%20redacted.pdf.

Feickert, Andrew. "U.S. Special Operations Forces (SOF): Background and Issues for Congress." Congressional Research Service, February 6, 2013.

Fridovich, David P., and Fred T. Krawchuk, "Winning in the Pacific: The Special Operations Forces Indirect Approach." *Joint Force Quarterly*, no. 44 (2007): 24–27.

Human Rights Watch. *"Just Don't Call It a Militia": Impunity, Militias, and the "Afghan Local Police."* New York: Human Rights Watch, 2011. Available at www.hrw.org/sites/default/files/reports/afghanistan-0911webwcover.pdf.

Jones, Seth G. "Reintegrating Afghan Insurgents." Occasional Paper OP-327-MCIA. Santa Monica, CA: RAND, 2011.

Lambert, Geoffrey, Larry Lewis, and Sarah Sewall. "Operation Enduring Freedom–Philippines: Civilian Harm and the Indirect Approach." *Prism* 3, no. 5 (2012): 117–135.

Lefèvre, Mathieu. "Local Defence in Afghanistan: A Review of Government-Backed Initiatives." Afghanistan Analysts Network, 2010. Available at http://aan-afghanistan.com/index.asp?id=763.

Malkasian, Carter, and J. Kael Weston. "War Downsized: How to Accomplish More with Less." *Foreign Affairs* 91, no. 2 (2012): 111–121.

Marrs, James R. "Findings and Recommendations of AR 15-6 Investigation: Credibility Assessment of Allegations of Human Rights Violations Appearing in a Human Rights Watch Report." USFOR-A-DJ2. United States Forces–Afghanistan, 2011.

Maxwell, David S. Statement to the House Committee on Armed Services, Subcommittee on Emerging Threats and Capabilities. Hearing on Understanding Future Irregular Warfare Challenges, March 27, 2012.

McRaven, William H. Statement to the House Committee on Armed Services, Subcommittee on Emerging Threats and Capabilities. Hearing on the Future of Special Operations Forces, September 22, 2011.

———. United States Special Operations Command Posture Statement to the Senate, Armed Services Committee, March 6, 2012.

Olson, Eric T. "U.S. Special Operations: Context and Capabilities in Irregular Warfare." *Joint Force Quarterly*, no. 56 (2010): 64–70.

Robinson, Linda. "The Future of Special Operations: Beyond Kill and Capture." *Foreign Affairs*, November/December 2012, 110–122.

———. "The Future of Special Operations Forces." Council Special Report No. 66. New York: Council on Foreign Relations, 2013.

———. Statement to the House Committee on Armed Services, Subcommittee on Emerging Threats and Capabilities. Hearing on the Future of Special Operations Forces, July 11, 2012.

Shurkin, Michael Robert. "Subnational Government in Afghanistan." Occasional Paper OP-318-MCIA. Santa Monica, CA: RAND, 2011.

United Nations Office of the High Commissioner for Human Rights. *Afghanistan: Annual Report 2012. Protection of Civilians in Armed Conflict*. Kabul: United Nations Assistance Mission in Afghanistan (UNAMA), 2013.

U.S. Army Doctrinal Publication 3-05. Special Operations. Washington, DC: US Department of the Army, 2012.

U.S. Army Special Forces, 1961–1971. Vietnam Studies. CMH Publication 90-23. Washington, DC: United States Army Center of Military History, 1989 [1973].

US Department of Defense. *Report on Progress Toward Security and Stability in Afghanistan*. Report to Congress in accordance with section 1230 of the National Defense Authorization Act. Washington, DC: US Department of Defense, 2009–2012.

"U.S. Special Operations Command Fact Book 2012." Tampa, FL: US Special Operations Command, 2012.

Wilder, Andrew R. "Cops or Robbers? The Struggle to Reform the Afghan National Police." Issues Paper Series. Kabul: Afghanistan Research and Evaluation Unit, 2007.

INDEX

Abbasin, Abdu Aziz, 74–75, 77–78, 86–87, 89
A Better War (Sorley), 26
Abu Sayyaf, 161, 183–184
Afghan Local Police (ALP), 177
  development of, 25–37
  and district support teams (DSTs), 28
  future of, 253–255, 257–258
  in Ghazni Province, 205–206
  growth of, 124–127, 130, 131, 241, 249–253
  in Kandahar Province, 41, 138–139
  in Kunar Province, 95–97, 99–103, 217, 219, 221, 224–225
  in Maiwand District, 149–150
  in Marawara District, 227, 231, 234, 237
  in Paktika Province, 67, 81, 91, 181–183, 187–188, 190–191, 194–195, 201
  in Uruzgan Province, 159–160, 166–167
  in Wardak Province, 209, 212
  in Zabul Province, 159–160, 166, 174
  See also Community Defense Initiative
Afghan Militia Force (AMF), 9, 11, 12, 68, 82, 125
Afghan Ministry of Defense, 257
Afghan Ministry of the Interior, 25, 57, 91, 125, 205, 226, 249–251, 253, 257
Afghan National Army Special Operations Command (ANASOC), 258–259
Afghan Public Protection Program (AP3), 15–16, 209
Afghan Security Forces Funds, 91
Afghan Security Guard force, 68
Afghan special operations forces, 124, 130, 175, 257
  competency of, 127–128
Afghanistan-Pakistan (AFPAK) Hands, 24, 32

Ahmadzai, Ali Shah "ASA," 249, 251
Air Force Special Operations Command's Combined Joint Special Operations Air Detachment–A (CJSOAD-A), 129–130
Allen, John, 124, 133, 134, 151, 177, 208, 223, 255
  and Operation Sayaqa, 117–120
  and "SOF Tribes," 120–121
Al Qaeda, 1, 11, 17, 22, 95, 102, 117, 228, 245, 248, 262
  in Afghanistan, 124, 256
  in Philippines, 184
Ambrose, Tim, 230–231
Andar District, 205, 207–208
Anderson, J. R., 160
Apocalypse Now, 219
Arghandab District, 19, 40–44
Asadabad (Afghanistan), 94, 105, 108, 114, 217–218, 228, 236
Asim Gul, 225–226
Aslamuddin, Asadullah, 212

Bagram Airfield (Afghanistan), 11, 68, 91, 103, 105, 164, 173, 178, 200, 235, 236, 245, 256
Bales, Robert, 145–148, 220
Balkh Province, 35
Barack, Fazil Ahmad, 45, 54
Barfield, Thomas, 14
Barwari, Obaidullah, 48, 53, 57, 139
Basic Underwater Demolition/SEAL (BUD/S) training, 137
Bergdahl, Bowe, 18
Biden, Joe, 24
bin Laden, Osama, 40, 245
  death of, 116, 117
Bishop, John, 214
Bismullah Khan "BK" Mohammedi, 29, 35
  and Afghan Local Police, 133–134

303

Bolduc, Don, 31, 125, 246, 249–250, 253, 258
Bradshaw, Adrian, 118
Brennan, John O., 199
Bush, George W. (and administration of), 161
Buzzard, Curtis, 30

Call of Duty (video game), 240
Camps (Afghanistan)
  Belambay, 145–148
  Bostick, 236
  Brown, 177
  Dyer, 104, 105, 222, 234
  Falcon, 236
  Honaker-Miracle, 236
  Integrity, 245–246
  Maholic, 178
  Monti, 236
  Morehead, 12
  Simmons, 176
  Vance, 105
  Wright, 233, 235–236, 238
Carter, Nick, 42
Carty, Bill, 61–62, 64
Castelli, Robert "Chris," 5–7
  See also Operation Adalat
Cavendish, Julius, 89
Central Intelligence Agency (CIA), 9, 13, 116, 117, 122
  and Counterterrorist Pursuit Teams (CTPTs), 67, 86, 197–199
  and Shamsi Airfield, 119, 120
Chak District, 210–211, 215
Chora District, 163–164
Clark, Stephen, 120
Clarke, Jason, 206
Colombia, 16, 128, 157–158, 160, 178, 184, 257–258, 262, 267
Combat Outposts (COP)
  Deqobad, 151–155
  Fortress, 221
  Margah, 81, 196
  Penich, 95–96, 109, 219, 221, 227
  Syadabad, 210
Combined Forces Special Operations Component Command–Afghanistan (CFSOCC-A), 14, 118, 242
Combined Joint Special Operations Task Force–Afghanistan (CJSOTF-A), 9–10, 11, 31, 95, 105, 125, 129, 235, 247

Commander Nazir Group, 66, 90
Commander's Emergency Response Program (CERP), 85, 131
Community Based Security Solutions (CBSS), 131
Community Defense Initiative, 16–17, 21–25, 26, 249
  See also Afghan Local Police
Critical Infrastructure Protection program, 131
Crocker, Ryan, 123–124
Cultural Support Teams, 54–55

Dadullah Lang, Mullah, 1–2, 4
Dahla dam, 5
Dawlat Khan, 89, 91, 194
Day Kundi Province, 17, 30
De Rawood (Afghanistan), 7
Development Alternatives, Inc., 85
Diciwal, Mohammed Kasim, 207–208
Dinter, Heinz, 118–119, 121, 125, 127, 135
District Augmentation Teams (DATs), 32, 187
Dunford, Joseph, 208, 212, 213, 214, 255, 257
Duskin, Michael, 211

8th Commando Kandak, 170–171
82nd Airborne Division, 148–149
  and 1-505 Battalion, 30
  and 1-508 Battalion, 2
Eikenberry, Karl, 12
  as US ambassador, 22, 63, 123
El Salvador, 10, 16, 238, 267
Eshqabad (Afghanistan), 47, 141, 142, 145
Evans, John, 127
Ezabad (Afghanistan), 45–48, 50–54, 58, 138, 154

Fahim Khan, Mohammed Qasim, 29, 35
Faizi, Aimal, 237
Fareed, Omar, 256
Fidai, Mohammad Halim, 209
Firebase Anaconda (Afghanistan), 7–8
1st Afghan Commando battalion, 104
1st Battalion, 8
1st Commando Kandak, 222
1st Infantry Division
  and 1-16 Infantry Battalion, 30, 96, 98
1st Special Forces Group, 30, 75, 183, 191, 192
5-2 Stryker Brigade, 40

503rd Infantry Regiment
  2nd Battalion of, 229
Fletcher, Tony, 235, 247
foreign internal defense (FID) mission,
  160, 170
4th Battalion, 192
Forts (US)
  Bragg, 11, 30, 49, 76, 128, 220, 240, 257
  Lewis, 147
  Riley, 30
Forward Operating Bases (FOB)
  Joyce, 105, 114, 115, 231, 232
  Super, 182, 186
  Tillman, 81, 88, 196
Fox, Chris, 215, 235

Gant, Jim, 81, 219–221, 227
  and "One Tribe at a Time," 95, 219
Ganjgal (Afghanistan), 222–223
Gates, Robert, 16
Gelan Province, 204
General Order Number One Bravo, 148
Ghaki Pass and Valley, 228–234
Ghazni Province, 29, 202, 203
  Afghan Local Police in, 205–206, 248
  Taliban in, 204, 206
Ghazni Provincial Response Company,
  204
Gizab (Afghanistan), 17–18
Green, Dan, 167–168
Grissom, James, 200–201
Guantanamo Bay detention camp, 18

Haas, Chris, 10, 11, 123, 125, 129, 157,
  172, 210, 220, 242, 246
  and Afghan Local Police 124,
    126–127, 132, 134–135
  and Bales massacre, 146–147
  and Maiwand District, 150–151
  and Operation Sayaqa, 118, 120–121
Hagel, Chuck, 213–214
Haiti, 26, 225
Hakim, Abdullah, 142–144, 263
Hansell, Brad, 137–140, 142–144
  and Bales masacre, 145–146, 148
  and Maiwand District, 148–154, 156
Harmon, Rob, 68
Haqqani network, 90
  in North Waziristan, 66–67, 117, 199
  and Pakistan, 119
Hauser, Ben, 234–235
Hayes Dan, 44–45, 48–51, 53–59,
  137–139

Hayes, Mike, 159, 163–170, 172, 174–176,
  178
  background of, 161
  ethics of, 162
Hekmatyar, Gulbuddin, 210
Helmand Province, 6, 44, 131, 209
  Afghan Local Police in, 125, 132
  British in, 2, 4, 30–31
  Taliban in, 3, 28
Helmand River, 40, 45
Herat Province, 2, 4, 130, 177
Hezb-e Islami Gulbuddin (HIG), 204,
  210, 214
Hindu Kush, 93–94, 209, 228, 233
Holahan, Rick, 222–223, 228
Hotak, Ghulam Mohammad, 15, 209
Howell, Scott, 246
Huggins, Jim, 151
Human Rights Watch, 130
Hutal (Afghanistan), 44–46
Hutchinson, Michael "Hutch," 69–70,
  73–78, 80–84, 86–91, 181, 192, 194,
  200
  background of, 65–66

Indonesia, 184, 185
Initial Accession (IA) or "X-Ray," 76
Interim Security Critical Infrastructure
  Program, 131
International Assistance Security Force
  (ISAF), 25, 31–32, 117, 123, 130, 209,
  213, 215, 218, 242–243
  Joint Command (IJC) of, 14, 120,
    132, 212, 235
  and Operation Nish, 3
Iran, 124
  and Afghan Shia, 18
Iraq, 14, 23, 30, 60, 120, 131, 167, 170–
  171, 204, 242, 245, 256–258, 262
  See also Sons of Iraq
Islamic Movement of Uzbekistan, 66

Jabbar, Hero, 45, 55
Jackson, Terrence, 205, 207
Jalalabad (Afghanistan), 94, 103,
  217–218
Jamaat Islamiya (JI), 184
Janan, Haji Hazrat, 213
Jan Mohammed, 55, 57–58, 142–144, 156
  and Bales massacre, 148
Jan Mohammad Khan, 10, 18, 55, 61
  assassination of, 167–168
Jimenez, Eddie, 103, 105, 122

Joint Asset Allocation Meetings
(JAAM), 247
Joint Prioritized Effects List (JPEL), 84
Joint Special Operations Task Force–
Philippines (JSOTF-P), 184
Jones, J. R., 156–157
Jones, Seth, 14, 17

Kabul (Afghanistan), 3, 12, 24, 178
CIA in, 13
ISAF in, 32
Taliban attack on, 14
US embassy in, 21, 28, 32, 123, 220,
239
Kabul Bank, 268
Kajaki (Afghanistan), 4
Kala Khan, 138, 143
Kandahar Airfield (Afghanistan), 2, 41,
148, 154, 177
Kandahar City (Afghanistan), 1, 2, 3,
44, 138
Airfield in, 10–11
offensive on, 4, 7
Taliban in, 39–40
Kandahar Province, 4, 148, 175, 248
Afghan Local Police in, 125, 138
Canadians in, 2
Dutch in, 5, 6, 7
Taliban in, 4–5, 39–41, 60–61, 159,
163, 176
Kandahari, Zakeria, 212
Karim, Abdul, 258
Karimi, Sher Mohammed, 128, 259–260
Karzai, Ahmed Wali, 10, 41–42, 44, 61
Karzai, Hamid, 5, 10, 44, 89, 90, 167,
237
and Afghan Local Police, 25
and Community Defense Initiative,
17, 18, 22, 25
and corruption, 22
and Kandahar, 61, 62, 63
and Nerkh District, 212–213
as Pashtun, 35–36
and US relations, 123–124, 213–214
Karzai, Qayum, 5, 10, 18, 63
and Bales massacre, 145
and Community Defense Initiative, 22
Kayani, Ashfaq Parvez, 117
Kearney, Frank, 11
Kettman, Mary, 84–86
Khalid, Asadullah, 8–9, 63, 134, 204
Khas Uruzgan District, 130, 168, 251, 254

Khost Province, 67, 85
Khyber Pass, 94
Kim, Jae, 192–196, 199–201
Krongaard, Alex, 33
Kteh Khas, 259
Kunar Province
Afghan Local Police in, 95–97,
99–103, 122, 217, 219, 221, 224–225,
229
battles in, 93, 248
CIA in, 236–238
Mohmand tribe in, 99
and N2K, 94, 103
and Pakistan, 217–218
Taliban in, 97, 217–218, 224–226
withdrawal from, 234–235
Kunar Provincial Response Company,
232
Kunduz Province, 35

Laghman Province, 140
Lawrence, T. E., 219, 267
Lodin, Zia, 68
Lord of the Rings, The (Tolkien), 55, 193

Mahaney Jr., Patrick J. "Pat," 1, 4, 11,
16, 33, 37, 62
and Firebase Anaconda, 8
and NATO Defense College, 9
and Operation Nish, 2–3
Maholic, Thom, 178
Maiwand District, 40, 44–64, 113,
137–138, 142
Taliban in, 143, 148–149
Mann, Scott, 31, 33–34
Marawara District, 230, 233–234, 237
Afghan Local Police in, 227, 231, 234,
237
Taliban in, 228–229
Marquez, Justin, 211
Martinez, Angel, 157, 177
Matiullah Khan, 5, 7, 8–9, 167–168
Mattis, James, 112
Maya (Afghanistan), 97, 104, 106–111,
118, 122, 227
See also Operation Sayaqa
Mazar-e Sharif (Afghanistan), 30, 34, 35
McChrystal, Stanley A., 4, 16–17, 27, 33
and counterinsurgency, 22
and Karzai, Hamid, 22–23
and *Rolling Stone* article, 24
and special mission units, 23, 244–245

McDonough, Denis, 161
McKenzie, Alec, 132
McKiernan, David D., 14–15, 16, 209
McRaven, William H. "Bill," 129, 161, 244–245, 248
Meyer, Dakota, 222
Military Information Support Operations (MISO), 74–75
Miller, Austin Scott, 21, 44, 96, 246, 249, 257
  and Afghan Local Police, 25–27, 30–32, 126–127, 132
  background of, 23
  leadership of, 33–36
  at Pentagon, 27
  and special mission units, 23–24, 25
Ministry of Rural Reconstruction and Development, 32
Miran Shah (Pakistan), 18
Mohammed, Haji Yar, 187, 189
Mohammed, Saleh, 138
Mohammed, Sultan, 138–139, 156
Mohseni, Ayatollah Shaikh Mohammed, 18
Mojaddedi, Sibghatullah, 15
Moro Islamic National Liberation Front, 183–184
Moses, Brad, 15, 209
Moshak (Afghanistan), 47, 142
Mulholland, John, 9
Mullah Dadullah Front, 175
Mullah Gulam Ali, 211
Mullah Nazir, 66–67, 199
Mullah Omar, 39
Mullen, Mike, 32
Mundagak Palace, 62
Munoz, Pedro, 177–178
Musahiban dynasty, 14

Nangahar Province, 10–11, 19, 53, 94, 114, 203, 234–235
Naqib, Karimullah, 19
National Directorate of Security (NDS), 15, 243–244
National Solidarity Program, 268
NATO, 9, 249
  and AP3, 15
  in Kandahar Province, 2
  in Kunar Province, 218
  Special Operations Component Command–Afghanistan, 243
Navarro Richard, 147, 151, 157, 247

Nawi Kalay (Afghanistan), 72–73, 194–195, 199
Nerkh District, 212–214
New Kabul Compound, 32–33
Newsom, Alex, 222
New York Times, 237
Niazi, Abdullah, 59, 138, 144–145
9/11 attacks, 2, 23, 66, 161, 197
Noor, Atta Mohammad, 35
Noriega, Manuel, 10
Nur Mohammed, 99–101, 217, 221–222, 224, 226–227, 251
Nuristan Province, 95, 102, 103, 209, 218, 228

Obama, Barack (and administration of), 16, 161, 255–256
  and drone strikes, 116
  and policy review in Afghanistan (2009), 22
Olson, Eric, 13, 14, 29, 95
101st Airborne Division, 68
187th Infantry Regiment, 78, 79
  2nd Brigade of, 41
Operations
  Adalat, 5–7, 12
  Anaconda, 68, 125
  Haymaker, 248
  Sayaqa, 103–116, 117, 121, 222
Operational Coordination Group (OCG), 256
Operational Detachment Alpha (ODA)
  112, 140
  1112, 183, 191
  1114, 182–183, 186, 189, 200
  1326, 205
  1411, 192, 200
  3124, 215
  3131, 225–228, 230–231, 234–238, 240
  3313, 104
  3314, 44–45
  3316, 95, 100
  3325, 65, 69, 74, 80–81, 89, 90
  3436, 224
  7233, 137, 148
opium trade, 40, 44–45, 50, 54, 143
Orgun District, 74, 78–85, 87–89, 91, 189, 191–193, 197, 201

Pakistan, 2, 71, 94, 101, 162, 165, 169, 187, 189
  Al Qaeda in, 1, 11, 66

Pakistan (*cont'd*)
  Bergdahl, Bowe in, 18
  Dadullah Lang, Mullah in, 2–4
  and Haqqani network, 119
  and India, 119
  and South Waziristan, 66, 70, 199
  Taliban in, 66–67, 81, 200, 217–218
  and US relations, 111–116, 117, 119, 122
  See also Maya; Operation Sayaqa
Pakistan-Afghanistan Coordination Cell
    (PACC), 23, 27
Paktia Province, 67
Paktika Province, 18, 218, 236
  Afghan Local Police in, 67, 81, 91,
    181–182, 187–188
  CIA in, 197
  and Loya Paktia (P2K), 67
  Taliban in, 66–75, 77–80, 82–84, 86,
    88–91, 188, 190, 194, 196
Paluso, Geno, 33
Panjwayi District, 41, 44, 59–60, 145,
    152
  Taliban in, 63–64
Parwan Detention Facility
    (Afghanistan), 123, 214
Parwan Province, 133–134
Pashtun, 2, 10, 29, 35, 89, 124, 135
  and armed defense groups, 21–22
  feuding among, 159, 167
  network of, 18
  and self-rule, 14, 83
  and education, 59
Patterson, Jess, 90, 190
Pederson-Keel, Andrew, 215
Persistent Ground Surveillance System
    (PGSS), 152
Peterson, Jake, 96
Petraeus, David, 33, 44, 95, 121
  and Afghan Local Police, 29–30, 36,
    101
  and Community Defense Initiative,
    24
  in Iraq, 24–25
Philippines, 128, 160–161, 183–185
  See also Abu Sayyaf
Pirkowti (Afghanistan), 74–76, 78–80,
    85–90, 192, 196, 199–200, 201
Pittman, Hal, 118
Polish Army, 203–204
  and Task Force White Eagle, 203
Popal, Ahmadullah, 170–171, 173–174
Provincial Augmentation Teams (PATs),
    32, 167

Provincial Response Company (PRC),
    201–202

Qaddafi, Muammar el-, 128
Qadir, Haji, 238
Quetta (Pakistan), 2, 39

Rabbani, Burhanuddin, 124
Rahman, Abdul, 250
Rahman, Haji Hazrat, 231
Rahman, Qari Zia "QZR," 218,
    227–229, 231–234, 238
RAND, 26, 34, 126, 250, 253
Rarey, Brian, 141
Raziq, Abdul, 42–43, 61–63, 140
  and Bales massacre, 147
Red Cross, 123
Reeder Jr., Edward M. "Ed," 21, 23, 31,
    49, 246
  and Afghan militia forces, 12
  and AP3, 16–17
  background of, 10
  as commander of CFSOCC-A, 14–16
  and Community Defense Initiative,
    16–19
  and Karzai network, 10–11
  and Pashtun, 10
  and Taliban, 12–14
Regional Command–East, 115–116, 211,
    235, 243
Regional Command–South, 41, 148,
    151, 156
Registan Desert, 40
Riga, Chris, 41–44, 61
Rotsaert, Pat, 103, 105
Russell, Jason, 183, 187, 190–191

Said Mohammed, 227
Salang Tunnel, 29
Samad, Abdul, 169
Samim, Mohibullah, 89
Sangin (Afghanistan), 3, 5
Sar Howza (Afghanistan), 81, 191
Sayadabad District, 215
Sayagaz (Afghanistan), 171–174
Sayyaf, Rasul, 183
Scaparrotti, Curtis, 120, 121, 133–134
Schad, Rex, 215
Schiro, Joseph L., 210–211
Schrader, Jay, 98
Schwartz, Mark, 125, 127
  and human rights abuses, 130–131
Schweitzer, Marty, 148

and Zhari District, 149–151
SEAL Team Six, 23, 116, 160, 170
SEAL Team Two, 161
Second Anglo-Afghan War, 44
Shah Wali Kot District, 176
Shah Wali Kot Valley, 5, 6
Shamsi Airfield (Pakistan), 119, 120
Sharana (Afghanistan), 71, 81, 82, 90,
    91, 200
Shigal District, 237
Shirzai, Gul Agha, 10–11, 234
Shkin (Afghanistan), 66–67, 71–72,
    79–83, 85–86, 197
6th Commando Kandak, 211
Soda Khan, 55
SOF Academic Week, 34
Solheim, Kent, 223
Sons of Iraq, 24–25
Sorley, Lewis, 26
Special Forces Groups
    1st, 30–31, 75, 183
    3rd, 30, 49
    7th, 8, 16, 49
    20th, 32
special mission units, 25, 84, 123–124,
    206, 235, 242, 244–246, 248, 262
    and Dadullah Lang, Mullah, 4
    reorganization of, 23
Special Operations Aviation Regiment,
    127
Special Operations Task Force–North
    (SOTF-N), 30–31
Special Operations Task Force–South
    (SOTF-S), 247
Special Operations Task Force–
    Southeast, 30–31, 159–160
Special Operations Teams–Alpha (SOT-
    As), 46–47, 73, 105
Spedar Pass, 71
Spence, Wes, 127
Stephens, Riley Gene, 210
Stigall, Jeff, 127
Stigall, J. R., 25, 33
Strickland, Brian, 167, 168
Strong Eagle III, 229
Sullivan, Mike, 43, 44
Swindell, Sean, 257–259

Tajik, 29, 35, 36, 83, 89–90, 124
    and Afghan Local Police, 132
    and Pashtun, 135
Taliban, 5, 83
    and Afghan Local Police, 125, 255

raids on, 12–13, 124
resurgence of, 1–2, 13
tactics of, 4, 6, 60–61
and tribal dynamics, 13–14
weapons of, 3, 109, 111
Tarin Kowt (Afghanistan), 5, 7, 8
    SEALs in, 160, 162–163, 170
Task Forces
    16, 26
    310, 86
    535, 29, 129, 245, 246
    714, 23
    and Delta task force, 23
Terry, James, 41, 63, 130
Thailand, 185
Thomas, Tony, 208, 210, 212, 242–249,
    252–253, 256
Tillman, Pat 196
Time, 89
Tolkien, J. R. R., 55, 193
Townsend, Steve, 94
Triple Action, 208, 248
Tunnel, Harry, 40–41
Tyson, Ann Scott, 220

Ua, Cameron, 75–76
United Nations, 9, 89
    blacklist of, 86
    and prisoner abuse, 123
United Nations Assistance Mission in
    Afghanistan (UNAMA), 251
Uruzgan Province, 5, 30, 175, 224
    Taliban in, 3–4, 7, 28, 159, 162–164
US Agency for International
    Development (USAID), 26–27, 28
    and Office of Transition Initiatives
    (OTI), 84–85, 194, 239
US Army Special Forces Qualification
    Course, 137
US Central Command, 11, 24, 34,
    111–112, 119
US Department of Agriculture, 28
US Special Operations Command, 13,
    29, 129, 208, 210
US Special Operations Joint Task
    Force–Afghanistan, 243
US State Department, 28
Uzbek, 29

Vietnam, 37, 93, 129, 151, 157, 161, 185,
    196, 222, 238–239, 263
    Civilian Irregular Defense Group in,
    13, 252

Village Stability Coordination Centers
(VSCCs), 31–32, 33
Village Stability Operations/Afghan
Local Police (VSO/ALP). *See*
Afghan Local Police
Votel, Joseph, 245

Wardak Province, 15, 29, 178, 203, 208,
211, 248
and Afghan Local Police, 209, 212
Taliban in, 210, 214
Washington Post, 199, 220
West Point, 66
White, Scott, 59–60
Wikileaks, 116
Wilson, Bob, 66
and Kunar Province, 94, 102
and Operation Sayaqa, 103, 105, 107,
109, 115–116

World Bank, 268
World Trade Center, 2
World War II, 3
Wright, Jeremy, 233

Yahya Khel District, 186, 188–190
Yarborough, William P., 73

Zabul Province, 2, 30
Afghan Local Police in, 133, 170
Taliban in, 28, 36, 159, 164–165, 168,
171
Zarghun Shah District, 185
Zarqawi, Abu Musab al-, 1
Zeegers, Randy, 32
Zerikow Valley, 4
Zhari District, 41, 44, 57, 60
and Afghan Local Police, 149–150

LINDA ROBINSON is a senior international policy analyst at RAND. She has been an adjunct senior fellow at the Council on Foreign Relations and Public Policy Scholar at the Wilson Center. Her book about the U.S. Army Special Forces, *Masters of Chaos*, was a *New York Times* bestseller; *Tell Me How This Ends*, which is about the Iraq War, was a *Foreign Affairs* bestseller and a *New York Times* notable book. She received the Gerald R. Ford Prize for Reporting on National Defense in 2005. She has conducted field research on special operations in Afghanistan, Iraq, Latin America and elsewhere over the past twelve years.

PublicAffairs is a publishing house founded in 1997. It is a tribute to the standards, values, and flair of three persons who have served as mentors to countless reporters, writers, editors, and book people of all kinds, including me.

I. F. STONE, proprietor of *I. F. Stone's Weekly*, combined a commitment to the First Amendment with entrepreneurial zeal and reporting skill and became one of the great independent journalists in American history. At the age of eighty, Izzy published *The Trial of Socrates*, which was a national bestseller. He wrote the book after he taught himself ancient Greek.

BENJAMIN C. BRADLEE was for nearly thirty years the charismatic editorial leader of *The Washington Post*. It was Ben who gave the *Post* the range and courage to pursue such historic issues as Watergate. He supported his reporters with a tenacity that made them fearless and it is no accident that so many became authors of influential, best-selling books.

ROBERT L. BERNSTEIN, the chief executive of Random House for more than a quarter century, guided one of the nation's premier publishing houses. Bob was personally responsible for many books of political dissent and argument that challenged tyranny around the globe. He is also the founder and longtime chair of Human Rights Watch, one of the most respected human rights organizations in the world.

·　　·　　·

For fifty years, the banner of Public Affairs Press was carried by its owner Morris B. Schnapper, who published Gandhi, Nasser, Toynbee, Truman, and about 1,500 other authors. In 1983, Schnapper was described by *The Washington Post* as "a redoubtable gadfly." His legacy will endure in the books to come.

Peter Osnos, *Founder and Editor-at-Large*